STUDIES IN EARLY MODERN CULTURAL,
POLITICAL AND SOCIAL HISTORY

Volume 21

ALEHOUSES AND GOOD FELLOWSHIP
IN EARLY MODERN ENGLAND

T0355746

Studies in Early Modern Cultural, Political and Social History

ISSN: 1476–9107

Series editors

Tim Harris – Brown University
Stephen Taylor – Durham University
Andy Wood – Durham University

Previously published titles in the series
are listed at the back of this volume

ALEHOUSES
AND GOOD FELLOWSHIP
IN EARLY MODERN ENGLAND

Mark Hailwood

THE BOYDELL PRESS

First published 2014
The Boydell Press, Woodbridge
Paperback edition 2016

ISBN 978-1-84383-942-2 hardback
ISBN 978-1-78327-154-2 paperback

The Boydell Press is an imprint of Boydell & Brewer Ltd
PO Box 9, Woodbridge, Suffolk IP12 3DF, UK
and of Boydell & Brewer Inc.
668 Mt Hope Avenue, Rochester, NY 14620–2731, USA
website: www.boydellandbrewer.com

A CIP catalogue record for this book is available
from the British Library

The publisher has no responsibility for the continued existence or
accuracy of URLs for external or third-party internet websites referred
to in this book, and does not guarantee that any content on
such websites is, or will remain, accurate or appropriate

This publication is printed on acid-free paper

Contents

Illustrations

Acknowledgements

I feel extremely privileged to have received various awards of funding that have allowed me to write a book on a subject I find so fascinating. My thanks go the the Arts and Humanities Research Council for funding my MA, to the University of Warwick for funding my Ph.D., to the Institute of Advanced Study at Warwick for a post-doctoral fellowship, to the Francis Bacon Foundation for awarding me a fellowship to conduct research at the Huntington Library, San Marino, and also to the University of Cambridge for employing me on a twelve-month contract when I was a Temporary Lecturer there. Had I been employed on a nine- or ten-month contract, which are becoming increasingly common, I would not have been in a position to complete revisions to this book over the summer of 2013. Year-long contracts are crucial to early career academics in temporary posts to allow them to produce the publications necessary to develop their career.

If I have been fortunate to receive such financial support, I have been luckier still to have benefited from working with some exceptional teachers without whose input I would never have been capable of this project. At my local state comprehensive Damien Keane encouraged my historical imagination, Keith Berridge provided invaluable and lasting advice on how to write history, and Paul Crossthwaite – my Physics teacher – taught me to 'worry' about how the world works. Andy Wood, who taught me as an undergraduate at the University of East Anglia, was an inspirational tutor who got me hooked on early modern history. My greatest mentor is my Ph.D. supervisor Steve Hindle. The energy, insight and enthusiasm that he has displayed in supporting me, both intellectually and personally, since taking me on in 2006, have been phenomenal. Above all, he has given me the Allman Brothers Band *Live at the Fillmore East*. I could not be any prouder to call myself a Hindleite. My fellow traveller under that banner, Brodie Waddell, has also been an invaluable source of both friendship and intellectual stimulation over the past eight years, and long may that continue.

Both Steve and Brodie deserve additional thanks for reading various full drafts of this book, as does Andy. I am also grateful for the valuable input and suggestions of Bernard Capp and Mark Knights, who read parts of the doctoral thesis, and of Beat Kümin and Phil Withington, whose examination of it provided me with valuable food for thought on how to expand it into book form. Countless conference audiences have provided helpful questions, comments and ideas, and I have benefited enormously from the opportunity to refine my ideas in dialogue with students who took my 'Drink and Disorder in Early Modern England' course, at Cardiff in 2010–11 and at Bristol in 2011–12, and those whom I supervised on 'Food and Drink in Britain and the Wider World, 1577–1773' at Cambridge in 2012–13. Conversations with Bill Brown and Rebecca Lemon during my time at the Huntington were particularly important in helping me to crystallise my arguments, and I would also like to acknowledge the influence on my work and thinking of fellow Warwick early modern drinking historians James Brown, Matthew Jackson and Angela McShane. Several individuals have been kind enough to share references or unpublished papers with me, and these are acknowledged in the footnotes.

I have been a fairly itinerant scholar over my short career so far, a fact that has afforded me the privilege of accumulating too many friends and colleagues to individually thank them for being good ones. The support and advice of a number of senior colleagues deserves special mention though, and I am especially grateful to John Morrill, Craig Muldrew, Selina Todd, Garthine Walker, Alex Walsham and Jane Whittle. Henry French, in particular, has been extremely generous in providing me with various forms of career support, and with pints. My travels have been smoothed by the kind hospitality of Ian and Aileen Fielding-Das, Debbie and Paul 'Tonehouse', Kev Passmore and Garthine Walker, Liz and Dennis Kneier, and Steve, Louise, Olivia, Tom and Joe Hindle. Thanks for the sofas/spare rooms/free dinners/glasses of wine and above all good company. Gary Love and Alexis Harasemovitch Truax were both invaluable friends who took me under their wing when I was in strange lands.

Finally, and most importantly, I would like to acknowledge four people without whom I would have achieved nothing, let alone this book. Laura Sangha is my rock. I wouldn't have got far without her. The unconditional love and support of my Mum and brother means the world to me. This book is dedicated to my Dad, who was a better friend and parent than he would ever take credit for. He is sorely missed.

Cowley Road Oxford
& Exeter Quayside
March 2014

Abbreviations

Bodleian	Bodleian Library Ballad Collection: facsimiles accessed online at <http://eebo.chadwyck.com/home> (Early English Books Online)
BL	British Library Ballad Collection: facsimiles accessed online at <http://eebo.chadwyck.com/home> (Early English Books Online)
Ches. Q.S. Recs	J.H.E. Bennett and J.C. Dewhurst (eds), *Quarter Sessions Records, with other Records of the Justices of the Peace for the County Palatine of Chester, 1559–1760* (Chester: Record Society of Lancashire and Cheshire, 1940)
CRO	Cheshire Record Office
EBBA	English Broadside Ballad Archive: <http://ebba.english.ucsb.edu/>
EBBO	Early English Books Online: <http://eebo.chadwyck.com/home>
ERO	Essex Record Office
Eyre	Adam Eyre, 'A dyurnall, or catalogue of all my accions and expences from the 1st of January, 1646–[7]', ed. H.J. Morehouse, in *Yorkshire Diaries and Autobiographies in the Seventeenth and Eighteenth Centuries* (Durham, 1877)
Leic. Boro. Recs	Mary Bateson, W.H. Stevenson and J.E. Stocks (eds), *Records of the Borough of Leicester, Being a Series of Extracts from the Archives of the Corporation of Leicester. Vol. III: 1509–1603; Vol. IV: 1603–1688* (Cambridge, 1905–23)
Lowe	Roger Lowe, *The Diary of Roger Lowe*, ed. William Sachse (London, 1938)
Nott. Boro. Recs	W.H. Stevenson (ed), *Records of the Borough of Nottingham: Being a Series of Extracts from the Archives of the Corporation of Nottingham*, Vol. IV, King Edward VI to King James I, 1547–1625 (London, 1889); and T.W. Baker (ed), Vol. V, 1625–1702 (London, 1900)

ODNB	*Oxford Dictionary of National Biography*, online edition: <http://www.oxforddnb.com/>
Pepys	The Pepys Ballad Collection, facsimiles accessed online at <http://ebba.english.ucsb.edu/> (English Broadside Ballad Archive, University of California, Santa Barbara)
Read. Boro. Recs	J.M. Guilding (ed.), *Reading Records: Diary of the Corporation*, Vol. II, 1603–1629; Vol. III, 1630–1640; Vol. IV, 1641–1654 (London, 1895–96)
Roxburghe	The Roxburghe Ballad Collection, facsimiles accessed online at <http://ebba.english.ucsb.edu/> (English Broadside Ballad Archive, University of California, Santa Barbara)
SHC	Somerset Heritage Centre. *Please note, the Somerset Quarter Sessions Rolls contain two sets of numbering, the second added when the rolls were transferred to microfilm. In all cases I have provided the second, most recent number, with one exception. Due to an error, the reference in Chapter 2, note 131, p. 92, refers to the older numbers.
Som. Q.S. Recs	E.H. Bates Harbin (ed.), *Quarter Sessions Records for the County of Somerset*, Vol. I, James I, 1607–1625; Vol. II, Charles I, 1625–1639; Vol. III, Commonwealth, 1646–1660 (London: Somerset Record Society, 1907–12); and M.C.B. Dawes (ed.), Vol. IV, Charles II, 1666–1677 (London, 1919)
VCH	*Victoria County History*: available online at: <http://www.victoriacountyhistory.ac.uk/>
Wilts. Q.S. Recs	E.B.H. Cunnington (ed.), *Records of the County of Wilts: Being Extracts from the Quarter Sessions Great Rolls of the Seventeenth Century* (Devizes, 1932)
Worc. Q.S. Recs	J.W. Willis Bund (ed.), *Worcestershire County Records: Calendar of the Quarter Sessions Papers*, Vol.1, 1591–1643 (Worcester: Worcestershire County Council, 1900)
WSHC	Wiltshire and Swindon History Centre
York Cast. Deps	James Raine (ed.), *Depositions from the Castle of York; Relating to Offences Committed in the Northern Counties in the Seventeenth Century* (Durham: Publications of the Surtees Society, 1861)

Introduction

'Bifil that in that seson on a day,
In Southwerk at the Tabard as I lay ...'
Geoffrey Chaucer, *Canterbury Tales* (c.1380–1400)

'They goe ten times to an Ale-house, before they goe once to
a Church.'
Thomas Young, *Englands Bane: or, The Description of
Drunkennesse* (1617)

'Tourists coming to England will have a number of cultural
signposts telling them what makes England 'England': high
on the list will be 'the pub' as a must-see ...'
Steven Earnshaw, *The Pub in Literature* (2000)[1]

From the starting point for Chaucer's pilgrims – and thus arguably for
English literature – through Thomas Young's complaint that it was 'too
much frequented by yong and old of all conditions', to its prominent place
on twenty-first century lists of 'what makes England "England"', the pub
has played a defining role in English social and cultural life. It has done
so over many centuries, and eulogies to its significance as an integral
strand in the fabric of English society often accord a sense of timeless-
ness to that role. But the place of the pub in English life is not timeless:
it has a history. Indeed, the term 'pub' only came into common usage in
the nineteenth century, as a shortened version of 'public house', which
itself was not used until the end of the seventeenth century. Before this
time England's drinking establishments were described as three distinct
institutions: inns, taverns and alehouses. This book charts the history of
the most common of these, the alehouse, during that formative period in
its history – between the middle of the sixteenth and end of the seven-

---

[1] Geoffrey Chaucer, *The Canterbury Tales*, in F.N. Robinson (ed.), *The Complete Works
of Geoffrey Chaucer*, 2nd edn (Oxford, 1976), General Prologue, ll.1–2; Thomas Young,
Englands Bane: or, The Description of Drunkennesse (London, 1617), sig. F; Steven
Earnshaw, *The Pub in Literature* (Manchester, 2000), p. 2.

teenth centuries – when it first came to achieve its centrality in the social and cultural lives of English men and women. There was nothing inevitable about this historical development. It involved a considerable struggle, but one from which the alehouse emerged as a key institution in early modern England. In large part this was because it facilitated one of the most important processes of social bonding in this society: participation in a form of recreation that contemporaries called 'good fellowship'.

The significance of the early modern period in the history of the alehouse is best brought out by sketching out developments in the period that preceded it. Whilst no dedicated studies of the alehouse exist for the medieval period, what evidence we do have indicates that the institution was not particularly prominent.[2] The years before 1500 constituted an important era in the history of the inn. These were large, purpose-built establishments whose main function was to provide lodging, stabling and refreshment for travellers – such as Chaucer's pilgrims – and they first began to appear in the twelfth and thirteenth centuries, and were fairly numerous by the fifteenth century, though mainly located in towns.[3] The tavern, whose main function was more explicitly as a drinking house, specialising in the retail of wine to the upper and middling ranks of society, appears in the historical record from the twelfth century onwards. In the thirteenth and fourteenth centuries many were substantial and prosperous establishments, run by prominent individuals within the community. These too, however, were mostly located in towns, and even throughout the early modern period their number remained small relative to inns and alehouses, and concentrated in London and larger urban centres.[4] The alehouse was the most humble of this triumvirate of drinking establishments. They retailed low-cost ale on a small scale, usually from the rooms of a private dwelling rather than purpose-built premises. They do not appear to have had substantial roots prior to the Black Death.[5] Although ale formed an essential

---

[2]   The most useful guides are Peter Clark, *The English Alehouse: A Social History, 1200–1830* (London, 1983), which contains a chapter on the period 1200–1500, and Judith Bennett, *Ale, Beer and Brewsters in England: Women's Work in a Changing World, 1300–1600* (Oxford, 1996), whose account of developments in the brewing industry also offers insights into ale-selling and alehouses.

[3]   Clark, *The English Alehouse*, p. 6.

[4]   *Ibid.*, pp. 11–12.

[5]   Historians often refer to the inns, taverns and alehouses of these periods of history as constituting a 'victualling hierarchy' arranged in this order to reflect their declining order of size and status. See Clark, *The English Alehouse*, pp. 5–15; James Brown, 'The

part of everyday diets for men, women and children, it was generally produced and consumed domestically. Any surplus might be sold to neighbours or passers-by – a branch or bush placed outside alerted potential customers – but such retailing was generally temporary, and 'out of doors', rather than involving on-site recreational drinking in the manner seen at taverns. In the two centuries between the Black Death and the Reformation this situation began to change as brewing became increasingly commercialised. Crucial here was the introduction of hops to the brewing process, which technically distinguished beer (hopped) from ale (unhopped), though the terms were often used interchangeably throughout the early modern period. Hops acted as a preservative, so whereas ale spoiled quickly and was thus produced in small batches, beer kept for longer, could be brewed in larger quantities, and transported over longer distances. This led to larger-scale commercial brewing operations, less domestic production, and an increased role for commercial retailing. Some of those who had sold ale occasionally began to do so on a more permanent basis as a business venture, though still generally retailing out of homes rather than purpose-built premises. The more permanent 'alehouse' began to get a foothold in English society.[6]

From this foothold in the late medieval period, the century or so between the Reformation and the Civil Wars saw the alehouse come to occupy a central place in early modern English society. Although we do not have evidence of their numbers from the earlier period, a government survey of drinking establishments in 1577 has allowed historians to estimate their frequency from this date forward. Already by this time there were around 24,000 alehouses in England, a ratio of roughly 1 to every 142 inhabitants – though this varied significantly across the country.[7] In the following half-century their total number is estimated to have doubled, and by the 1630s there were around 50,000. Numbers then

---

Landscape of Drink: Inns, Taverns and Alehouses in Early Modern Southampton' (Ph.D. diss., University of Warwick, 2008), *passim*; Paul Jennings, *The Local: A History of the English Pub* (Stroud, 2007), ch. 2. The concept is avoided here, as it is not clear that inns necessarily had a more exclusive clientele than taverns, though alehouses were certainly of a lower status and generally smaller than both. On the scarcity of alehouses before the Black Death see Clark, *The English Alehouse*, p. 23; Bennett, *Ale, Beer and Brewsters*, pp. 20–1.

6   This is a broad-brush picture of the key changes in this period. For more detail see Bennett, *Ale, Beer and Brewsters*, *passim*; Clark, *The English Alehouse*, ch. 2.

7   In Nottingham it has been estimated at 1:33; for York 1:69; for Somerset 1:279; for Cheshire 1:51. For these and estimates for other towns and counties see Clark, *The English Alehouse*, pp. 42–3.

levelled off, and estimates put the total at 58,000 by 1700. This pattern was to some extent driven by a period of major population growth, and over the longer period of 1540 to 1650 the population had itself doubled, from around 2.7 million to 5.2 million, before it too levelled off in the second half of the seventeenth century.[8] But the rate of increase in the number of alehouses outstripped the pace of population growth, and the ratios of alehouses to inhabitants accordingly decreased. By the 1630s the ratio was one alehouse to every 95 inhabitants nationally, down from 1 to 142 in 1577. By 1700 the ratio was closer to 1 to 87. In Shrewsbury the ratio fell from 1 to 70 in 1570, to 1 to 29 by 1630.[9] In Southampton there was a particularly concentrated 'leap' in alehouse numbers between 1595 and 1604, when the ratio went from 1 to 108 to 1 to 61.[10] As we will see in Chapter 1, this proliferation did not go unremarked by contemporaries, and both the central government and many local communities were both aware of, and often unsettled by, the growing prominence of the alehouse in the English landscape.

It is difficult to be precise about the causal process behind this rise of the alehouse in the second half of the sixteenth and first half of the seventeenth centuries, but there are a number of factors whose contributions are clear enough. The process of commercialisation in brewing continued apace, as it did in English society more generally in these years.[11] Increased levels of alcohol consumption do not, however, appear to have been a major factor, and if anything annual per capita consumption of ale and beer may actually have been falling in the early modern period. Although the available evidence from before 1684 – when

---

[8] E.A. Wrigley and R.S. Schofield, *The Population History of England 1541–1871: A Reconstruction* (London, 1981).

[9] Clark, *The English Alehouse*, pp. 44–7.

[10] James Brown, 'Alehouse Licensing and State Formation in Early Modern England', in Jonathan Herring, Ciaran Regan, Darin Weinberg and Phil Withington (eds), *Intoxicants and Society: Problematic Pleasures of Drugs and Alcohol* (Basingstoke, 2013), p. 120. In the Lancashire towns of Prescot, Clitheroe, Manchester, Liverpool and Wigan the seventeenth-century ratios have been estimated to have ranged between 1:15 to 1:78: see W.J. King, 'Regulation of Alehouses in Stuart Lancashire: An Example of Discretionary Administration of the Law', *Transactions of the Historic Society of Lancashire & Cheshire* 129 (1980 for 1979), p. 41. Thirty south Lancashire villages surveyed in 1647 contained on average 1:57; twenty-five Essex villages in 1644 had a ratio of 1:95: see Keith Wrightson, 'Alehouses, Order and Reformation in Rural England, 1590–1660', in Eileen Yeo and Stephen Yeo (eds), *Popular Culture and Class Conflict 1590–1914: Explorations in the History of Labour and Leisure* (Brighton, 1981), p. 4.

[11] See Craig Muldrew, *The Economy of Obligation: The Culture of Credit and Social Relations in Early Modern England* (Basingstoke, 1998), ch. 1.

Customs and Excise records begin – is far from compelling, the best estimates yet made suggest that in the fourteenth and fifteenth centuries
people consumed on average eight pints of ale per day, but this gradu-
ally fell to a figure closer to two pints by the end of the seventeenth
century.[12] The proliferation of alehouses may have had little to do with
a growing thirst for beer, and rather more to do with increased demand
for a site of communal recreation at a time when other alternatives were
coming under attack. The late medieval period could boast a rich culture
of communal feasts and festivals that were intimately connected with the
church, and these recreational events often involved the consumption of
large quantities of ale. Especially brewed for the purpose, this ale was
then sold to provide funds for church infrastructure or alms for the poor,
and such communal drinkings were often situated in the churchyard,
or in church houses that were specially constructed to host communal
social events.[13] After the Reformation such events came under hostile
attack from Protestant reformers, who had some degree of success in
reducing their occurrence and in effecting a greater separation between
'sacred' and 'profane' space, forcing those festivals that did remain out
of the churchyard.[14] The dissolution of the monasteries was also significant, removing a traditional supplier of hospitality for travellers at a
time when high inflation was causing growing landlessness and labour
migration, a process which also provided plenty of would-be alehousekeepers looking for a means of staving off poverty.[15] Taken together,
these processes stimulated the emergence of the alehouse as a crucial
supplier of more than just ale: it could provide incomes, cheap lodgings,
and a much-needed space for recreation within the local community. As
such, it came by the seventeenth century to rank alongside the house-

[12] A.L. Martin, *Alcohol, Violence and Disorder in Traditional Europe* (Kirksville, MO,
2009), pp. 61–72; see also J.A. Spring and D.H. Buss, 'Three Centuries of Alcohol in
the British Diet', *Nature* 270 (1977), pp. 567–72.

[13] For the richness of late medieval festive culture see Ronald Hutton's classic account,
The Rise and Fall of Merry England: The Ritual Year, 1400–1700 (Oxford, 1994); on the
role of communal recreation in local systems of charity see Judith Bennett, 'Conviviality
and Charity in Medieval and Early Modern England', *Past and Present* 134 (1992), pp.
19–41; on 'church houses' see Beat Kümin, *The Shaping of a Community: The Rise and
Reformation of the English Parish, c.1400–1560* (Aldershot, 1996), p. 60.

[14] For these attacks and their success see Hutton, *Rise and Fall of Merry England*, esp.
pp. 260–2. For an example of the 'privatisation' of church houses after the Reformation
see Eamon Duffy, *The Voices of Morebath: Reformation and Rebellion in an English Village*
(London, 2001), pp. 125–6, 146.

[15] On the role of monasteries in providing hospitality see Felicity Heal, *Hospitality in
Early Modern England* (Oxford, 1990), ch. 6.

hold, the church, the law courts, the manor and the parish, as one of the key institutions that did so much to structure the lives of early modern English men and women. Apart from the household it was arguably the institution most directly and regularly encountered by the majority of villagers and townspeople.

It is with the emergent recreational function of the alehouse that this book is, above all else, concerned. Practices of sociability are central to understanding the character and development of all societies. Decisions regarding with whom to voluntarily associate beyond the contexts of work and the home are central to the development of social bonds, social networks, collective identities and forms of community. Such communities can be structured by institutions – a medieval manor, an early modern parish, a modern school, a tribe – that necessitate practices of association that are relatively or even exclusively involuntary, but many more are forged through unconstrained sociability: through the active choice to spend time in the company of others. In an age before social media, or in societies and cultures with low levels of literacy that preclude engagement in networks of letter writers, physical co-presence and the availability of suitable sites in which to gather were essential to such forms of voluntary association. Voluntary association could take on a formal, even quasi-institutional, character – clubs, societies, religious congregations, guilds and unions – and historians have, of course, dedicated considerable attention to the formation of such types of purposeful interaction. But less formal, and especially recreational, practices of sociability are ubiquitous and arguably more important. Their informality, and their status as 'leisure', tends to mean that they are understood to be less purposeful, and less historically consequential. They have certainly received far less attention from historians. Yet some of the most potent bonds in any society, those that motivate people's decisions and actions, develop from choices made about with whom time should be spent informally, and for pleasure. These bonds and these choices might, of course, overlap with connections made through more formal or involuntary forms of association – they often do – but this should not detract from their significance: rather, forms of recreational sociability are regularly an expression of, and serve to enhance and reinforce, those forms of community and the social bonds that individuals feel most deeply. The study of recreational sociability – of which alehouse sociability, or 'good fellowship', was one of the most regular and widespread forms in early modern England – promises to reveal a great deal about the motivations and allegiances of historical actors, both individual and collective.

This book is not then just a history of an institution during a key

6

period of its development. It is also a history of an important social practice. And it connects these histories to wider historical processes. Indeed, drinking houses have recently been described by one of their leading historians as 'microcosms of early modern society' whose study can shed light on a number of the period's central developments and characteristics, and the same can be said for the practices of sociability that they hosted.[16] The process of state formation, the development of a 'public sphere', the nature of popular politics, the operation of gender norms, the formation of social identities, the growing polarisation between social classes, and the changing basis of notions of community: all of these are implicated in the analysis that follows. The book seeks, then, to make contributions to a number of strands of existing historical literature, but its agenda is perhaps best illuminated by considering it as an attempt to bring together the two main traditions of writing about the history of drinking in early modern England. The earlier of these – what we might term 'the social history of the alehouse' tradition – constitutes a body of work published in the first half of the 1980s, of which Peter Clark's monograph *The English Alehouse* is the most significant and enduring.[17] The authors of these works – influenced by a growing interest in the social history of early modern England that was turning its attention to administrative and legal archives – identified a significant body of material that reflected attempts by the early modern English authorities to regulate and police the dramatically growing number of alehouses. They used these records to examine the role of the alehouse in society, focusing on its functions, services and clientele, and devoting special attention to what the regulatory campaign against the alehouse could reveal about social relations and even class conflict: their conclusions will be examined in more detail in Chapters 1 and 2. After this first burst of serious academic interest in the alehouse in the early 1980s, very little work on the institution followed in the 1990s – in part, perhaps, because Clark's extensive research had seemed to put the relevant issues to bed, though it was certainly not his intention to close the field down – until

---

[16] Beat Kümin, *Drinking Matters: Public Houses and Social Exchange in Early Modern Central Europe* (Basingstoke, 2007), pp. 3–4.

[17] Clark, *The English Alehouse*; Peter Clark, 'The Alehouse and The Alternative Society', in Donald Pennington and Keith Thomas (eds), *Puritans and Revolutionaries: Essays in Seventeenth-Century History Presented to Christopher Hill* (Oxford, 1978), pp. 47–72; Wrightson, 'Alehouses, Order and Reformation'; Anthony Fletcher, *Reform in the Provinces: The Government of Stuart England* (London, 1986), ch. 8; S.K. Roberts, 'Alehouses, Brewing and Government under the Early Stuarts', *Southern History* 2 (1980), pp. 45–71; King, 'Regulation of Alehouses'.

a broader 'cultural turn' in the study of history raised a new set of questions which reignited interest in early modern drinking.[18] The focus of a new 'cultural history of drinking' approach that has emerged in the past decade has been less on drinking places and more on drinking practices, and the concern has been to recover the meanings and values that were associated with sociable and recreational drinking, and what this can tell us about early modern identities and cultural norms.[19] The source base for such approaches also represents a shift from the earlier tradition, with literary sources – and literary scholars – coming to occupy a central place in recent analyses, alongside an intensified interest in a particular type of legal record relatively neglected by those earlier historians who were primarily interested in regulation – witness testimony containing accounts of drinking practices and rituals.[20]

This book combines elements of both traditions to produce a history of the alehouse, and of the sociability that took place within it, that is

[18] The lull in interest in the alehouse may also owe something to a wider process in which 'the history of pleasure and recreation . . . become increasingly removed from the academic mainstream', itself a result of powerful critiques warning of 'the real danger of over politicising leisure as an arena of struggle'. See Emma Griffin, 'Popular Culture in Industrialising England', *The Historical Journal* 45 (2002), pp. 619–35, quote at p. 620; Gareth Stedman Jones, *Languages of Class: Studies in English Working Class History, 1832–1982* (Cambridge, 1983), pp. 76–90, quote at p. 88.

[19] See for instance Phil Withington, 'Company and Sociability in Early Modern England', *Social History* 32 (2007), pp. 291–307; Alexandra Shepard, '"Swil-bols and Tos-pots": Drink Culture and Male Bonding in England, c.1560–1640', in Laura Gowing, Michael Hunter and Miri Rubin (eds), *Love, Friendship and Faith in Europe, 1300–1800* (Basingstoke, 2005), pp. 110–30. This development in early modern English studies has been preceded and inspired by important works in a similar vein in European contexts: see in particular Thomas Brennan's pioneering *Public Drinking and Popular Culture in Eighteenth-Century Paris* (Princeton, 1988) and 'Towards the Cultural History of Alcohol in France', *Journal of Social History* 23 (1989), pp. 71–92; also B. Ann Tlusty, *Bacchus and Civic Order: The Culture of Drink in Early Modern Germany* (Charlottesville, 2001). For more on the development of the European historiography see the essays in, and introduction to, Beat Kümin and B. Ann Tlusty (eds), *The World of the Tavern: Public Houses in Early Modern Europe* (Aldershot, 2002). The most important recent contribution on this area is Kümin, *Drinking Matters*. See also A.L. Martin, *Alcohol, Sex, and Gender in Late Medieval and Early Modern Europe* (Basingstoke, 2001); Martin, *Alcohol, Violence and Disorder*; Mack Holt (ed.), *Alcohol: A Social and Cultural History* (New York, 2006).

[20] For the importance of literary approaches to drinking culture in this period see the essays in Adam Smyth (ed.), *A Pleasing Sinne: Drink and Conviviality in Seventeenth-Century England* (Cambridge, 2004); and also Phil Withington, 'Renaissance Drinking Cultures and Popular Print', in Herring *et al.* (eds), *Intoxicants and Society*, pp. 135–52; and the references in Chapter 3 below. For depositions see in particular Withington, 'Company and Sociability'.

genuinely social *and* cultural. It shares 'the social history of the alehouse' tradition's concern with the regulatory campaign that was fought against the alehouse, and argues that it is important for cultural historians interested in the meanings of drinking practices not to lose sight of the fact that for many in early modern English society the right to participate in recreational drinking was highly contested. Where it goes beyond existing accounts of the campaign against the alehouse is in emphasising that to a considerable extent this was a struggle fought out precisely over this right: whereas older histories tended to portray the motivation behind alehouse-going as the straightforward pursuit of narcotic release, this account shows that the popularity of the alehouse owed more to the attractions of sociability than to the physiological effects of alcohol. It was the fact that the alehouse facilitated a meaningful and important form of social interaction that rallied many contemporaries to defend it from regulatory attacks. Indeed, it will be argued here that the social history of the alehouse tradition underestimated the force of this opposition to regulatory campaigns. Early historians of alehouses tended to see the history of these institutions and their patrons as a passive one, in which they 'simply responded to larger-scale processes of change' rather than influenced them, or were 'forced on the defensive' and subjected to the assertion of the 'cultural hegemony' of their opponents.[21] This account accords rather more historical agency to alehouses and their patrons, and argues not only that they fought hard against their opponents, but that through doing so they ultimately won a place for the alehouse and for recreational drinking at the centre of English social and cultural life, a victory that represents a considerable historical achievement.

This development can only be understood by also drawing on elements of the recent 'cultural history of drinking' approach. Through an examination of the meanings contemporaries attached to recreational and sociable drinking in alehouses, and of the role of such 'good fellowship' in the formation and maintenance of social identities and bonds, we can come to appreciate how and why the alehouse was able to take on such significance and centrality in early modern England. This book therefore combines analysis of the records of alehouse regulation with an examination of the literary and depositional sources that have come to form the raw materials of recent cultural histories of drinking. The argument advanced here nonetheless makes some important departures from

---

[21] Clark, 'The Alehouse and the Alternative Society', p. 67; Wrightson, 'Alehouses, Order and Reformation', p. 20.

this emerging body of work, especially in turning away from the recent emphasis on relatively elite social groups, on the literate and educated, on men, and on those living in major urban centres.[22] Its primary focus is, rather, on the recovery of the importance of alehouse sociability to the 80% to 90% of the population – male and female – who lived outside of early modern England's handful of large cities, and who fell comfortably within the ranks of the 'non-elite'. The argument advanced here is situated much more obviously in the tradition of 'history from below'.[23]

This agenda underpins the decision to focus by and large on alehouses, which were far more prevalent and less exclusive than either inns or taverns in this period. They were still generally, as they had been in the late medieval period, run out of the rooms of people's homes. Indeed it was individuals, rather than premises in which they lived or worked, that were licensed to sell ale and beer. They were generally humble buildings, but there was some variation in their size. Evidence from probate inventories – a source type that probably over-represents those at the larger, wealthier end of the scale – suggests the average alehouse contained five rooms, including lofts, cellars, outbuildings and lodging rooms. Although some ran into double figures, and most seem to have offered a choice of separate chambers to drinkers, many would have been run out of a single room. Furniture was rudimentary – a few tables and benches – but the atmosphere was enhanced by pasting printed broadsides to the walls, and a fire for customers to warm themselves beside was an essential feature.[24] There were two main types of ale or beer for sale, which could be taken away or consumed on the premises: the small beer that was consumed by all men, women and children as part of their diet, which it has been estimated had an alcohol content in the region of 2%; and the strong

---

[22] For a focus on educated, elite, urban men see, for instance, Phil Withington, 'Intoxicants and Society in Early Modern England', *The Historical Journal* 54:3 (2011), pp. 631–57; Michelle O'Callaghan, *The English Wits: Literature and Sociability in Early Modern England* (Cambridge, 2007). Other work does not necessarily focus on all of these categories together, but in both the English and European contexts there is a tendency to focus exclusively on one category from a list of social elites, men, or urban areas. The intention here is to complement, rather than to dismiss or necessarily critique, the work of those whose focus is on more socially exclusive or urban contexts.

[23] For the recent revival of interest in the 'history from below' tradition see Mark Hailwood and Brodie Waddell (eds), 'The Future of History from Below: An Online Symposium' (2013) <http://manyheadedmonster.wordpress.com/history-from-below/> [accessed 1 May 2014].

[24] For more on the material culture of alehouses see Brown, 'The Landscape of Drink', ch. 2; Clark, *The English Alehouse*, ch. 4. For the estimates of the average numbers of rooms see Brown, p. 59; Clark, p. 65.

beer that was consumed by those engaged in hard labour, and for recreation, which could range from anywhere between 5% and 12% depending on how much malt the brewer chose to use.[25] Some fairly basic food, and lodgings, had also become part of the package of services offered by the alehouse as it developed into a more permanent institution in the early modern period, and this range of services will be discussed at greater length in Chapter 1.

This institution, and the recreational sociability it facilitated, lies at the heart of this study, but the lines between alehouses and the other types of drinking establishments were not always clear cut to contemporaries. The boundary between a larger or well-established alehouse and a smaller rural inn in particular could be blurred: we will see in Chapter 2 that some alehousekeepers claimed, for legal reasons, to be running inns, and the comment of a judge at the end of our period, that 'if an inn degenerate to an alehouse, by suffering disorderly tippling . . . it shall be deemed as such', shows that the tone of behaviour within an establishment could also muddy the waters on its precise status.[26] Moreover, the typology of drinking establishments is not always precisely stated in archival records. Many drinking establishments are simply referred to by a name, such as 'the signe of the Nag's Head', or 'the Red Lyon', without specifying whether this is an inn, tavern or alehouse. In other cases records might make reference to drinking at a site referred to simply by the name of its occupant, such as 'Widow Barrington's house', where it is not always clear if this place was operating as an alehouse or not. A case from Nettlecombe, Somerset, from 1663, highlights the porous lines between private dwellings and alehouses, with two drinkers describing their call 'into the dwelling house of ... Chrystable Baker who kepeth an alehouse there by lycence'.[27] In practice, then, the archival record does not always sort the sites of alcohol consumption neatly into inns, taverns, alehouses and private dwellings. The approach adopted here has been to combine a common-sense approach with an inclination to be inclusive: mentions of the sale of ale, for instance, are taken to distinguish an alehouse context from an instance of private sociability in an individual's home; reference to the presence of an 'innkeeper' rather than an 'alehousekeeper' has been taken to demarcate an inn from an

---

[25] For these estimates of strengths see Craig Muldrew, *Food, Energy and the Creation of Industriousness: Work and Material Culture in Agrarian England, 1550–1780* (Cambridge, 2011), p. 80.

[26] See Earnshaw, *The Pub in Literature*, p. 5.

[27] SHC, Q/SR/104/5.

alehouse in cases where this is not stated; and sites of drinking where the supporting evidence offers no clear clues as to their precise status have generally been included in the analysis. The distinctions between drinking establishments followed by this book are not dissimilar then to those made by early modern contemporaries: important, but not absolute.

If the institutional focus of the book is narrowed onto the alehouse, its geographical focus is a broad one: England. London – whose size relative to any other settlement in this period gave it, and its landscape of drinking establishments, a unique character – is excluded. Other large cities – York, Norwich, Newcastle, Bristol, Exeter – feature occasionally, but the principal focus is on the settlements in which the vast majority of the population lived the majority of their lives, ranging from 'country towns' – at the top end, county centres with populations of up to 5,000 or so; at the lower end, market towns which could have as few as 600 inhabitants – to rural villages and hamlets.[28] Evidence is drawn from a wide range of counties and boroughs, though Somerset, Wiltshire, Cheshire and Essex for counties, and Reading and Nottingham for boroughs, feature most prominently as these were the main focus of documentary research. The analysis avoids ironing out local variations and peculiarities – many are highlighted in what follows – but the overall aim is to delineate the broader contours in the history of alehouses and alehouse recreation in England in this period within which localised patterns took shape.[29] Chronologically, the book forwards an argument about the long-term development of the alehouse from the medieval period through into the eighteenth century, although in practice the discussion of the years before c.1550 and after c.1700 are bookends, based on a reading of the work of others, designed to supplement an analysis of primary material drawn from a front-heavy 'long' seventeenth century. It was the years between 1550 and 1700 that saw an explosion in alehouse numbers, the pursuit of an ambitious national legislative and regulatory campaign, the development of new genres of print that were intimately connected to drinking culture, and a relative absence of competition from alternative

[28] On this categorisation of early modern towns see Peter Clark and Paul Slack, *English Towns in Transition, 1500–1700* (Oxford, 1976).

[29] For recent studies that adopt a local focus see Brown, 'The Landscape of Drink'; Phil Withington, 'Intoxicants and the Early Modern City', in Steve Hindle, Alexandra Shepard and John Walter (eds), *Remaking English Society: Social Relations and Social Change in Early Modern England* (Woodbridge, 2013), pp. 135–63; Matthew Jackson, 'Cultures of Drink: A Comparative Case Study of Early Modern Bristol and Bordeaux' (Ph.D. diss., University of Warwick, in progress).

sites of communal recreation. It was in these years that the alehouse took on a centrality in English social, cultural and even political life that it had not enjoyed before, and arguably neither it nor its successor the pub has done so to the same extent since.

What follows is divided into two sections, each of two chapters. The first section, 'The Alehouse in the Community', assesses the services and functions that alehouses provided to their host communities, and how 'battles' over their appropriate role reflect social and power relations both in those communities and in society as a whole. Chapter 1 examines the legislative and regulatory framework that was developed in this period to police the role played by the alehouse, and argues that whilst alehouses were widely accepted as essential institutions, they were officially prohibited from facilitating recreational drinking. Chapter 2 explores the extent to which this framework was enforced, and resisted, on the ground, and argues that in practice the relationship between the authorities and the alehouse was rather more ambivalent than allowed for in existing historiographical accounts. It will be suggested that this ambivalence had much to do with the role the alehouse played in facilitating recreational drinking. The second section, 'The Community in the Alehouse', focuses on the nature and character of that recreational drinking. Chapter 3 examines a particular type of literary source that was intimately connected to alehouse culture, the broadside ballad, to reconstruct the key meanings and values that contemporaries associated with what they called 'good fellowship'. Chapter 4 draws on depositional and diary material to produce an account of the quotidian practice of alehouse recreation, and uses an analysis of the patterns of who drank with whom to argue that 'good fellowship' was an activity that served to both express and reinforce meaningful social bonds between those who participated in it together, and that it was from this fact that the alehouse drew its importance in the lives of early modern English men and women. The conclusion considers the significance of these findings for the way we understand a number of the central processes and features often associated with the history of early modern England, and reflects on how the history of alehouses and good fellowship developed into the eighteenth century. Ultimately the book aims to demonstrate the significance of the history of drinking to the history of early modern England. The alehouse was not a place where historical actors went for a brief hiatus from the historical stage. Rather, gatherings around the alebench both reflected and influenced the character of society and wider processes of historical change. As such, they demand our attention.

Part One

The Alehouse in the Community

1

'True and Principal Uses'
The Role and Regulation of Alehouses

John Noyes was a prominent figure in the early-seventeenth-century economic and political spheres of the Wiltshire town of Calne. He was a clothier – a trader in the town's main commodity, woollen cloth – and served as a Member of Parliament for the borough in 1604, and between 1599 and 1630 was several times Burgess Steward, the chief executive of the town's corporation.[1] In 1612, he took his turn to act as town constable, a role that made him responsible for the keeping of the peace. Here, like so many of the office-holders in the towns and villages of early-seventeenth-century England, Noyes perceived the main impediment to his task to be the disorder emanating from local alehouses.[2] At the meeting of the Wiltshire quarter sessions in April 1612, the court responsible for issuing and revoking alehouse licenses, Noyes and his fellow constable John Killinge made a plea to their superiors, the county magistrates, for assistance in subduing these noisome institutions:

> We desyre to have the nomber of Alehowses to be diminished in the Towne of Calne for they doe all brewe a[nd] vie who maye brewe the strongest Ale and thither do resorte all the great drinkers bothe of the Towne and Countrie to spende theyer tyme in idleness and theyer monie in excessivie drinkinge.

The challenge of policing the town's alehouses was made more acute by an uncooperative disposition on the part of their patrons, who

---

1 VCH, *Wiltshire*, V, pp. 111–32; A.W. Mabbs (ed.), *Guild Stewards' Book of the Borough of Calne, 1561–1688* (Devizes, 1953), pp. xxi–xxii.
2 The prominence of alehouse regulation within the portfolio of duties of office-holders in this period can be seen in the 1594 Leicester Mayoral Oath, which bound the officeholder to the duty of 'the repression and putting downe of ... alehowses': *Leic. Boro. Recs*, III, p. 302.

Beinge partly drunke and halfe mad, no officer can well iudge whether they be drunke yea or no, and therefore can not punishe [them] according to the Lawe, and all me[n] for the most p[ar]te love these cupp companions so well, that no man will take uppon him to be a sworne witnes against any drunkard.

The suggested remedy was to target ale-sellers, and request them to lower the strength of their offerings:

It were greatly to be wisshed that all Ale sellers might be compelled to make theyer Ale a great deale smaller and to sell a full Quart for a pennie, otherwise this sinne of drunkennes will never be avoyded men are so bewitched w[i]th the sweetness of stronge Lycoure.[3]

This example represents just one drop in an ocean of archival material produced by the tensions surrounding the proliferation and role of alehouses. Indeed, so prominent were such concerns in the late sixteenth and early seventeenth centuries that historians have argued that 'no social institution caused more heart-searching and dispute in Stuart England than the alehouse', and have described a 'battle' over the alehouse that was 'one of the most significant social dramas of the age'.[4] It was a battle in which John Noyes and many similar local office-holders were joined, and one in which the lines of conflict have been seen by historians as intimately related to deeper fissures in early modern society: struggles over the role of drinking houses are thought by historians to 'mirror nearly all the tensions of their time'.[5] But what tensions, exactly, should we see reflected in pitched battles such as that between John Noyes and the 'cup companions' of Calne? What were the battle-lines over which this great social drama was fought out?

The historiography of the early seventeenth century suggests a number of major fault-lines in this society which have served as frameworks for interpreting the struggle over the alehouse. 'Recreation', for instance, is thought to have become at this time 'an issue which divided men, forcing them to take a stand for either traditionalism or reform'.[6] In a compelling account, David Underdown situated the issue of recreation

---

[3] WSHC, 1612/E/177.

[4] Fletcher, *Reform in the Provinces*, p. 229; Keith Wrightson, *English Society, 1580–1680* (London, 1982; 2nd edn, Bury St Edmunds, 2003), p. 175. This and all subsequent references are to the second edition.

[5] Kümin and Tlusty, eds, *The World of the Tavern*, p. 11.

[6] Robert Malcolmson, *Popular Recreations in English Society, 1700–1850* (Cambridge, 1973), p. 13.

at the centre of a 'cultural conflict', one that pitted the proponents of a traditional, communal culture centred on festivals, church ales and revels, on the one hand, against a new, post-Reformation reforming impulse, deeply hostile to this festive culture, and closely associated with the 'hotter sorts of Protestants', or 'Puritans', on the other.[7] The battle over the alehouse does not, however, fit quite so neatly into this model of conflict over popular recreations between 'reformers' and 'traditionalists'. Whereas traditional recreations such as dancing around the Maypole divided the aristocracy, gentry, clergy, parish notables and local officials of early modern England amongst themselves – a cultural division that Underdown saw as finding its ultimate expression in Civil War allegiances – historians have tended to see these groups as united by their shared hostility to the alehouse. If traditional festive sociability had its Puritan opponents amongst the upper and middling sorts, it could also count some of their number as loyal supporters – not least James I and Charles I. The alehouse, by contrast, rarely found such friends in high places, and found its enemies across the cultural and religious divide. Peter Clark, for instance, identified a 'broad consensus of opinion' among the middling and upper ranks of society that alehouses were a 'dangerous force' that fostered 'opposition to the established religious and political order'.[8] Likewise, Keith Wrightson identified an alliance between magistrates, ministers, and those 'better sorts' within the local community who often acted as parish officials – minor gentlemen, yeomen and substantial craftsmen – which 'crystallised around the focal issue of controlling the alehouses', and whose collective antipathy to the institution came close to a 'militant hostility'.[9] Condemnations of alehouses by magistrates and ministers as 'nests of Satan' that fuelled 'the horrible and loathsome sin of drunkenness' are familiar to all students of early modern England. These sentiments are epitomised in Sir Richard Grosvenor's 1625 denunciation of alehouses as

> The very bane of this countrey; a receptacle for knaves and harlotts; the robbers counsell chamber; the beggars nurserye; the drunkard's academye; the theeves sanctuarye. Here are you deprived of the obeydience of your sonnes, of the duetye of your servants.[10]

---

7 David Underdown, *Revel, Riot and Rebellion: Popular Politics and Culture in England* (Oxford, 1985), ch. 3.

8 Clark, 'The Alehouse and the Alternative Society', p. 48.

9 Wrightson, 'Alehouses, Order and Reformation', pp. 18, 21.

10 Richard Cust and Peter Lake, 'Sir Richard Grosvenor and the Rhetoric of Magistracy', *Bulletin of the Institute of Historical Research* 54 (1981), p. 45.

'Puritan' zeal doubtless provided some of the impetus for such attacks on the alehouse, and Grosvenor was himself a staunch Calvinist. But on the issue of alehouses historians have viewed 'the hotter sort of Protestantism' as complementing a widely shared concern with 'order' amongst all stripes of the middling and upper ranks of early modern society, rather than the divisive creed it represented on the issue of more traditional communal recreations.[11] It is important to keep in mind, therefore, a distinction between traditional 'churchyard' recreations and those centred on the alehouse; a distinction that was certainly meaningful to contemporaries engaged in 'battles' over both. If churchyard recreations were for Underdown a source of vertical cultural and religious conflict in early-seventeenth-century England, for Clark and Wrightson the battle over the alehouse was more distinctly one of horizontal divisions and even class conflict.

If the enemies of the alehouse have been portrayed as a broad alliance of the upper and middling ranks of early modern English society, what has been written about those whom we can count as its supporters and patrons? For Peter Clark, the alehouse was an institution 'run by the poor for the poor', the main appeal of which was its offer of 'alcoholic release' to the downtrodden: he depicted it as a hub for poor men for whom it facilitated 'the desperate pursuit of drunken oblivion', serving the alcohol that offered them 'an anaesthetic against a harsh, oppressive world and their own route march of misery'.[12] There was more to the appeal of the alehouse than this, of course, and several of its historians have sought to emphasise that it was not simply the drink – the bewitching strong liquor that John Noyes identified – that attracted customers, but rather the fact that it offered a wide range of other services. Indeed, alehouses have recently been described as multi-functional institutions that played an indispensable role in their host communities. They offered rudimentary lodging to travellers – sometimes no more than a place on an ale-bench, or a bed shared with the alehousekeeper and alewife. Many provided food – ranging from bread and cheese, pies and pasties, to broiled herring suppers, or the service of cooking 'bring your own' food for customers who lacked their own facilities. Alehouses were also crucial to the local poor in their retail of 'take-away' small beer to those who

---

[11] For Grosvenor's Calvinism see *ODNB*; on the campaign against the alehouse as part of a widespread concern with 'order' in early modern England see Wrightson, *English Society*, pp. 175–8.

[12] Clark, 'The Alehouse and the Alternative Society', p. 53; Clark, *The English Alehouse*, pp. 126, 215, 111.

did not have the means to brew at home. Beyond these subsistence functions alehouses acted as important centres of economic exchange where people traded goods, sealed business deals, or enquired about available work. They could act as pawnbrokers and provide a source of credit to the local poor, serve as relatively safe settings for courtship, play host to various rites of passage celebrations, and function as a neutral venue for the amicable settling of disputes between neighbours. Not to mention, of course, providing a public space for more routine forms of recreational and sociable drinking – a role to which we will return at length.[13]

Catering for this impressive array of local needs has helped to earn the alehouse a reputation amongst a number of its historians as 'an essential village institution', that was 'anything but marginal', and which occupied a 'central place in the village society of pre-industrial England'.[14] This emphasis on the integral place of the alehouse in the fabric of local communities has also been used to call into question the notion that a broad alliance of the middling and upper ranks of society were 'militantly hostile' to it. Anthony Fletcher has instead argued that the 'strong sense that the alehouse was an essential village institution was often promoted by substantial parishioners and was usually accepted by JPs'.[15] Likewise, Beat Kümin has recently encouraged historians to recognise the widespread ambivalence of early modern attitudes towards the functions of drinking establishments, suggesting that a complex mix of both negative and positive reactions to their role was more characteristic than 'militant hostility', even amongst the upper and middling ranks of society.[16] Indeed, we might note here that John Noyes, for all his concern with Calne's alehouses, called for their number to be diminished, rather than eradicated, and for ale to be brewed 'a great deal smaller', rather than prohibited. There was a grudging acceptance here of some role for alehouses in the community.

---

13 On the range of services provided by the alehouse see Wrightson , 'Alehouses, Order and Reformation', pp. 1–11; Clark, *The English Alehouse*, esp. ch. 6; Fletcher, *Reform in the Provinces*, esp. pp. 229–52; Kümin, *Drinking Matters*, esp. chs 3–4; Brown, 'The Landscape of Drink', ch. 4; Sara Pennell, '"Great quantities of gooseberry pye and baked clod of beef": Victualling and Eating Out in Early Modern London', in Paul Griffiths and Mark Jenner (eds), *Londonopolis: Essays in the Cultural and Social History of Early Modern London c.1500–c.1750* (Manchester, 2000), pp. 228–59.

14 Fletcher, *Reform in the Provinces*, p. 234; Kümin, *Drinking Matters*, p. 31; Wrightson, 'Alehouses, Order and Reformation', p. 1.

15 Fletcher, *Reform in the Provinces*, p. 234.

16 Kümin, *Drinking Matters*, p. 126.

This brief summary of existing explorations of the 'battle' over the role of the alehouse in early modern English society leaves a certain tension unresolved: it presents us with a broad alliance of magistrates, ministers and 'better-sort' parishioners who were both militantly hostile toward, and yet generally accepting of, the alehouses within their communities. It may be that we accept that many of those within these groups held contradictory positions on alehouses, and it may be that there were some important differences of opinion within this very broad swathe of society: we will revisit these issues as we progress. Here, though, I want to offer a third explanation that helps to resolve this tension by focusing in particular on the way opposition to, and indeed support for, alehouses was manifested in the regulatory framework that governed the licensing and operation of the institution. The argument that follows confirms ambivalence in the attitudes of the middling and upper ranks towards the role of the alehouse when its various functions are taken as a whole, but at the same time finds unequivocal attitudes when we dissect the role of the alehouse into its component functions. A useful way of disaggregating the 'bewildering array' of alehouse services has recently been provided by Beat Kümin, who suggests that the various social, economic, political and cultural uses of drinking houses cluster around two core functions: 'Public houses catered for the material and physical needs of publicans and patrons on the one hand, and facilitated social interaction on the other.'[17] An acceptance that the alehouse should provide the first of these functions is unanimous within the regulatory framework. The second function, on the other hand – and especially the facilitation of sociable, recreational drinking – is not accepted as a legitimate alehouse service. In other words, it is alehouse sociability, rather than the alehouse *per se*, that was targeted by the official regulatory campaign. To understand the struggle against the alehouse we need to recognise it, therefore, as first and foremost a struggle against alehouse sociability.

The next section of this chapter demonstrates that the legislation passed in the early years of the seventeenth century was underpinned by this intention to restrict all alehouses from facilitating recreational drinking, a development that was a departure from earlier efforts to only target particularly disorderly alehouses. The following section examines two forms of quarter sessions business: the presentments of alehouse offences by local officials, and petitions sent to the magistrates calling for specific alehouses to be licensed or suppressed. This section argues

[17] Kümin, *Drinking Matters*, p. 85.

that those members of the local middling sort that played a key part in the enforcement of national laws 'on the ground' recognised this distinction between legitimate and illegitimate alehouse services. The final two sections look at how this attack on alehouse sociability was founded on an inherent tension in the way the role of the alehouse was understood: its legitimacy derived from the essential role it played in the domestic economy of the poor, but its intimate association with poverty created considerable anxiety both about its legitimate patrons and about its appropriate proprietors.

Legislation

The earliest piece of national legislation to concern itself with the selling of ale dates from 1266, when the Assize of Bread and Ale was introduced.[18] This created stipulations on the price, measure, and quality of ale sold, and was exercised under the jurisdiction of local manor and borough courts. The principal purpose of the assize was to police fraudulent practices on the part of retailers, who were fined for offences, but the regularity with which many offenders were presented suggests that such fines acted less as a deterrent and more as an informal licensing fee that underpinned an 'embryonic licensing system'.[19] Nonetheless, there were no national legislative restrictions on who could sell ale, or how they ran their houses, until an Act of Parliament of 1495 granted authority over ale-selling to the Justices of the Peace, empowering them to 'reject and put away' ale-sellers wherever they thought it convenient, and to take surety from them for their 'good behaviour'.[20] This marked a shift from the regulation of *what* was sold to restrictions on *who* was permitted to sell it. This reflected a growing concern with a perceived link between alehouses and disorder, and in particular criminal activity, which found

---

18 51 Henry III c. 6.

19 Judith Hunter, 'English Inns, Taverns, Alehouses and Brandy Shops: The Legislative Framework, 1495–1797', in Beat Kümin and B. Ann Tlusty (eds), *The World of the Tavern: Public Houses in Early Modern Europe* (Aldershot, 2002), p. 65. For examples of assize amercements acting as 'licensing fees' see A.F.C. Baber (ed.), *Court Rolls of the Manor of Bromsgrove and King's Norton, 1491–1504* (Kineton: Worcestershire Historical Society, 1963), p. 103; David Noy (ed.), *Winslow Manor Court Books, 1327–1377, 1423–1460* (Aylesbury: Buckinghamshire Record Society, 2011), p. xxiv. King, 'Regulation of Alehouses', pp. 31–46.

20 11 Henry VII c. 2.

full expression in the preamble to the 1552 Act that introduced the first mandatory licensing system:

> For as much as intolerable hurts and troubles to the Commonwealth of this Realm doth daily grow and increase through such abuses and disorders as are had and used in common alehouses and tippling houses.[21]

Justices of the Peace had been granted discretion to close alehouses by the 1495 Act, but this new measure stipulated that all alehouses must have a licence. Such licences were to be granted at meetings of the quarter sessions, or by two magistrates acting together outside of sessions; were to be limited at the Justices' discretion to a number deemed appropriate to serve a given area; and licensees were to be bound by recognizance with two sureties for maintaining 'good order' in their houses. The precise terms of 'good order' were not detailed – save for the stipulation that no unlawful games, such as dice, cards or skittles, be permitted[22] – but county benches and borough authorities had some autonomy to introduce their own conditions to the recognizances. By the time central government sought to offer more detailed guidelines in a proclamation of 1619, mandatory conditions came to include prohibitions of operating during divine service, buying or pawning stolen goods, and harbouring 'rogues, vagabonds, sturdy beggars and masterless men'.[23]

By the turn of the seventeenth century there existed a regulatory framework for alehouses designed to stamp out those that were disorderly and to license a controlled number that kept good order. In itself, this fact may seem to resolve that tension between hostility and ambivalence on the part of the upper and middling ranks of society: disorderly alehouses were loathed; orderly alehouses were tolerated, even supported. Yet the raft of further legislation passed in the early part of the seventeenth century – four new Acts were passed between 1603 and 1609, followed by the detailed Royal Proclamation of 1619, and three further Acts in the 1620s – changed the nature of the regulatory framework in significant ways.[24] These measures are generally seen as 'consolidating', 'clarifying' or 'codifying' the licensing agenda laid out in

---

[21] 5/6 Edward VI c. 25.

[22] Those games stipulated in the Unlawful Games Act of 1541, 33 Henry VIII c. 9.

[23] P.L. Hughes and J.F. Larkin (eds), *Stuart Royal Proclamations*, I (Oxford, 1973), pp. 409–13.

[24] 1 James I c. 9; 4 James I c. 4; 4 James I c. 5; 7 James I c. 10; 21 James I c. 7; 1 Charles I c. 4; 3 Charles I c. 4.

1552, measures taken to make that system more effective.[25] In fact, they marked a number of important innovations. For instance, the 1604 'Act to restrain the inordinate haunting and tipling in inns, alehouses and other victualling-houses' went beyond the distinction between orderly and disorderly alehouses to specify that only certain alehouse *functions* were legitimate:

> The ancient true and principal use of inns, ale-houses and victualling houses was for the receipt, relief and lodging of wayfaring people travelling from place to place, and for such supply of the wants of such people as are not able by greater quantity to make their provision of victuals, and not meant for entertainment and harbouring of lewd and idle people to spend and consume their money and their time in lewd and drunken manner.[26]

Here then, for the first time, was a statement that whilst alehouses were permitted to serve and lodge travellers, and provide essential victuals to the local poor, they were explicitly *not* permitted to facilitate recreational drinking. The Act went further to delineate this distinction, forbidding alehousekeepers from permitting anyone – with the exception of travellers or workmen lodging at the establishment – to 'continue drinking or tipling' in their establishment above a period of 'one houre at dynner tyme, to take their Diet in an Alehouse'. The 1606 'Act for repressing the odious and loathsome sin of drunkenness' criminalised drunkenness for the first time, introducing a five shilling fine for anyone convicted of drunkenness, and further extended the punitive measures of the 1604 Act so that persons who 'remain or continue drinking' in their own city, town or village beyond the one hour stipulation were subject to a fine of 3s 4d, rather than the alehousekeeper bearing sole responsibility for the offence as in the original Act.[27] The 1619 proclamation further added that no 'Tipling or drinking after nine of the clocke in the night time' was to be permitted.

These measures were not simply an extension or codification of a regulatory system designed to weed out the disorderly alehouses from the orderly. Instead, they represented a novel and ambitious attempt on the part of the national government to prohibit all recreational drinking

---

[25] For summaries of their content see Hunter, 'English Inns, Taverns, Alehouses and Brandy Shops', pp. 68–9; James Nicholls, *The Politics of Alcohol: A History of the Drink Question in England* (Manchester, 2009), pp. 14–16.

[26] 1 James I c. 9.

[27] 4 James I c. 5.

in all alehouses. They stipulated that whilst subsistence functions were the 'true and principal uses' of alehouses, extended periods of drinking for pleasure – or for that matter for drunken oblivion – were illegitimate, and they sought to micro-regulate alehouse sociability by introducing time limits, cut-off times, and fines not only for those who had over-indulged to the stage of palpable drunkenness, but even to those who were deemed to 'tipple' for longer than was absolutely necessary for diet and nourishment. The legislative measures of the early seventeenth century marked an escalation from a war against disorderly alehouses to a war against all forms of recreational drinking in all alehouses.

Historians such as Marjorie McIntosh and Margaret Spufford have warned against attributing too much novelty to campaigns of social regulation pursued around the turn of the seventeenth century, arguing that many of the concerns expressed by the authorities at that time had significant medieval precedents and roots.[28] In the case of alehouse regulation, campaigns conducted under the jurisdiction of the manor courts from the late thirteenth to the mid sixteenth centuries do not generally appear to have shown much concern for policing social behaviour, instead restricting themselves to enforcing the assize of ale.[29] There were some exceptions to this pattern though, with a rising concern with disorderly alehouses emerging in major market towns and urban centres across the fifteenth and sixteenth centuries that preceded the shift in national legislation in this direction.[30] Moreover, we can also detect some precocious efforts to micro-regulate recreational drinking in alehouses at the manor and borough court level well before national legislation adopted such an agenda. For example in Broughton, Huntingdonshire, in 1465, the constable was told that if he found people in the alehouse after 8.00p.m. he should put them in the stocks, regardless of whether their behaviour was disorderly, and an order from the jurors of Basingstoke, Hampshire, specified in 1516 that no alehousekeeper should serve apprentices after 7.00p.m. and servants after 9.00p.m.[31] The borough of Leicester was also ahead of national legislation when it introduced a bylaw in 1563 stipu-

---

[28] M.K. McIntosh, *Controlling Misbehavior in England, 1370–1600* (Cambridge, 1998); M. Spufford, 'Puritanism and Social Control', in A.J. Fletcher and J. Stevenson (eds), *Order and Disorder in Early Modern England* (Cambridge, 1985).

[29] For examples see Baber (ed.), *Court Rolls of the Manor of Bromsgrove and King's Norton*; Noy (ed.), *Winslow Manor Court Books*; M. Clare Coleman (ed.), *Court Roll of the Manor of Downham 1310–1327* (Cambridge: Cambridgeshire Records Society, 1996).

[30] McIntosh, *Controlling Misbehavior*, pp. 74–8.

[31] *Ibid.*, pp. 76–8.

lating that town dwellers should not be permitted in any alehouse to 'sytt drynking or typling above the space of one hower', and iterated that the alehouse was not intended as a space for recreational drinking: 'if he or they will drynke any ale of bere, beyng townes men, shall send for the same to their o[w]ne howse or howses'.[32]

Several features of the early-seventeenth-century legislation can be shown to have precedents in initiatives taken by local manor and borough authorities – and for that matter in the church courts, which had a jurisdiction over drunkenness before it was criminalised in secular law[33] – and to some degree the national regulatory framework should be seen as having developed in dialogue with the local authorities and officials that were dealing with the alehouse problem on the ground.[34] In fact, some manor courts appear to have continued to play a key role in alehouse regulation long after official jurisdiction had passed to the magistrates and the quarter sessions. A 'booke of the penell laws' agreed by the jurors of the manor of Ashby de la Zouch, Leicestershire, in 1620, suggests that many of the recent stipulations on alehouse-keeping laid out in the early-seventeenth-century legislation were being policed at the manor court level:

> It is agreed by the jury that noe alehousekeep or victualler shall suffer or p[er]mit any p[er]son or p[er]sons whatsoever (travaiilers & strangers excepted) to tiple or drinke in their house above the space of one houre or to stay in theire house at prayer tyme or any other unseasonable tymes vizt. After nyne of the clocke at night not haveing some lawfull necessaty & iust occasion soe to doe.[35]

That offences were to result in a fine paid to the local lord of the manor, rather than to the under-officers of the magistrate as stipulated in national legislation, suggests that the control of alehouse licensing was not always readily accepted as under the jurisdiction of the quarter sessions, and may again be evidence that a manor had introduced such measures prior to

---

[32] *Leic. Boro. Recs*, III, pp. 108–9.

[33] See the section on 'Drunkenness and Swearing' in F.G. Emmison, *Elizabethan Life: Morals and the Church Courts* (Chelmsford, 1973), pp. 68–72. Presentments tended to focus on those whose drunkenness was connected with other offences, rather than reflecting a concerted campaign against all recreational drinking.

[34] A similar process of national legislation developing in dialogue with local initiatives can be seen in the establishment of the poor laws. See Paul Slack, *Poverty and Policy in Tudor and Stuart England* (London, 1988), chs. 6 and 7.

[35] Henry E. Huntington Library, Hastings Manorial Records (HAM), Box 2, Folder 1.

national law-making. Indeed, W.J. King has demonstrated that the court leet jurors of Prescot, Lancashire, worked to exclude the magistrates from alehouse regulation there, as they sought to preserve their own system of licensing that helped to raise revenue locally.[36] As a growing body of recent work has begun to emphasise, manor courts continued to play a role in 'implementing the sorts of "moral regulation" that so excited many previous social historians' well into the seventeenth century and possibly beyond.[37] It is important to concede, therefore, that aspects of the national legislative framework for alehouse regulation based on the operation of a licensing system administered through the quarter sessions had precedents in bylaws made by local manor and borough courts, courts which continued in many places to play an important role in regulation on the ground.

That said, the fact that in the early years of the seventeenth century a *nationwide* regulatory system was in place, and had been set on a footing to micro-regulate recreational drinking in all alehouses and not just to eliminate disorderly alehouses, provides a crucial and historically novel backdrop against which the battle over the alehouse played out in the seventeenth century. That framework did not change significantly across the century, or indeed well into the eighteenth.[38] The 1650s witnessed a period of particular vigour in attempts to suppress alehouses under the Republican regime, but no new legislation was deemed necessary: a more zealous attempt to enforce that already on the statute books was the strategy adopted.[39] After the Restoration, historians have suggested that a relaxation of alehouse concern and regulation occurred – a point taken up in Chapter 2 – but whether this was the case or not, the framework remained in place, and those local authorities that did still target alehouses continued to draw inspiration from the early-seventeenth-century legislation. When the Buckinghamshire magistracy sought a clampdown on alehouses in 1702 they issued a court order encouraging officers to put into practise existing laws against 'the loathsome sin of drunkenness' and against 'tippling', referring officers to the specific

---

[36] King, 'Regulation of Alehouses'.

[37] Brodie Waddell, 'Governing England through the Manor Courts, c.1550–1850', *Historical Journal* 55:2 (June 2012), p. 287; Brown, 'Alehouse Licensing and State Formation', p. 116.

[38] Hunter, 'English Inns, Taverns, Alehouses and Brandy Shops', p. 69.

[39] For more on efforts in the 1650s see Bernard Capp, *England's Culture Wars: Puritan Reformation and its Enemies in the Interregnum, 1649–1660* (Oxford, 2012), pp. 152–62.

statutes passed between 1603 and 1623.[40] If the drive behind alehouse regulation began to wane in many quarters as the century progressed, the national regulatory framework – geared up to prohibit recreational drinking in alehouses – remained relatively unchanged.

Presentments and petitions

As recent work on the early modern English polity has clearly demonstrated, 'parliamentary legislation, conciliar order, or royal proclamation were not the end of the law-making process but merely its beginning'.[41] National laws had to pass through a filter of more localised governmental structures and processes before being implemented in local communities, and an army of office-holders played their part in the administration of central policy on the ground – and, indeed, as we saw in the previous section, often took the initiative in developing new policies and measures which came from the 'bottom-up' as much as from the 'top-down'.[42] That the polity operated in this way led, of course, to considerable local variations in the operation of the law. We have touched already on the ways in which jurisdictional overlaps may have complicated the operation of alehouse regulation in certain communities, and the following chapter will examine in greater depth the considerable variation in the efforts and achievements of those magistrates and local officials charged with implementing the legislation against alehouses. In short, the letter of the law and the law in practice were two different animals, and the historian needs to explore the relationship between the two.

Here, then, the focus will be on one particular aspect of that relationship that can help to illuminate the attitudes of the middling ranks of local society toward the alehouse: what complaints did they bring against those alehouses which they sought to have suppressed by magistrates? In

---

[40] William Le Hardy and Geoffrey L. Reckitt (eds), *Calendar to the Sessions Records, County of Buckingham, II, 1694–1705* (Aylesbury: Buckinghamshire County Council, 1936), pp. 350–2.

[41] Steve Hindle, *The State and Social Change in Early Modern England, 1550–1640* (Basingstoke, 2000), p. 20.

[42] For the participatory nature of the early modern English polity, and the extent to which 'the state' relied on local office-holders for the implementation and administration of the law, see *ibid.*; Michael J. Braddick, *State Formation in Early Modern England, c.1550–1700* (Cambridge, 2000); Mark Goldie, 'The Unacknowledged Republic: Officeholding in Early Modern England', in Tim Harris (ed.), *The Politics of the Excluded, c.1500–1850* (Basingstoke, 2001), pp. 153–94.

part this will be gleaned from those presentments of offences that local officials delivered to magistrates to support their appeals for alehouses to be suppressed – presentments such as those by John Noyes. Considerable attention will also be paid to another aspect of law-making and implementation, one that is perhaps unduly marginalised by a focus on formal office-holding: the role of petitioning. Within the alehouse regulatory framework ultimate authority for granting or revoking licences lay with the county magistracy, and the responsibility for detecting breaches of licence conditions primarily with the parish or town constable. In practice, however, many non-office-holders played a key role in the process of alehouse regulation and licensing. Quarter sessions records contain a sizeable body of petitions calling for the magistrates to suppress given alehouses. Such petitions were supported by anything between a single individual to as many as fifty or sixty members of the local community, generally drawn from the ranks of the local better sort. Petitioners were more often than not functionally literate – that is, they could write their own name rather than simply signing with a cross.[43] It was also common for such petitioners to hold or have held some form of local office – constable, churchwarden or overseer of the poor – and they were likely to be amongst the more prominent landholders of their village.[44] Occasionally they even explicitly identified themselves as the 'better sort' or 'chief inhabitants' – or in the case of a petition from Glastonbury in 1635, the 'men of best quality' – though more commonly they simply claimed to speak for, and as, the collective body of 'the inhabitants' of their locale.[45] These petitions can help us understand the way such groups saw the role of the alehouse in their communities, but they also reveal more than the views of proactive alehouse opponents. A number of surviving petitions are appeals *for* alehouse licences to be granted. These were usually in the name of, or on behalf of, named individuals within the community who claimed to be poor – though these too were often supported by a large number of more substantial fellow parishioners or townsmen. Those that were so supported provide insight into the arguments that local chief inhabitants were prepared to accept as legitimating the presence of an alehouse in the community.

[43] On the relationship between literacy and social status see David Cressy, 'Levels of Illiteracy in England, 1530–1730', *The Historical Journal* 20:1 (1977), pp. 1–23; on the literacy of anti-alehouse petitioners see King, 'Regulation of Alehouses', p. 34.

[44] Wrightson, 'Alehouses, Order and Reformation', p. 19.

[45] *Som. Q.S. Recs*, II, p. 248.

The place occupied by alehouses in local communities was not, then, something that was determined and policed solely by 'the authorities'. It was a matter that mobilised both supporters and opponents of the alehouse without formal office, who sought to influence and direct the decisions made by those with it. The remainder of this chapter will draw upon a combined sample of presentments and petitions to explore how the regulatory framework established by central legislation was utilised at a local level by those involved in the 'battle' over the alehouse. The arguments petitioners made, both to support and to attack local alehouses, provide us with another window onto contemporary understandings of the role of the institution. It is a window that perhaps offers us a view of the attitudes of those who lived cheek-by-jowl with alehousekeepers and patrons that is clearer than that provided by the more abstract principles behind central law-making.

One area in which national legislation did not offer precise prescription was in regard to what the appropriate number of alehouses in any given community should be. It was left to the Justices to determine how many they thought 'convenient'. Petitioners were often more than happy to give magistrates a steer here, and we can usefully ask how many alehouses – if any – they thought necessary to serve the needs of the local community. Considering the prominent strand of hostility towards the alehouse identified earlier, we might ask whether an alehouse was generally considered a necessary or desirable facet of communal infrastructure at all. There were some petitioners who saw their role as entirely dispensable. Take, for example, the 'well affected' inhabitants of the parish of Westonzoyland, Somerset, who informed their JPs in 1651 of their 'desire to bee free from Alehowses there not beinge occasion for anie within the same parishe, but on the contrary it beinge very inconvenient to have anie there'.[46] The jurymen of the hundred of Whorlsdown, Wiltshire, presented Edward Swaine of Hinton for unlicensed ale-selling in 1646, and urged the magistrates to suppress his house, 'there beinge noe need in that hamlet for any alehouse at all'.[47] This example may indicate that a belief that no alehouses at all were ever necessary in a parish or settlement was primarily restricted to the smallest communities, as such a call was not common in petitions to the quarter sessions. Indeed, in an effort to provide greater clarification on appropriate numbers to the

[46] *Som. Q.S. Rec*, III, p. 159.
[47] WSHC, 1646/T/128.

Norfolk magistrates, in 1604 Chief Justice Popham wrote suggesting that 'populous' towns should have a maximum of four alehouses, and that the appropriate number for a village was one.[48]

The 1628 petition of the parishioners of Bradford-on-Avon, Wiltshire, was much more typical than a call for all alehouses to be removed. The parishioners complained that a disorderly 'company of alehouses' encouraged idleness, drunkenness and fighting, to 'the greate disturbance of other [...] neighbours and the great dishonor of Almightie god, and the great impoverishment of the same towne'. The petitioners desired that these alehouses 'may be all suppressed by order of Sessions there beinge an Inn & some other Alehouses besides that are fit to give entertainement to strangers'.[49] Whilst clearly demonstrating that these petitioners felt the alehouse could play a very disruptive role within the town, they stopped short of calling for the suppression of all drinking houses, and effectively endorsed the inn and other alehouses which they deemed to be providing the valuable function of entertaining strangers. A similar line was taken by a presentment to the Wiltshire quarter sessions at Warminster in 1646, which emphasised the threat posed by the institution whilst simultaneously conceding that not all alehouses could be conveniently suppressed: 'Wee desire that the multitude of Alehouses, the common enimies to the peace & prosperity of this kingdome may bee supprest that sell ale & beere without lisence, And [tha]t as many of those who have lisence [tha]t may be convieniently spared may bee put downe.' This was followed by a more specific, but equally pragmatic request, that 'whereas wee have five lisensed Alehouses in our towne of Steepleashton, Our request is, that wee may have but two Alehouses there, or 3 at the most'.[50] Likewise, the jurymen of the hundred of Bempstone in Somerset desired in 1616 that 'some of the tipplers in the parish of Wedmore might be suppressed, for that they are too many, being six in number, and they account one or two to be sufficient'.[51] The self-styled 'men of the best qualetie' of Glastonbury petitioned the Somerset Justices in 1635 in the conviction that their town had become 'much prejudiced and decaied' by the 'multitude of Alehowses' there. Yet their request was not for a total purge of these institutions, but rather that there should be a restriction to the customary number of eight licensees

---

[48] Fletcher, *Reform in the Provinces*, p. 231.
[49] WSHC, 1628/E/121.
[50] WSHC, 1646/T/100.
[51] *Som. Q.S. Recs*, I, p. 161.

in Glastonbury.[52] Similarly, several of the inhabitants and parishioners of Bunbury, Cheshire, complained in 1638 that their town was 'oppressed with seven Alehouses', whereas they felt that 'in truth one or two at the most were sufficient'.[53] In general, then, even those members of the community who regarded alehouses as 'common enemies' to 'peace and prosperity' were prepared to accept that the institution could not be abolished altogether. If these petitioners showed signs of a 'militant hostility' to alehouses, they nonetheless accepted that a small number were necessary.

Another aspect of the local alehouse problem that preoccupied petitioners was the precise location of those alehouses that were to be tolerated. The national regulatory system again afforded discretion to magistrates on this issue, but according to Michael Dalton's *Country Justice* – a popular handbook for seventeenth-century magistrates – a Star Chamber speech by King James I in 1616 had offered clear guidance. Dalton related James's concern with 'the aboundance of Alehouses, and more specially against the infamous, and blinde Alehouses, as being haunts and receipts for robbers, theeves, rogues, vagabonds, and other idle, loose, and sturdie fellowes'. 'Blind' alehouses were those out of the way, tucked down side-streets or on the periphery of a village, and Justices were advised in particular to prohibit these, as Dalton noted: 'the alehouses to bee allowed are meetest to bee about the middest of the towne; but not to be in anie corners, or places out of, or distant from the towne, except upon the rivers side, & where there is great need'.[54] Indeed, the rule of thumb for a magistrate to remember was 'that in allowing of Alehouses they have a regard as well to the person, as the place; for all persons are not fit to be allowed for Alehouse-keepers; neither are all places meete for an Alehouse'.[55] The main concern of government here was that such places were much more difficult for officers to keep a close eye on and to police. Many local officials shared such concerns. In an order of 1607 the Somerset bench went as far as to forbid the licensing of any tippling or alehouses on the entire 'hill of Mendipp' – a notoriously unruly mining area – in response to complaints that such places harboured 'thieves and other Lewde vagrant wandering persons' because they were 'remote from the eye and view of such officers

---

52 *Som. Q.S. Recs*, II, p. 248.

53 *Ches. Q.S. Recs*, pp. 94–5.

54 Michael Dalton, *The Countrey Justice* (1619), pp. 27–8.

55 *Ibid.*

as have the charge of government'.[56] 'The Inhabitants' of the tithing of Monksilver and Bicknoller in Somerset petitioned the same bench in 1631, requesting that Robert Brewer's alehouse be suppressed as it stood 'remote from the Inhabitants of the said tythinge . . . by the space of two miles or more'.[57] Petitioners from Corsham, Wiltshire, asked their JPs to suppress an alehouse, the Red Lion, that had been 'set up anew' by one Christopher Nott 'in a remote place in the skirts of the towne where is daylye used greate abuses by drunkards common haunters of alehouses & idlers'.[58] Even existing licensees might share – or perhaps play upon – these anxieties over peripheral alehouses. The widow Edith Pearce, who ran an 'ancient inn' in the centre of Paulton, Somerset, petitioned the JPs in 1627 to complain that her livelihood had been prejudiced by a rival alehouse set up by a man 'dwellinge farr remote from the hart of the towne being the outmost house thereof'.[59]

Concerns about the location of alehouses were not solely motivated by issues of surveillance. In 1654 the mayor, burgesses and other inhabitants of Taunton petitioned the Somerset magistrates to suppress an alehouse not only because it was 'att that distance from the view of the Officers . . . that manie irregularities are there mainteyned uncontrolled', but also because the house stood 'in a place noe way fitting . . . for travellers'.[60] In 1612, the constables of the parish of Westbury-sub-Mendip, Somerset, were also uneasy with the alehouse of Henry Bendell, as he lived 'oute of the towne in the fi[e]ld', a location 'out of the most usuall way for travellers'.[61] Whilst petitions undoubtedly do reflect some anxiety over issues of alehouse surveillance, the importance placed on a central location was as often informed by concerns over alehouses fulfilling their legitimate role of providing lodging for travellers. Indeed, attacks on alehouses did not simply label them as disorderly; they stressed just as often that alehouses were not fit to fulfil their 'true and principal' uses.

---

[56] SHC, Q/SR/2/125. On the particularly truculent nature of mining areas see R.W. Malcolmson, '"A set of ungovernable people": the Kingswood Colliers in the Eighteenth Century', in John Brewer and John Styles (eds), *An Ungovernable People: The English and their Law in the Seventeenth and Eighteenth Centuries* (New Brunswick, 1980), pp. 85–127; Andy Wood, *The Politics of Social Conflict: The Peak Country, 1520–1770* (Cambridge, 1999); Simon Sandall, *Custom and Popular Memory in the Forest of Dean, c.1550–1832* (Saarbrücken, 2013).

[57] SHC, Q/SR/65:2/137.

[58] WSHC, 1608/T/92.

[59] SHC, Q/SR/58:2/196.

[60] *Som. Q.S. Recs*, III, p. 242.

[61] SHC, Q/SR/16/79.

Inhabitants from the township of Hunsterston, Cheshire, complained in 1646 that none of the four alehouses there kept 'any victualling or lodging'.[62] In 1587 the jury of Mickletorn, Nottingham, presented two alehousekeepers 'because they are nott able to lodge straungers'.[63] This concern worked both ways – it may have been another stick with which 'militants' could attack alehouses, but it also reinforced the sense that certain alehouse functions and alehouses were indeed legitimate. Petitioners seeking a licence often also placed the weight of their appeal on the provision of 'true and principal uses', stressing that the location of a premises was indeed suitable for travellers needing refreshment or overnight lodging. Thomas Shenton of Bickerton, Cheshire, petitioned the magistrates in 1646 to grant him a licence to sell ale from a dwelling he had recently taken, on the grounds that it was situated 'neere the rodes between Nantwich and Wrexham, & betweene Warrington & Salop [Shropshire]'.[64] The parishioners of Bawdrip, Somerset, made an appeal in the same year for the widow Mary Nunny to be granted a licence to keep an alehouse and 'house of entertainem[en]t for travellers', because her house was 'neere the kings high way'.[65] That year also saw an appeal by nineteen of the inhabitants of Hackleton, Wiltshire, to allow Robert Dowse to keep an alehouse in the parish as 'there is comon and usuall rode through the sayd parish from the west partes of this kingdom to London and Oxford, in w[hi]ch respect there is a greate necessitie for continnueinge this house for entertaynment for travellers and passengers'.[66] That a main road was the preferred location of an alehouse was not only to allow for their easier surveillance – it was also the most practical option for the fulfilment of their duty to serve travellers.

Petitioners seeking to secure a licence for an alehouse also often made their service of victuals to the local poor – the other 'true and principal' function – a cornerstone of their argument. In 1608, John Runnye of Queen Camel, Somerset, was able to gather twenty-four signatures to support his appeal to have his licence continued by stressing his history of both providing 'very clean and sufficient lodging ... for passengers or wayfaring men' and 'relieving and supplying of the wants and necessities of divers of the poor neighbours there inhabiting'.[67] Ellis Pawley,

---

62 CRO, QJF/74/2/27.
63 *Nott. Boro. Recs*, IV, pp. 215–16.
64 CRO, QJF/74/2/32.
65 *Som. Q.S. Recs*, III, p. 5.
66 WSHC, 1646/M/228.
67 SHC, Q/SR/3:2/170.

of Martock, Somerset, was able to muster considerable support for his appeal to be licensed in 1627, securing forty-one signatures by emphasising that 'he doth p[ro]vide good small beere for the poor people'.[68] A 1609 petition from the inhabitants of Wanstrow, Somerset, requested a licence for Thomas Allyn on the grounds that this would be in accordance with 'a statute made for allowing a "typler" in every parish needful for the poor of the same parish and other passengers travelling or going through'.[69] In fact, despite the range of services the alehouse could offer – as a centre of economic exchange, communication and social interaction – the arguments requesting a licence that were put before Justices of the Peace tended to be restricted in focus to their two most basic functions – lodging travellers and providing victuals to the local poor – and their ability or record with regard to delivering these services. This no doubt reflects a pragmatic legalism on the part of petitioners: these may well have been the only arguments that would persuade their more influential and substantial neighbours to lend their signature to the appeal, and of course were the only services that were authorised by legislation. In general, petitioners for licences told the justices exactly what they wanted to hear.

If petitioners regularly constructed claims around the 'true and principal uses', they also adhered to the official line that recreational drinking was not one of them. Some historians of drinking houses have argued that contemporaries often accepted the sociable function of alehouses: Anthony Fletcher has suggested that not only did contemporaries believe that 'their role in the domestic economy of the poor was vital', but also that 'their recreational function was generally accepted'.[70] Yet, if the inhabitants of seventeenth-century communities were tolerant of the alehouse's role in accommodating sociability, this was not reflected in petitions to the quarter sessions, and few petitioners, if any, made a case for a licence on the grounds that the alehouse played a vital role in facilitating social interaction. Indeed, even Fletcher found that 'the nearest that villagers normally came to a candid demand for a public drinking place for their own use rather than the use of outsiders was in the stress upon the need for somewhere to transact parish business'.[71] Even cases such as this were rare, though the inhabitants of Seend, Wiltshire, did

---

[68] SHC, Q/SR/58:1/112.
[69] SHC, Q/SR/6/15.
[70] Fletcher, *Reform in the Provinces*, p. 229.
[71] *Ibid.*, p. 235.

include in their 1646 appeal for the continuation of the licence of John Stokes the argument that 'his said house is usually resorted unto for making of Rates for the parish [setting the levels of local taxes] And is resorted unto upon Arbitracons for thending [the ending] of differences betwene man & man'.[72] Such claims that the alehouse could play a role in social cohesion, rather than increasing tensions within the community, were unusual in petitions to the quarter sessions.

More common were petitions that used the illegitimacy of sociability as an argument against the alehouses in their community. A favoured approach in such petitions was to contrast the inappropriate facilitation of recreational drinking with a failure to provide essential victuals to the local poor. In their 1605 petition against John Bindley's alehouse, the 'honest men' of Audlem complained that the alehousekeeper – inverting his legitimate role – was happy to serve drunken revellers but refused to sell victuals to his neighbours: '[when] theire honest neighbowers do at any tyme send to his house for a quart of ale then there is non ready but [when] lewd company come in as roges dronkerdes . . . then there is no want'.[73] Complaints from 1612 against Henry Bendell's out-of-town alehouse in Westbury-sub-Mendip, Somerset, included the accusation that he had 'refused to serve the poore for theire redie mony, when he hathe had bothe ale and breade in his howse', but he had been happy to ply 'the children and servants of the inhabitants' of the parish with ale in his house for 'so longe that they have fowght and comitted bludshed'.[74] The Swindon alehousekeeper Edward Feantrell was presented in 1635 because he refused to sell any drink to the poor to take and consume at home, but if they would drink it in his house 'they shall have it by the stone pott', and he regularly suffered 'poore men & idle persons to sitt tippling and drinking in his house' for the 'great parte of the night'.[75] In 1612 John Noyes had presented John Scotte, 'Tipler', not only because he and his wife did not have 'sufficient beddinge to lodge poore travelers when neede shall be', but also because Scotte would often 'be tipmirrie ['tip-merry'; intoxicated] himselfe'. In fact, the promotion of recreational drinking by alehousekeepers in Calne had, for Noyes and his fellow constable, got out of hand: as we have seen they complained that the alehouses there did 'all brewe a[nd] vie who maye brewe the strongest Ale'

---

72 WSHC, 1646/M/236.
73 CRO, QJF/34/2/91.
74 SHC, Q/SR/16/79.
75 WSHC, 1635/E/139.

in an attempt to attract 'all the great drinkers bothe of the Towne and Countrie to spende theyer tyme in idleness and theyer monie in excessivie drinkinge'. This had created the nightmare scenario that contemporaries feared, with alehouse sociability seemingly poised to undermine local law and order. The constables revealed that they 'can not punishe them according to the Lawe' because 'all me[n] for the most p[ar]te love these cupp companions so well, that no man will take uppon him to be a sworne witnes against any drunkard'.[76] The constables of Calne would no doubt have been glad to endorse the licence appeal of Robert Fay of Collingbourne, Wiltshire – as eighteen of his neighbours and the local minister did in 1605 – as, unlike their local alehousekeepers, he was a man not given to the maintenance of 'pot companions'.[77]

All of this seems to suggest a certain consensus within the petitions and presentments as to the appropriate role of the alehouse in the local community. Complainants regularly pointed to the disruptive and disorderly influence alehouses could have – they were 'common enemies of the peace' that created violence and bloodshed – but there was nonetheless a grudging acceptance that a certain number were necessary. As was the case with legislation, the line between alehouses that were deemed necessary and those that were not was not simply drawn between orderly and disorderly alehouses. The legitimacy of a given alehouse also hinged on its provision of services. Those that failed to provide the 'true and principal' functions of lodging travellers and serving the local poor could expect appeals for them to be suppressed; those that could convince their neighbours and the magistrates that they were suitably located and prepared to offer such services – and maintained 'good order' – could make a strong claim to a licence. There was an additional, crucial, proviso: whether an alehouse attracted the support or approbation of the chief inhabitants of a locale was dependent on the role it played in facilitating recreational drinking. Those engaged in the 'battle over the alehouse' through local office-holding and petitioning mirrored national legislation in organising their offensives as attacks on alehouse sociability, not alehouses per se. If the latter was perceived as a necessary evil, the former was not.

Perhaps the seeming consensus in such sources was instrumental. It would have made sense for petitioners and officers to keep their arguments over alehouse licensing tightly bound within the principals of the

---

[76] WSHC, 1612/E/177.
[77] Fletcher, Reform in the Provinces, pp. 234–5.

national legislative framework, for it was this framework that governed the decisions taken, ultimately, by the magistrates. These sources may not, then, offer a transparent window onto the way local 'better sorts' viewed the appropriate role of the alehouse in their communities. Their nature may only reveal the arguments that were relevant in a legal context, rather than the full range and complexity of attitudes towards alehouses, and in particular towards recreational drinking in alehouses. Nonetheless, this analysis shows that the notion at the heart of the regulatory framework – that alehouses were necessary, but alehouse sociability was not – represented a widely circulating discourse that informed – strategically or otherwise – the way local petitioners joined the battle over, and defined the role of, the alehouse.[78] Moreover, on further analysis we can begin to see a certain internal logic within the arguments made by petitioners and local officials that helps to explain the seemingly widespread view that recreational drinking should be off-limits. For even the legitimate functions of alehouses created anxiety, and there existed an inherent fear that the group for whom the alehouse was deemed necessary – the poor – could not be trusted to utilise the institution in the 'true and principal' ways for which it was intended. To achieve a fuller picture of the way contemporaries understood the role of the alehouse, and of the tensions that role produced, we need to interrogate the ways petitioners and officialdom viewed the patrons and proprietors of alehouses.

Legitimate patrons

The apparent consensus regarding legitimate alehouse services provided a clear identification of who were regarded as the institution's legitimate patrons: travellers and the local poor. At a time of growing inland trade and a rise in the number of landless labourers it must have been fairly common in many communities to find chapmen, tinkers, pedlars, travelling tradesmen, migrant labourers and soldiers seeking overnight accommodation.[79] Although such sojourns represented an official and

[78] Petitions for poor relief provide another context in which petitioners were well acquainted with, and sought to some extent to work strategically within, legal frameworks: see Steve Hindle, *On the Parish? The Micro-Politics of Poor Relief in Rural England c.1550–1750* (Oxford, 2004), esp. pp. 405–28.
[79] Clark, *The English Alehouse*, pp. 128–131; David Rollison, 'Exploding England: The Dialectics of Mobility and Settlement in Early Modern England', *Social History* 24

routine use of the alehouse they still aroused some degree of unease from contemporaries, as is evident from the conditions of an alehouse licence granted to Annacletey Plumbly by the Somerset magistrates in 1617. The conditions stated that Plumbly was required to be 'continually provided and furnished with meate drinck … and other provision to serve all such waifaringe p[er]sons and passengers as shall uppon lawfull cause repaire to you[r] house'.[80] Plumbly was required to receive such individuals into her alehouse, but she was also expected to keep a close eye on their activities. It was stipulated that such 'wayfaring persons' were not to be lodged for more than one night without notice being given to the constable or tithingman, and that local officials should be informed of any trading that took place with such individuals: 'you shall not receive or keepe buy or contract for any lynnen apparrell goods or other chattells … of any waifaringe p[er]son except you make the same knowen to the constable or officer'. These stipulations were insisted upon because local officials, and no doubt the local community more generally, were anxious about the crucial but often imperceptible distinction between respectable travellers and 'vagabonds or suspicious persons'.[81] The latter were believed to target alehouses as suitable bases for criminal activity, especially the fencing of stolen goods.[82] Indeed, alehousekeepers were charged with the difficult task of discerning who fell into this latter category and were required to report them immediately to the constable. Failure to do so could lead to the suppression of their alehouse, a fate that befell Charles Matthews of Wincanton, Somerset, in 1676. Matthews was disabled from keeping an alehouse for three years for 'harbouring vagrants', and especially for failing to report the would-be burglar Bartholomew Romane, who had been convicted 'as a common vagrant and wandering rogue, it appearing upon evidence that he carried about with him several unlawful picklock instruments'.[83]

The degree of trepidation with which an alehouse lodger was greeted by a potential host community should not be overstated.[84] Travellers

---

(1999), pp. 1–16. See also Andrew McRae, *Literature and Domestic Travel in Early Modern England* (Cambridge, 2009).

[80] SHC, Q/SR/28/95.

[81] See David Hitchcock, 'A Typology of Travellers: Migration, Justice, and Vagrancy in Warwickshire, 1670–1730', *Rural History* 23:1 (2012), pp. 21–39.

[82] Clark, *The English Alehouse*, pp. 145–7.

[83] *Som. Q.S. Recs*, IV, p. 205.

[84] For a later period Keith Snell has argued that 'foreigners' from other parishes could expect a very hostile reception: 'The Culture of Local Xenophobia', *Social History* 28

might receive a warm welcome, such as the two seamen who stopped to lodge in Shrewton, Wiltshire, in 1654, en route from Plymouth to Portsmouth, and were bought drinks by a local husbandman, William Richards, who himself 'had a son at sea'.[85] No doubt the majority of stopovers occurred without arousing so much as a ripple of tension or apprehension in the community. Yet suspicion of travellers was never far from the surface and when a crime took place strangers who patronised alehouses were always high on any list of suspects. Indeed, another of the conditions of Annacletey Plumbly's licence was the requirement that:

> if knowledge come to you of any robbery murder or fellony donne you shall imediately declare to the constable or other officer as neere as you can the names apparrell and dwellinge places of all such p[er]sons as have lodged in your house in two daies or more before and in two daies or more after the same robbery murder or felony was committed.[86]

The volatility of attitudes towards travelling alehouse patrons is also clear from the above-mentioned events in Shrewton in 1654. After spending several hours drinking with the seamen, William Richards and his new companions fell asleep at the ale bench. When Richards awoke he saw that the seamen had left, and upon checking his pockets found himself light of 10s and 6d. Richards pursued the strangers to the 'Grinding Stone' alehouse in nearby Amesbury, where the constables willingly arrested the pair at his request despite finding that one of the men 'had about him being searched four shillings, two pence but the other being searched had not any money found about him'. Whilst the guilt of the two seamen may be uncertain, it is clear from this example that attitudes towards travellers could quickly shift from a sociable welcome to heavy-handed suspicion when the anxieties of the local community were stoked by reports of criminal activity.[87]

If the attitudes of contemporaries towards travelling alehouse patrons appear from these sources to have been characterised by latent suspicion, attitudes towards the patronage of alehouses by the local poor

---

(2003), pp. 1–30. Peter Clark, on the other hand, has suggested that for the early modern period alehouses did not witness as much friction between 'locals' and itinerants as might be expected: Clark, *The English Alehouse*, pp. 130–1.

[85] WSHC, 1654/M/200.

[86] SHC, Q/SR/28/95.

[87] For further examples of travelling alehouse patrons suspected of criminal activity see: SHC, Q/SR/152/4, 9; WSHC, 1655/H/159; ERO, Q/SR/410/55.

provoked an anxiety amongst the opponents of alehouses that was both more explicit and proactive. Of course, the local poor were in legislative terms the only members of the local community permitted to patronise alehouses, to purchase the ale and other victuals that were a necessary part of their diet. As Dalton advised – in a guideline that reflects once again the important role played by the petitions of local chief inhabitants in licensing decisions – an alehouse could be deemed necessary in a community where provision for travellers was not essential if it was thought meet to serve the local poor:

> In towns which are no through-faire, the Justices shall doe well to be sparing in allowing of any alehouses, (except it be at the suit of the chiefe inhabitants there, and to supply the wants of their poore).[88]

At times petitioners and local officials complained to the magistracy that an alehouse was serving members of the local community who had no right to patronise it, especially those younger members of the community who would have been able to fulfil their dietary needs under the roofs of their masters. One offender on this front was, once again, Henry Bendell of Westbury-sub-Mendip, whose many misdemeanours included the fact that 'he hathe usually kept in his howse the children and servants' of local inhabitants.[89] Annacletey Plumbly's licence instructed that 'you shall not suffer your neighbours theire children apprentices nor servants to eate or drinck in your house att any time'.[90] The parishioners of Paulton, Somerset, petitioned the magistrates in 1636 to suppress the alehouse of Richard Bourne as he allowed 'his neighbours servants and children to continue tiplinge in his howse all night', with the result that 'they neglect their parents and master's service'.[91] Yet complaints about members of the local community making inappropriate visits to the alehouse were not restricted to their illegitimate patronage by disobedient youth: as often they made reference to their patronage by groups who had every right to be there according to statutory provisions – poor workmen and day labourers. Rightful or otherwise, their patronage still caused concern, especially when their visits shaded into the recreational rather than the subsistence-oriented. The petition of the inhabitants of Pewsey, Wiltshire, claimed in 1646 that 'pore labourers' were

---

88 Dalton, *The Countrey Justice*, p. 28.
89 SHC, Q/SR/16/79.
90 SHC, Q/SR/28/95.
91 *Som. Q.S. Recs*, I, p. 269.

often drawn into the premises of local alehousekeepers 'to spend theyr moneyes and time'.[92] Petitioners from Bradford-on-Avon were concerned with the alehouse patronage of such workmen, complaining in 1628 that alehouses were 'entertaineinge poore worke men and day labourers and sufferinge them to spend theire money'.[93] This highlights a major tension within contemporary attitudes: whilst the poor were the only members of the local community who could legitimately patronise the alehouse, it was their patronage which aroused the most anxiety and concern.

Historians have long recognised that the concern for 'order' in early modern English society led to the widespread assumption that 'any popular gathering was a potential source of disorder, particularly if it took place in an alehouse', and that whilst 'the unruly rich were only sometimes a problem, the poor were unruly by definition'.[94] Such prejudices were reflected in the wide array of derogatory terms that early modern elites used to describe collective gatherings of the poor, who they perceived of as 'the many-headed monster'.[95] So, whilst on the one hand it was accepted that it was necessary and legitimate for the poor to patronise the alehouse to purchase essential victuals, on the other, such activity was inevitably a source of angst for many sections of the community who feared it could shade easily into unruly drunkenness. Their fears were not only of drunken disorder: in the eyes of many petitioners, when the poor did step through the alehouse door to drink for recreation they embarked on a downward trajectory that could only lead to greater impoverishment both for the individual and subsequently for the community as a whole. A common complaint in petitions was that the alehouse induced and indulged idleness amongst poor workmen and servants, an attitude that seems to have taken on an almost proverbial status in the seventeenth century.[96] In the private correspondence of the Smyth family of Ashton Court, Bristol, Florence Smyth wrote

---

92 WSHC, 1646/M/215.

93 WSHC, 1628/E/121.

94 Susan Amussen, *An Ordered Society: Gender and Class in Early Modern England* (New York, 1993), pp. 168, 170.

95 Christopher Hill, 'The Many-Headed Monster in Late Tudor and Early Stuart Political Thinking', in C.H. Carter (ed.), *From the Renaissance to the Counter-Reformation: Essays in Honour of Garrett Mattingley* (New York, 1965), and reprinted in Hill, *Change and Continuity in Seventeenth-Century England*, rev. edn (New Haven, 1991), pp. 181–204.

96 For the classic exploration of growing concern with the balance between work and leisure in the time-use of early modern workers see E.P. Thompson, 'Time, Work-Discipline, and Industrial Capitalism', *Past and Present* 38 (1967), pp. 56–97; reprinted

to Thomas Smyth in 1641 to report the slow progress being made by agricultural workers on the estate, complaining that 'threshers and mowers' were 'wild rascals [that] cannot be gotten out of the alehouse be the weather never so fair'.[97] The 1607 order against alehouses on the Mendips in Somerset was not untypical in expressing concern that the poor's patronage of the alehouse disrupted their work. It complained that labourers and men's servants spent their time in alehouses 'tippling and bowsing [boozing] there upon the Sabbath and holy days at the time of divine service, as at and on other days and times when they should be at their work'.[98]

The 1646 petition of the inhabitants of Pewsey, Wiltshire, saw the alehouse patronage of labourers and servants there as resulting in 'great preiudice in neglectinge our husbandry … w[hi]ch is likely to be the utter ruine of our said Children, servants, pore labourers & our selves'.[99] Not only were these workmen neglecting to fulfil their vital role in the economy and failing to maximise their earning potential, they were also spending money in the alehouse that was essential to family provision. The inhabitants of Bradford-on-Avon criticised alehousekeepers in 1628 for allowing poor workmen and day labourers 'to spend theire money when as theire wife and children are ready to starve for want of food'.[100] The 'men of best qualetie' in Glastonbury believed a similar process was at work in the alehouses of their town in 1636, with the 'meaner sort' becoming 'much impoverished through their dayly resorte unto them by meanes whereof Diverse of their Children become chargeable unto the said parish'.[101] In a presentment of 1673, the constables of Kingswood, Wiltshire, also blamed the alehouse for inducing idleness and poverty in the local community, with adverse consequences for the poor rates – a local tax levied on the 'chief inhabitants' of parishes to raise funds to aid the parish poor.[102] They suggested that due to 'the abounding of alehouses' in the parish 'we are very poore and beggerly the greatest part

---

in his *Customs in Common: Studies in Traditional Popular Culture* (London, c.1991), pp. 352–403.

[97]   J.H. Bettey (ed.), *Calendar of the Correspondence of the Smyth Family of Ashton Court, 1548–1642*, Bristol Record Society 35 (Gloucester, 1982), p. 174. I am grateful to Dr Jason Peacey for this reference.

[98]   SHC, Q/SR/2/125.

[99]   WSHC, 1646/M/215.

[100]   WSHC, 1628/E/121.

[101]   *Som. Q.S. Recs*, II, p. 248.

[102]   On this system of poor relief see Hindle, *On the Parish?*

of us, whereas our poores booke was formerly but at [£]50 a yeer these two last years it was now a hundred and fifty pounde a yeer which is by the means of so much drunkenness amongst us'.[103]

For some contemporaries the degenerative impact on the community that resulted from the poor's participation in alehouse sociability did not stop at an increase in the poor rates. The 'honest men' of Audlem, Cheshire, petitioned the quarter sessions in 1605 to suppress the alehouse of one John Bindley for allowing 'unthrifty' persons to frequent his alehouse with the consequence that 'manie houses are broken in the night tyme' and 'gates and hedges in the night tyme torne pulled up and carried awaie, by reson of manteninge of such [unthrifty persons]'. The petitioners pleaded for the house to be put down so that 'honest men maie lyve in peace and enioye ther house and goods in saffetie'.[104] Sixteen of the inhabitants of Little Bedwin, Wiltshire, petitioned the JPs to take action against alehouses in their town in 1648, building a similarly forceful argument about the role the alehouse played in increasing poverty and in provoking conflict over local resources: 'the keeping up [of] soe many Alehouses doth make soe many theeves, who rob and steale to maintaine themselves in money to spend lewdly, that wee cannot keepe our sheepe in our folds nor in our grounds, whereby our arable lands are uterly decaied, there having been stollen from us w[i]thin these three or fower yearers last aboute fower or five hundred sheep'. They also accused alehousekeepers of buying stolen wood from 'lewd persons who cut downe our young oakes, our quick sett hedges & coppice woods to brew beere to maintaine them in their drunkeness'.[105] For some contemporaries, then, the frequenting of alehouses by the poor led not just to rising poor rates, but to high levels of theft that threatened both private property and natural resources.

From these petitions we can observe a prevalent understanding of the relationship between alehouses and the poor: a fear that institution and patron had the potential to become locked in a vicious spiral in which the proliferation of one fed that of the other, putting pressure on poor rates and resources until the sustainability of the entire local community was itself under threat. A petition sent to the Somerset magistrates by the burgesses of Yeovil in 1618 suggested that this destructive pattern was observable in their town. They described a bygone era in the history

---

103 WSHC, 1673/E/98. See also Wrightson, 'Alehouses, Order and Reformation', pp. 16–17.

104 CRO, QJF/34/2/91.

105 *Wilts. Q.S. Recs*, p. 194.

of the town when 'many poore men w[hi]ch were of small meanes' rented houses in which to practise their trades, whereby they were able to provide for their families, and – possibly – even contribute to the poor rates, they 'beinge rather helpful to others then any wayes desiringe any helpe from the Towne'. This section of the community had since, however, 'fallen into decaye', as the rents of these houses had been pushed up by a high demand to acquire them as alehouses. Unable to afford the increased rents, and thus disabled from plying their trades, these poor men had instead themselves become regular patrons of these alehouses, where they 'always spend, and never gett any thinge towards their mayntenaynce, but by way of prigging [stealing] … and their poore wives and children Complayne for want in the meane tyme'.[106] The burgesses of Yeovil understood the cause of growing poverty in their town to be the increase in the number of alehouses, with the rising number of poor men providing a growing trade for the institutions, and with knock-on effects on crime and poor rates. Yet, despite their ability to provoke spiralling poverty, the burgesses of Yeovil still accepted the necessity of alehouses, calling for a reduction in their number to previous levels rather than for an outright ban. Likewise, the inhabitants of Little Bedwin felt that one alehouse should be retained, even though the institution had been pinpointed as the root cause of a spate of thefts of wood and sheep, and the utter decay of the community's arable lands. Again, then, we return to the inherent tension in attitudes towards the poor's patronage of the alehouse: it was seen as legitimate and necessary, but contemporaries nonetheless feared that it had the potential to undermine the very sustainability of the community if essential drinking shaded into recreational drinking. Such concerns lay bare the logic behind the seemingly widespread consensus that the latter should be strictly prohibited and policed. The principal agent of such policing was the alehousekeeper.

Alehousekeepers

Petitioners and the authorities were keen to ensure that the poor patrons of alehouses came under a watchful eye. There were, of course, officials responsible for this, and we will come to their role in more depth in Chapter 2. The front line here though was the licensee, who in principle had full control over the provision of services and the prohibition

---

[106] SHC, Q/SR/30/73.

of recreational drinking, and licence conditions made it clear that he or she bore responsibility for preventing anyone 'to continue tiplinge above one houre att the most in one daie'.[107] However, if the government and local chief inhabitants did not trust patrons to adhere to this prescription, nor did they have much confidence in the capacity of alehouse-keepers to do so, for they too were generally drawn from the ranks of the poor. Indeed, as we have seen, it has become a historiographical commonplace that the alehouse was an institution 'run by the poor for the poor', and licensing records confirm that contemporaries thought it appropriate that the institution should be run by poorer members of the community.[108] In particular, it was thought that ale-selling could provide a valuable source of income to those who might otherwise become chargeable to the parish.[109] The widow Edith Pearce of Paulton, Somerset, for example, pleaded for a licence in 1627 on the grounds that she was 'a sole woman havinge foure small children and noe other livinge to give her selfe and Children mayntenance but such profitts as is yelded unto her by travaylinge and wayfaringe men'.[110] Thomas Shenton of Bickerton, Cheshire, informed the magistrates in 1646 that 'having but very small meanes to maynteine himself his wife & children, hath, for their better subsistence, taken a mesauge [a cluster of buildings]' for which he hoped to obtain a licence to sell ale.[111] Running an alehouse could therefore plausibly be represented as a means by which the poor could provide for their own maintenance.

That a licence was intended only as a lifeline for the poor can also be seen in reactions to those alehousekeepers who seemed to be only too comfortable financially. The inhabitants of Westbury, Wiltshire, called in 1670 for the suppression of an alehouse being run by a father and son who had 'inriched themselves by impoverishing of many honest families by drawing them to spend theire estates in theire alehouse'.[112] If running an alehouse was intended to stave off poverty rather than bring prosperity, it was also seen as the exclusive privilege of those deemed unable to maintain themselves through more conventional labour or

---

107   SHC, Q/SR/28/95.

108   Clark, 'The Alehouse and the Alternative Society', p. 53.

109   This stands in contrast to recent work on Germany and central Europe which has suggested that publicans were usually one of the wealthiest non-elite groups in society: Kümin, *Drinking Matters*, pp. 50–63; Tlusty, *Bacchus and Civic Order*, pp. 41–3.

110   SHC, Q/SR/58:2/197.

111   CRO, QJF/74/2/32.

112   *Wilts. Q.S. Recs*, p. 246.

work in a trade. The constables of Calne presented the alehousekeeper William Bush in 1612 because he was 'a Carpenter by crafte, and is able to live w[i]thout Ale Keepinge and therefore we desyre that they maye be forbidden to sell ale any more'.[113] The 'well-affected' inhabitants of Barford St Martin in the same county appealed in 1647 for certain alehousekeepers in their town to have their licences revoked as they were 'otherwise able of themselves to provide for themselves & for theyr families by labouring with theyr hands (as other men)'.[114] A similar case was made by the inhabitants of Hockwold-cum-Wilton in Norfolk during the first Civil War, who appealed for Edward Miller to be suppressed from selling ale as he was a blacksmith and 'able in both body and purse to use his trade'.[115] In an attempt to restrict the numbers of these institutions, running an alehouse was only seen as a legitimate activity for the very poorest members of the community who had no other means to provide for themselves and their families.

Whilst to be in a condition of serious poverty may have been necessary for licence applicants, it was not in itself sufficient to secure permission to run an alehouse. The parishioners of Steeple Ashton, Wiltshire, wrote to the JPs on behalf of their 'poor aged neighbour William Burgis' in 1646. Burgis was 'verry ould and his labour quite done', and he only possessed a small copyhold which was no longer sufficient to maintain him and his aged wife and their family.[116] In the face of such 'troublesome times' Burgis had resorted to selling beer, but was quickly warned against doing so by the constable of the hundred – a command which, as his neighbours were keen to stress to the magistrates, the old man had dutifully obeyed. Despite his poverty, inability to work, and eagerness to cooperate with the local authorities, this appeal for Burgis to be licensed to resume his ale-selling fell on deaf ears and his house was ordered to be suppressed. Perhaps Burgis's initial illicit ale-selling had cast a doubt over his reputation – a doubt the licensing authorities were not prepared to overlook. Another illustrative example comes from a letter written in 1602 by one Edmund Thursteons to an Essex magistrate, to complain on behalf of his neighbours about an 'alehouse of great misorder', the 'Blowe Lyon' at Runsell. Thomas Ingram, the alehousekeeper, had been commanded to cease ale-selling, but pleaded poverty in refusing

---

[113] WSHC, 1612/E/177.

[114] *Wilts. Q.S. Recs*, p. 215.

[115] Norfolk Record Office, C/S 3/42A(2). I am grateful to Peter Smith for this reference, and for a transcription of this case.

[116] WSHC, 1646/M/227.

the order: 'he maketh povertie his colour to contynne his course'. His neighbours were not convinced by his claim of poverty, but nor did they accept that it gave him the right to run an alehouse, and stated that they would rather 'contribute to his charge, being a dead [deed] of charitie, then that he should maynteyne himselfe by this … [it being] very hurt-full and offensive to all the neighbors'.[117] To this community, then, this alehouse was so disruptive that they would prefer to have Ingram as a charge on the rates than to countenance the continuation of his licence. It was a dilemma no doubt faced by many communities.

In addition to being in a condition of poverty, licensing officials and the local community also had to be assured that an individual could be trusted to keep order in their alehouse. Petitioners were therefore keen to get members of their local community to testify to their reputation; a reputation based around the contemporary notions of 'honesty' and 'credit'.[118] John Runnye of Queen Camel, Somerset, was able to include in his 1608 appeal for a licence the endorsement of twenty-three of his neighbours – including a gentleman, Mr John Young – that he was a man of 'very good and honest behaviour' who had lived in the same house for over forty years and had an unblemished history as a victual-ler.[119] John Tucker of Wellington was able to secure a certificate from his neighbours to send to the magistrates in 1609, which declared that

> we have known the said John … from his youth hetherto, to be an honest man and born in Wellington aforesaid, and that during his dwelling and abode there he hath behaved and demeaned himself in good and honest sort, and also that he hath from time to time since he became a married man and 'hoseholder' been of a good conversation and governed his house in good order and therefore think him a fit and mete man to keep brewing and selling of drink.[120]

Securing the verification of his reputation by his neighbours may have been more straightforward for Tucker than for many would-be alehouse-keepers. Tucker could point to his marriage and subsequent householder

---

[117]   ERO, Q/SR/159/35.

[118]   See Muldrew, *The Economy of Obligation*; Alexandra Shepard, 'Manhood, Credit and Patriarchy in Early Modern England, c.1580–1640', *Past and Present* 167 (2000), pp. 75–106; Alexandra Shepard, 'Honesty, Worth and Gender in Early Modern England, 1560–1640', in Henry French and Jonathan Barry (eds), *Identity and Agency in England, 1500–1800* (Basingstoke, 2004), pp. 87–105.

[119]   SHC, Q/SR/3:2/170.

[120]   SHC, Q/SR/6/16.

status as evidence of his standing, the latter being the central pillar of respectability in seventeenth-century local communities. As the work of Alexandra Shepard has shown, a large number of those men who ranked amongst the poorest in this society found it increasingly difficult in the seventeenth century to afford, and therefore achieve, the setting up of their own independent household of which they were the head. This created a very real and serious set of constraints upon such men's claim to 'credit', 'worth' or social standing, and trying to establish reputability must have been a difficult task for many of the poor who pursued an alehouse licence. Indeed, Shepard has argued that one alternative pillar upon which poor men might attempt to build their claims to 'worth' was their ability and willingness to work, yet even this avenue was closed to alehousekeepers, who were technically forbidden from ale-selling if they were capable of labour or practising a trade.[121]

The task was especially difficult for prospective female alehouse-keepers, for whom the problems of establishing a good reputation could be further compounded by suspicions over their sexual conduct.[122] The constables of Kingswood sought to have the alehouse of Elizabeth Fords suppressed in 1673, not only because she allowed illicit tippling in her house, but also on the grounds that she was 'a young widow and also a whorish woman for she hath had a bastard within these three quarters of this yeer past and many in our place and out of it too doth resort to her to the great dishonour of God'.[123] The task was not, however, impossible. Joan Brown, a widow, of Somerford Magna, Wiltshire, fared better in 1683 when she secured a letter of support from the rector stating that 'she has allways had ye repute of a civil honest person among her neighbours & to the best of my knowledge keeps as good orders in her house as any one w[ha]tsoever'.[124] It may be, of course, that Joan Brown was much older than the 'young widow' Elizabeth Fords, and thus escaped some of the anxiety of the local community regarding her sexual reputation. These additional difficulties in proving their reputability to the authorities may explain the relative lack of petitions for licences by females, although other evidence suggests that female alehousekeepers

[121] Shepard, 'Manhood, Credit and Patriarchy', pp. 75–106.

[122] See, for instance, the case of Margaret Knowsley, for whom suspicions that she ran a disorderly unlicensed alehouse and had miscarried an illegitimate child overlapped: Steve Hindle, 'The Shaming of Margaret Knowsley: Gossip, Gender and the Experience of Authority in Early Modern England', *Continuity and Change* 9:3 (1994), p. 397.

[123] WSHC, 1673/E/98.

[124] WSHC, 1683/T/89.

were common in seventeenth-century England.[125] The majority of these were widows, and perhaps their unlicensed alehouses were more likely to be tolerated because of the lack of alternative forms of employment and their diminished threat to father bastards onto the community in old age, meaning fewer were involved in licensing disputes.[126]

What emerges then is another area of tension at the centre of attitudes towards the role of the alehouse in the local community. In the interests of restricting numbers and serving the needs of the local poor, contemporaries believed that alehouses could only legitimately be run by the poorest members of the community. Furthermore, fears over the disruptive potential of the poor's patronage of the alehouse left contemporaries anxious that only individuals of good repute be entrusted to run these institutions. And yet, poverty and respectability were not natural or comfortable bedfellows in the seventeenth-century mindset. Nonetheless, the shrewdest applicants for a licence did their utmost to lay claim to both. John Bindley of Audlem, Cheshire, responded to appeals to have his alehouse suppressed in 1605 by suggesting they were malicious attempts to 'undo' him, he 'beinge but a very poore man who is heartely disyrous to live quiet, and at peace wherein I might the better Labour to defend an honest poore life w[i]th the love and favour of the Countrey'.[127] In an attempt to convince the magistrates that it was possible to lead 'an honest poor life', Bindley even sought to portray his ale-selling as labour. Thomas Addis, an alehousekeeper from the township of Castle Northwich, Cheshire, also presented himself as a man both poor and reputable. He complained to the quarter sessions in 1676 that he had recently been 'suppressed & deprived of his former priviledge of brewing & sellinge of ale by meanes whereof both he & his whole family are disabled to subsist & wilbe suddenly forced to begge their bread'. Addis was demonstrating that he clearly qualified for a licence on the grounds of poverty, but was also eager to stress that before the recent decision against him his reputation in the community was a good one: 'yor pet[itioner] hath kept good rule & order within his house & hath been of honest, inoffensive & peaceable behaviour amongst his neighbours & was never justly tainted by any for his miscarriage'.[128]

---

[125] Wrightson, 'Alehouses, Order and Reformation', p. 2.

[126] For more on female keepers see Martin, *Alcohol, Sex, and Gender*, pp. 70–3; Matthew Jackson, 'A Contested Character: The Female Publican in Early Modern England and France', *Brewery History* 150 (2013), pp. 16–27.

[127] CRO, QJF/34/2/95.

[128] CRO, QJF/104/1/170.

Whilst such appeals ticked the right boxes in terms of principles, they still did not guarantee a licence in practice. A petition of 1646 for the granting of a licence to sell ale to Robert Dowse of Hackleton, Wiltshire, secured nineteen signatures certifying that Dowse was 'a man of a sober and honest life and conversacon and free from suspicon of any irregular carryage in any indirect or unlawfull course for ought wee could ever see or heare'. Although there is no evidence of any question marks over Dowse's reputation, the licensing authorities of Wiltshire still decided to suppress his alehouse. They dealt similarly with the house of John Stokes of Seend, who appealed for a licence in the same year with the support of thirteen signatories who vouched for the fact that he had always 'kept good order in his house'.[129] These decisions demonstrate that, even when certain sections of the community were prepared to vouch to the contrary, the reputation of a poor man could never be entirely beyond question.

As with the patrons of alehouses, the poverty of alehousekeepers both legitimated their involvement with the institution whilst simultaneously serving as a source of anxiety for many contemporaries. There was a real concern that alehouses could easily transcend the boundaries of their essential and legitimate role and instead set in motion a vicious circle of poverty and disruption in local communities. Many contemporaries were eager to minimise the disruptive potential of alehouses by circum-scribing the types of activity that could legitimately take place within their walls. Restricting recreational, sociable drinking – an activity that was perceived to encourage excess, profligacy and disorder – was seen as particularly crucial by those who sought to keep alehouses on a right-eous course. Contemporaries saw the character of the alehousekeeper as central to determining which course a given alehouse might take, and yet the fact that the poor were 'unruly by definition' meant that their exclusive right to take on this task left many sections of the community unable to ever rest assured that their local alehouse was in safe hands.

Some contemporaries saw ways of minimising that disruptive poten-tial. The 'chiefest inhabitants' of Chard, Somerset, complained in 1616 that the town had 'many tipplers who do brew their own beer by reason whereof they doubt [fear] that wood and other fuel will in short time become very scarce and dear'. They further claimed that 'there is such strong drink brewed that drunkenness and much other inconveniences doth thereby ensue'. Their proposal, accepted by the JPs, was that

---

[129]   WSHC, 1646/M/228, 236.

Richard Munday be licensed as a common brewer, with the exclusive right to brew the beer and ale to be sold in the town. All alehousekeepers were therefore required to purchase their ale from the common brewer in the first instance.[130] The rationale behind this proposal was that the use of fuel and the strength of beer could be more easily regulated by a common brewer, keeping the pressure on resources and levels of drunkenness in check whilst still providing essential victuals to the poor. A common brewer could also refuse to sell ale to unlicensed or disreputable alehousekeepers. This type of scheme was popular with urban authorities: the Leicester burgesses, for instance, passed an ordinance in 1574 creating a clear division between brewers and retailers of ale and beer, with brewers forbidden from retail, but retailers to be supplied exclusively by the common brewers. These brewers, in turn, were to be controlled by a guild – 'a felloweshipp & brotherhode' – under the close supervision of the mayor and burgesses.[131] This way, the trade in ale and beer was to have additional layers of involvement and management from more prominent members of the community, and not just the poor.

An even more restricted system was implemented in the Somerset parish of Croscombe the following year, where all alehouses were to be replaced by a single common brewer. In response to a request from 'the greater part of the most sufficient inhabitants', the magistrates agreed that only one licence to both brew and sell ale be granted in Croscombe to one Thomas Delton, 'a fitt man for that purpose', to act as 'a Brewer to be alwaies furnished wth good wholesome drinke for the poore'.[132] The sort of men 'fit for that purpose' were likely to be drawn from the ranks of 'the most sufficient inhabitants' of their locale. Indeed, when the burgesses of Evesham introduced a common brewer scheme in 1611, requiring all alehousekeepers to receive their ale and beer from a common brewer and forbidding them to brew their own, they appointed a member of the common council, Mr Phillip Parsons, to take on the role.[133] A similar scheme introduced in Southampton in 1659 granted a monopoly on brewing to an alderman, Richard Walker.[134] There were a number of reasons for this. In part this was an attempt to introduce an added layer of regulation to the trade: if the reins of control over local

---

[130] *Som. Q.S. Recs*, I, pp. 174–5.

[131] *Leic. Boro. Recs*, III, pp. 153–4.

[132] SHC, Q/SR/28/125.

[133] S.K. Roberts (ed.), *Evesham Borough Records of the Seventeenth Century, 1605–1687* (Worcester, 1994), p. 10.

[134] Brown, 'Alehouse Licensing', p. 124.

ale production were in the hands of 'a fit man for that purpose' rather than poor alehousekeepers, then the disruptive potential of the alehouse could be constrained. There were also financial concerns. A common brewer needed considerably more capital than a single retailer to produce ale and beer on a scale to service a whole community, so wealthier individuals were needed. There was a profit motive at work too: the introduction of common brewers was no doubt part of a wider process of more substantial villagers and townsmen moving into the expanding and increasingly lucrative brewing industry – though in a number of towns there were attempts to direct the proceeds of brewing back into various forms of poor relief and provision.[135] Wherever the profits went, such schemes represented moves by the more substantial inhabitants of towns and villages to take control of ale and beer production from their distrusted poorer neighbours. The extent of common brewer schemes in the seventeenth century should not be overstated, however.[136] In most places the role played by the local alehouse still rested primarily on the shoulders of the poor members of the community that ran alehouses, a situation that fed the considerable anxieties that surrounded the role of the alehouse in early modern English communities.

Conclusion

As this chapter has shown, the 'battle over the alehouse' was not motivated by a 'militant hostility' to the institution on the part of its opponents amongst the upper and middling ranks of society. Alehouses were almost universally accepted as a necessary feature of communal infrastructure, albeit one whose role needed to be carefully circumscribed. This not only meant 'disorderly' alehouses were denounced; contemporaries also made a key distinction between legitimate and illegitimate patrons and services. That the legitimate patrons were deemed to be the local poor – a group who were potentially unruly by definition – meant that recreational drinking on their part was perceived as a dangerous

---

[135] For more on the growing potential for profit in the brewing trade in the seventeenth century, and the subsequent increased involvement of 'middling-sort' men, see Bennett, *Ale, Beer and Brewsters*. On attempts by certain urban authorities to divert the profits back into poor relief schemes see Brown, 'Alehouse Licensing', p. 124; Paul Slack, 'Poverty and Politics in Salisbury, 1597–1666', in Peter Clark and Paul Slack (eds), *Crisis and Order in English Towns 1500–1700* (London, 1972), pp. 182–3.

[136] Estimates suggest that in the early eighteenth century over two-thirds of publicans still brewed their own beer: see Jennings, *The Local*, p. 97.

and thus illegitimate function of the alehouse. A central and previously overlooked feature of the battle against the alehouse, therefore, is that this was in key respects a campaign against alehouse sociability.

Indeed, these petitions and presentments indicate attitudes towards alehouse sociability that were far from ambivalent. Petitioners very rarely made a case that social interaction in alehouses could legitimately serve as a 'stabilizing function' in local society. The situation in central Europe appears to have been very different. In the German city of Augsburg, Ann Tlusty found that 'those responsible for law enforcement recognised alcohol as a necessary part of social and professional life. The drunkenness that resulted was not viewed as sinful but as acceptable behaviour for male citizens.'[137] Recreational drinking was seen as central to fostering a shared sense of professional and civic identity, which in turn served to buttress the civic order of Augsburg. The greater legitimacy of sociability in Augsburg than in the local communities of England may be due to the fact that in Germany 'even the public tavern, which was open to all respectable members of society, had a measure of exclusivity. Beggars, persons taking alms, and ... irresponsible householders were banned from tavern company.'[138] That the poorest members of the community were excluded from the city's drinking establishments removed much of the anxiety over the disruptive potential of recreational drinking that plagued alehouse sociability in England.[139]

In England too, moreover, recreational drinking could be seen as a legitimate and positive activity in more exclusive social contexts. Alan Everitt has suggested that inns were central to the social and cultural activities of both urban and rural elites, which included a key role for conviviality, from at least the second half of the seventeenth century.[140] Michelle O'Callaghan has demonstrated that the tavern 'played a particularly prominent role in fostering new forms of sociability among an

---

137 Tlusty, *Bacchus and Civic Order*, p. 6.

138 *Ibid.*, p. 31.

139 The equivalent of the alehouse in early modern Augsburg appears to have been the 'tap landlords', who were licensed to sell beer on a retail basis for customers to take home, but were not licensed to seat guests or serve food. Tlusty suggests that 'although customers occasionally gathered in front of a tap landlord's shop for a drink or two, these shops did not have the character of a public tavern and will not be considered as such'. It may be the case that the problem of the poor's collective recreational drinking was marginalised in Augsburg by the lack of a potential location for it such as that provided by the English alehouse. *Ibid.*, p. 36.

140 Alan Everitt, 'The English Urban Inn, 1560–1760', in Alan Everitt (ed.), *Perspectives in English Urban History* (London, 1973), pp. 91–137.

urban elite' who were, especially in London, turning their attention to 'the formation of elite communal identities through sociable activity' and 'the pleasures of conviviality'.[141] Phil Withington has argued, in an echo of Tlusty's analysis of Augsburg, that legitimate sociability was not only a feature of elite London's tavern life, but in towns across the country recreational drinking and 'keeping company' were integral to the establishment of corporate and civic identities and solidarities.[142] Indeed, the burgesses of Calne – whose hostility to alehouse sociability was manifest in the presentments of John Noyes against 'cup compan- ions' – nonetheless saw their own convivial consumption of beer, wine and tobacco as an important adjunct to the proper functioning of civic governance. Their accounts reveal regular payments for such intoxicants to the proprietors of 'The Bear' and 'The Wheel': the inns in the town where they held civic meetings.[143] The ruling strata of rural communities might also engage in similarly convivial parish meetings. The vestry of East Hoathly, Sussex, for example, spent considerable sums consuming drinks at their regular meetings in a public house, where they considered the distribution of relief payments to the parish poor – no doubt paying close attention to the drinking habits of poor relief claimants as they themselves liberally imbibed.[144]

It is unsurprising that contemporaries saw some positive role for sites of recreational drinking, and recognised the importance of communal centres of sociability to the personal and social lives of their customers. As Tlusty argues, 'sociologists have long recognised that taverns serve certain social functions', providing a place to establish and pursue social relationships, to engage in games and recreation, and to discuss personal problems, and that 'all of these functions were served by early modern taverns as well'.[145] And yet, whilst early modern contemporaries

---

[141] Michelle O'Callaghan, 'Tavern Societies, the Inns of Court, and the Culture of Conviviality in Early Seventeenth-Century London', in Adam Smyth (ed.), A Pleasing Sinne (Cambridge, 2004), pp. 37–8.

[142] Phil Withington, The Politics of Commonwealth: Citizens and Freemen in Early Modern England (Cambridge, 2005), esp. pp. 131–7; Withington, 'Company and Sociability'.

[143] Mabbs (ed.), Guild Stewards' Book, passim.

[144] Naomi Tadmor, 'Where was Mrs Turner? Governance and Gender in an Eighteenth-Century Village', in Steve Hindle, Alexandra Shepard and John Walter (eds), Remaking English Society: Social Relations and Social Change in Early Modern England (Woodbridge, 2013), p. 89. On the role of claimants' drinking habits in decisions about poor relief see Hindle, On the Parish?, pp. 386–7.

[145] Tlusty, Bacchus and Civic Order, p. 182.

accepted that these important social functions were a legitimate part of the role to be played by inns and taverns in the lives of both national and local elites, they were not recognised as part of the appropriate role to be played by the alehouse in the lives of the poorest members of local communities. Recreational drinking *per se* was not unanimously condemned in seventeenth-century England, but those humble men and women who looked to socialise over a pot of ale in front of the alehouse fire had no place in ideals of a well-ordered commonwealth.

This reading of contemporary attitudes towards the legitimacy of alehouse sociability does, however, require qualification. First, whilst there was undoubtedly a class-based dimension to attacks on alehouse sociability, elite sociability did not go entirely uncensored in early modern England – a point to which we will return in Chapter 3. What is the case, however, is that it was only alehouse sociability that was subjected to attempts to micro-regulate it. Indeed, the relative legitimacy of sociability in taverns and inns is reflected in the fact that the regulatory campaigns against the alehouse in our period were never aimed at these institutions. Judith Hunter has found that, as regards licensing and orderly conduct, 'taverns remained largely outside the responsibility of JPs',[146] and although inns were briefly subjected to the ill-fated licensing monopoly scheme of Sir Giles Mompesson between 1617 and 1621, it was only alehouses of the three main types of drinking establishment that were 'systematically targeted by central legislation throughout the early modern period'.[147]

Second, as the example of the 'cup companions' of Calne shows, the alehouse did play an important role in facilitating sociability in local communities, despite the seeming consensus amongst national and local elites that such activity was illegitimate. As discussed above, the regulatory sources drawn upon here present a blinkered picture. No doubt many contemporaries – both amongst the poor petitioners seeking a licence, and the middling sort who signed such appeals – were far more accepting of recreational drinking in alehouses, but they did not see admission of such as the best way to win an argument in a licensing dispute at the quarter sessions. This would nonetheless suggest that there was no *official* legitimacy for alehouse sociability in seventeenth-century England, and that this was a central principle of the regulatory system which few members of local communities were prepared to challenge in a legal

---

146 Hunter, 'English Inns, Taverns, Alehouses and Brandy Shops', p. 72.
147 Brown, 'Alehouse Licensing', p. 113.

context. Whether such a circumscribed view of the role of the alehouse went uncontested on the ground, and whether the official prohibition of recreational drinking was enforceable in practice, are rather different matters, to which the next chapter will turn.

2

'Authority and Good Government Trampled Underfoot': Authority and the Alehouse

In 1656 the mayor of Salisbury, William Stone, opened a petition against 'needless alehouses' in his town with the following entreaty to the magistrates of Wiltshire:

> Lay to hart the great disorders & variety of sin & wickednesse comitted in alehouses dens of sathan in which most commonly god is highly dishonoured religion abused authority and good government trampled under foot.[1]

As the previous chapter showed, such concerns with the 'great disorders' that were feared to occur in alehouses were prevalent amongst the middling and upper sort opponents of the institution, and served to underpin a regulatory framework designed to closely police the role played by the alehouse in early modern English communities. Such an analysis provides an important backdrop to understanding the 'battle over the alehouse', highlighting the motivations of some of those engaged in this conflict, and delineating the contours of the terrain on which it was fought out. It reveals little, however, about the motives and tactics of the 'other side' in this conflict – those alehouse-goers allegedly responsible for all varieties of 'sin and wickedness' – or of the character of the fighting itself. This chapter brings these issues into focus.

Undoubtedly the complaints that were directed at alehouses in petitions and presentments tell us something about the institution and its clientele. Many alehouses were indeed sites of 'disorder' as their opponents saw it. Petty crime, sex, violent confrontations, and excessive and profligate drinking certainly all occurred in alehouses.[2] What is less clear is whether these examples constitute plausible evidence, as William Stone argued, that alehouse-goers respected no authority whatsoever, that they

[1] WSHC, 1656/H/135.
[2] Clark, 'The Alehouse and the Alternative Society'.

were enemies of church and state. As Peter Clark memorably put it, for opponents of the alehouse such transgressions instinctively aroused deeper fears that alehouses 'served as the stronghold of popular opposition to the established religious and political order' and as the 'command post of men who wanted to turn the traditional world upside down and create their own alternative society'.[3] If it seems sensible to accept that alehouses did play host to forms of what today might be labelled 'anti-social behaviour', it is important to explore at greater length whether it really did act as a centre of serious political and religious subversion. Was the 'battle over the alehouse' fought out between radically opposed religious and political worldviews, as some of the enemies of the institution suggested?

As well as exploring the views held towards authority by alehouse-keepers and alehouse patrons, this chapter examines those instances when they came into direct contact with the exercise of authority. As discussed in Chapter 1, the letter and operation of the law are different animals. We have seen how alehouse regulation was envisaged to work in national legislation, and to some extent how it was mobilised by local officials and petitioners. Here the attention moves on from the principles behind licensing legislation and the arguments mobilised for or against an alehouse licence, to consider the issue of enforcement. How did magistrates respond to the pressures on them, from legislation coming from above and from petitions coming from below, in reaching their decisions? How did the constables charged with enforcing such licensing decisions take to their task? And how did the targets of alehouse regulation respond to a decision to revoke their licence or issue them with a fine? In other words, this chapter will examine how alehouse regulation worked in practice rather than principle: how it was enforced – and, indeed, resisted – on the ground.

The following section on 'alebench politics' investigates the political culture of the alehouse. It draws on evidence of political discussion in alehouses to test the various theories that have been proposed about its allegedly subversive character, and argues that the political culture of the institution should be understood as less radical but nonetheless more sophisticated and heterogeneous than historians have hitherto characterised it. The two sections after that turn their attention to the enforcement of alehouse regulation, focusing first on the varied efforts of officials – both at the level of the magistracy and of the parish – and then on the

---

3   *Ibid.*, p. 48.

opposition to regulatory efforts mounted by alehousekeepers and patrons. Taken together they show that a degree of ambivalence on the part of officialdom, combined with a defiant disposition on the part of many of the targets of regulation, resulted in a rather patchy record of success and failure in the campaign against the alehouse. The final section offers a reconsideration of the relationship between the church and the alehouse that serves to reinforce the arguments of the preceding sections. It demonstrates that whilst the rhetoric of opponents of alehouses often condemned them as 'nests of Satan', in practice alehouse patrons were not especially unorthodox. Many combined church-going and alehouse-going, and refused to see an inherent dichotomy between being a good Christian and a 'good fellow'. Moreover, much like secular officials, the clergy were not unanimous in their 'militant hostility' towards alehouses, or even alehouse sociability. Many were keen to encourage the links between the church and the alehouse that seemed entirely natural to the majority of their parishioners. Overall, then, the chapter reveals that the alehouse was not a hub of radical anti-authoritarianism. Its relationship with authority was undoubtedly fractious, but it was one marked in practice by rather more ambivalence on both sides than the rhetoric of legislators and petitioners reveals. As such, the alehouse occupied a more mainstream place in early modern English communities than the carefully circumscribed role imagined for it in the dreams, or the radically subversive role feared in the nightmares, of its staunchest opponents.

Alebench politics

Those 'chief inhabitants' that petitioned the magistrates to suppress alehouses were often most fearful of the potential of such institutions to cause socio-economic dislocation in their local community and to feed a cycle of poverty. For the Crown, the principal fear was that the alehouse could serve as a breeding ground for sedition, subversion and irreligion, and feed a challenge to established authority. As early as 1545, in the last major address of his reign, Henry VIII expressed his concern that attempts to create a godly people through introduction of a vernacular Bible had been corrupted in the nation's alehouses: 'I am very sorry to know and hear how unreverently that most precious jewel, the Word of God, is disputed, rhymed, sung and jangled in every alehouse and tavern, contrary to the true meaning and doctrine of the same.'[4] The

---

4   Ethan Shagan, *Popular Politics and the English Reformation* (Cambridge, 2003), p. 232.

Elizabethan regime heard reports that questions of the Queen's own legitimacy, gender and sexual character were commonly discussed 'in alehouses and such like places, whereupon ensue dangerous or undutiful speeches of her majesty's most gracious government'.[5] The early Stuart monarchs shared the Tudors' fears that alehouse talk was a destabilising force. Indeed, the controversial 'Declaration on Sports', issued by James I in 1618 and reissued by his son Charles I in 1633 – permitting a variety of sports and recreations on Sundays that had been forbidden in some areas by Puritan local authorities – made this clear.[6] The Declaration complained that the prohibition of 'the common and meaner sort of people from using such exercises as may make their bodies more able for war', would encourage them 'in place thereof' toward 'filthy tipplings and drunkenness, and breed a number of idle and discontented speeches in their alehouses'.[7] A 1633 report on popular recreations and feasts in Somerset, by the Bishop of Bath and Wells, William Piers, made a similar case, arguing that 'if the people should not have their honest and lawful recreations upon Sundays after evening prayer', they would go instead to 'tippling houses, and there upon their ale-benches talk of matters of the church or state'.[8] Even those high ranking officials who supported some forms of popular communal recreation were fiercely opposed to the alehouse, fearing its role as a centre of anti-authoritarian conversation.

Such concerns waned to some extent after the Restoration, in part because the Crown's anxiety over the potent cocktail of alcohol and politics gave way to fears of a novel and even more dangerous mixture of caffeine and politics. Charles II came close to introducing an outright ban on coffeehouses in both 1666 and 1675, with a Royal Proclamation in the latter year denouncing coffeehouses as sites where 'divers False, Malitious and Scandalous Reports are devised and spread abroad, to the Defamation of his Majesties Government, and to the Disturbance of the Peace and Quiet of the Realm'.[9] In fact, this switch of concern to the

---

[5] David Cressy, *Dangerous Talk: Scandalous, Seditious and Treasonable Speech in Pre-Modern England* (Oxford, 2010), pp. 61–2.

[6] For more on the 'Book of Sports' see Alistair Dougall, *The Devil's Book: Charles I, The Book of Sports and Puritanism in Tudor and Stuart England* (Exeter, 2011).

[7] David Cressy and Lori Anne Ferrell, *Religion and Society in Early Modern England: A Sourcebook* (London, 1996), pp. 145–8.

[8] *Ibid.*, pp. 148–50.

[9] Markman Ellis, *The Coffee House: A Cultural History* (London, 2004) p. 86; see also Brian Cowan, *The Social Life of Coffee: The Emergence of the British Coffeehouse* (London, 2005), ch. 7.

coffeehouse created some space for alehouses to be re-evaluated as 'loyal' institutions. The ritual of drinking loyal 'healths' – toasts – to the King had become a central expression of royalist identity during the Civil War, to some extent reconfiguring the political symbolism of alcohol consumption.[10] A successor to William Piers as Bishop of Bath and Wells, Peter Mews, penned a tract in 1671 declaring that ale was a 'good friend' to 'the church and religion' and that alehouse-goers were 'good men and quiet, no dangerous plotters in the Common-weal'.[11] The association with sedition was not shaken off entirely. In 1695, an alehouse in Hereford, 'The Catherine Wheel', was suppressed amidst fears that 'divers persons disaffected to the present government do weekly and daily resort thither and read private, false and seditious newsletters to corrupt his majesty's subjects'.[12] In 1683 the Grand Jury of Northamptonshire demanded greater regulation of their inns and alehouses because of their 'great temptation in spreading seditious news'.[13] Yet Peter Clark has suggested that in the eighteenth century the association between the alehouse and political and religious dissent turned on its head: 'far from being regarded as the enemy of the political establishment, the popular drink trade was increasingly seen by 1750 as its ally. Relations with the Church likewise improved.'[14]

Nonetheless, when the 'battle over the alehouse' raged most fiercely in the first half of the seventeenth century its opponents certainly saw it as a hotbed of dissent. Was this justified? Historians have reached some starkly contrasting conclusions here. Peter Clark, whose work first planted the connection between the alehouse and an 'alternative society' in the historiographical landscape, actually argued that the institution's opponents vastly exaggerated its political radicalism. He concluded that most alehouse patrons were 'too concerned to keep themselves together body and soul to become radical activists', with the result that the

---

10 Capp, *England's Culture Wars*, pp. 162–71; Nicholls, *The Politics of Alcohol*, ch. 2; Angela McShane Jones, 'Roaring Royalists and Ranting Brewers: The Politicisation of Drink and Drunkenness in Political Broadside Ballads from 1640 to 1689', in Smyth (ed.), *A Pleasing Sinne*, pp. 69–87; Rebecca Lemon, 'Compulsory Conviviality in Early Modern England', *English Literary Renaissance* 43:3 (2013), pp. 381–414. My thanks to Dr Lemon for allowing me to see a pre-publication version of this piece.

11 Peter Mews, *The Ex-Ale-Tation of Ale* (London, 1671), pp. 9, 13, quoted in Steve Pincus, '"Coffee politicians does create": Coffeehouses and Restoration Political Culture', *Journal of Modern History* 67 (1995), p. 825.

12 Adam Fox, *Oral and Literate Culture in England, 1500–1700* (Oxford, 2000), p. 376.

13 Everitt, 'The English Urban Inn', p. 111.

14 Clark, *The English Alehouse*, p. 237.

alehouse's contribution to political resistance to the ruling class 'tended to be small . . . confined to the desperate seditious outbursts' of 'marginal people' with 'minimal political awareness' – isolated outbursts which 'seem almost invariably to have fallen on deaf ears'.[15] More recently, a rather different interpretation of 'seditious outbursts' has been offered by historians of early modern England under the influence of the work of anthropologist James C Scott. In a theorisation of power relations derived initially from his fieldwork in Malaysian peasant communities, Scott argued that subordinates in societies with a profoundly unequal distribution of power – 'the ruled' – rarely risk an open and public chal- lenge to the authority of the elite – 'the rulers'. Instead, he argued that they reserved their criticisms for expression in situations that were free from the usual constraints of power, and out of earshot of elites. In such contexts 'subordinates' developed a shared, radically subversive worldview that contrasts sharply with their public displays of deference. Scott labels this 'backstage' worldview the 'hidden transcript'. Particularly important to the development of the 'hidden transcript' in Scott's formulation are 'sequestered social sites', locations from which rulers are absent and 'in which the unspoken riposte, stifled anger, and bitten tongues created by relations of domination find a vehement, full-throated expression'. For early modern England, Scott identified the alehouse as such a space: 'a privileged site for the transmission of popular culture ... that was usually at odds with official culture'.[16] This analytical model received eager endorsement from a number of scholars of early modern England, to the extent that one historian has recently suggested that 'within the field, "alehouse gossip" [now] stands almost as a metonym for empow- ering subordinate verbalisations'.[17] Those 'desperate' and 'isolated' sedi- tious outbursts that Clark had in the late 1970s dismissed as impotent

---

[15] Ibid., p. 160; Clark, 'The Alehouse and the Alternative Society', pp. 66–8.

[16] James C. Scott, Domination and the Arts of Resistance: Hidden Transcripts (London, 1990), esp. pp. 120–1.

[17] For examples of the application of Scott's ideas by scholars of early modern England see Andy Wood, '"Poore men woll speke one daye": Plebeian Languages of Deference and Defiance in England, c.1520–1640', in Tim Harris (ed.), The Politics of the Excluded, c.1500–1850 (Basingstoke, 2001), pp. 67–98; Adam Fox, 'Ballads, Libels and Popular Ridicule in Jacobean England', Past and Present 145 (1994), p. 72; John Walter, 'Public Transcripts, Popular Agency and the Politics of Subsistence in Early Modern England', in Michael J. Braddick and John Walter (eds), Negotiating Power in Early Modern Society: Order, Hierarchy and Subordination in Britain and Ireland (Cambridge, 2001), pp. 123–48; Keith Wrightson, 'The Politics of the Parish in Early Modern England', in Paul Griffiths, Adam Fox and Steve Hindle (eds), The Experience of Authority in Early Modern England (Basingstoke, 1996), p. 35. The quote is from James Brown, 'Drinking Houses and the

were reconfigured around the turn of the century as evidence that the alehouse did indeed host a radically subversive political culture, albeit one that was strategically submerged from the view of elites.

To suggest that the alehouse could have hosted a shrewdly concealed political radicalism is not to project an entirely alien or anachronistic model onto early modern English power relations. Evidence supporting Scott's theorisation can be identified in the arguments of contemporaries, such as the seventeenth-century radical Roger Crab, who wrote in 1657:

> When the all-seeing eye looks into every alehouse of this nation, and seeth of which sort are most there … they will appear to be labouring poor men … [who] in times of scarcity pine and murmure for want of bread, Cursing the Rich behind his Back; and before his Face, Cap and Knee and [assume] a whining countenance.[18]

If it is possible to show that the existence of a 'hidden transcript' was plausible to contemporaries, it is much more difficult to actually try and recover it. If it existed, the majority of its expressions of radicalism will remain forever hidden, part of a 'dark figure' of exchanges lost to the historical record. That said, close analysis of those 'seditious outbursts' that do survive, those fragments of alebench talk that come down to the present, allows us to reach a number of conclusions about the political culture of the alehouse that cast serious doubt on the models offered by both Clark and Scott.

There are occasional glimpses of the kind of radicalism that haunted the worst nightmares of the opponents of the alehouse. In 1671 a band of men responsible for a spate of thefts, assaults and hedge-breaking in the Worcestershire parishes of Severn Stoke, Kempsey and Pirton – self-styled as the Levellers, and led by brothers known as Robin Hood and Little John – were known to use two unlicensed and 'very disorderly' alehouses as 'the chief places of their rendezvous'.[19] Andy Wood has also found evidence that labourers 'sitting in their alehouses spoke of how "rich men" starved the poor and imagined bloody day-dreams

Politics of Surveillance in Pre-Industrial Southampton', in Beat Kümin (ed.), *Political Space in Pre-Industrial Europe* (Farnham, 2009), p. 77.

[18] As quoted in Steve Hindle, 'Exhortation and Entitlement: Negotiating Inequality in English Rural Communities, 1550–1650', in Braddick and Walter (eds), *Negotiating Power*, pp. 116–17.

[19] State Papers, Domestic, Charles II. 287, no. 62. Thanks to Brodie Waddell for this reference.

of "knocking down" the "rich churls'".[20] Far more common than such examples of radical levelling principles is evidence of words spoken specifically against the monarch, especially, though by no means exclusively, at times of acute political tension.[21] In 1641 one Thomas Stafford was indicted for speaking seditious words at an alehouse in the Yorkshire village of Youlthorpe, where he was accused of declaring Charles I 'fitter to be hanged then to be a Kinge' and 'the Kinge and Queene was at masse together'.[22] In 1685, in an alehouse in Pitsea, Essex, Jon Stibbert levelled a similar accusation at Charles II, opining that 'the King went openly to Mass, and he did not know but he might prove a second Mary'.[23] In nearby Rochford, in the following year, a tailor named Francis Raw suggested the King was a Jesuit.[24] At Newall, Cheshire, in 1695, one Mary Winfield reported to the magistrates that a blacksmith, Robert Chester, had called King William 'a rogue', had asserted that he was 'noe Lawfull King, but that the Lawfull King was King James in France; And that King William had noe right but by the Queen's Apron Strings'.[25] Whether such expressions represented widely held plebeian critiques of the established political order, or were isolated opinions that fell on deaf ears, they nonetheless indicate a familiarity with the religious history and succession issues of their age that belies any suggestion that political awareness was minimal.

Another common category of alebench discourse involved expressions of contempt for more local figures of authority than the monarch. In an alehouse conversation in Great Durnford, Wiltshire, in 1665, a labourer named Andrew Waters confronted a miller, William Dawkins, after the latter declared, 'I care not a fart for a King, nor for never a Magistrate in England.'[26] Robert Simpson, a Nottingham scrivener, was presented by the constables to the borough authorities in 1620 as a man who 'useth in the alehouses amongst his companions base and contemptious terms against the magistrates'. They went on to specify that he had railed specifically against the mayor, saying 'let him kisse my arse, even the very nocke of my arse'.[27] In Wilton, in 1610, it was reported that Robert

---

[20] Wood, "'Poore men woll speke one daye'", p. 91.
[21] For examples from across the early modern period see Cressy, *Dangerous Talk*.
[22] *York Cast. Deps*, no. II.
[23] ERO, Q/SR/447/100.
[24] ERO, Q/SR/449/85.
[25] *Ches. Q.S. Recs*, p. 195.
[26] WSHC, 1665/H/178.
[27] *Nott. Boro. Recs*, IV, pp. 367–8.

Somison had been using 'filthy communicacion' about that town's mayor when an 'honest man' had 'apprehended him for itt'. Somison was undeterred, and responded by 'outragiously brak[ing] out against the maior saieng I had rather be a tankerd bearer in london then a maior in wilton & more creditt to be a tankard bearer then a maior'.[28] On occasion, this outright mocking of authority took the form of a communal, rather than isolated, expression. In Rayleigh, Essex, in 1589, John Badcocke led a drinking ritual in which key local authority figures were unfavourably impersonated:

> He, with others more (sitting upon their alebench and greatly abusing themselves at one Mother Larkinge's house), took upon him and was called by the name of Mr. Parson, another taking upon him and was called by the name of churchwarden, another by the name of a sworn man, another by the name of the honest men of the parish, and another by the name of an apparitor whose name was Thomas England; thus sitting, abusing themselves like drunken sots.[29]

It might be tempting to see such behaviour, as David Cressy has done, as evidence of 'conventional plebeian obstreperousness' or 'anti-authoritarian belligerence' on the part of the lower orders, calculated to irk, rather than to overthrow, authority.[30] But there were undoubtedly occasions when such critiques of authority represented more than simply 'cathartic release'. When the Wanstead brickmaker John Stephens told those with whom he was drinking in a Great Ilford alehouse in 1685 that at their last monthly meeting all the Justices of the Peace were drunk – he claimed that 'the table where they sat was so full of empty bottles that one could not lay a pipe betweene them' – it was intended to undermine the legitimacy of a decision they had made against him. Indeed, he complained that 'they would not do him justice and that he would complain of them to my lord Chief Justice'.[31] When Nicholas Wilkins of Warwick was convicted of keeping an unlicensed alehouse in 1615, he and a number of fellow townsmen – including a number of men of middling-sort rank – responded by holding a mock trial in an alehouse in which they impersonated the town magistracy, depicting them as corrupt 'greedy Cormorants' and 'old gouty whoremasters' in a ritual intended

28 WSHC, 1610/H/123.
29 Emmison, *Elizabethan Life: Morals and the Church Courts*, p. 70.
30 Cressy, *Dangerous Talk*, pp. 232, 75.
31 ERO, Q/SR 449/87.

'not only to ridicule but to harm as well', and to discredit the authority of the magistracy and their decision.[32] That attempts to undermine local authority figures might go beyond individual verbal expressions can also be seen in their expression in forms intended to reach a wider audience. In Kirkby Malzeard, Yorkshire, in 1602, Stephen Proctor, local Puritan gentleman and Justice of the Peace, was the subject of a rumour 'which identified him as a source of a recent levy on alehouses, a rumour that caused his likeness to appear on alehouse doors accompanied with "a paire of Gallowes"'.[33] In Reading, in 1636, an anonymous letter, 'full of base and scandalous wordes, tendinge to the defamacion of the Maiour' was left in the tavern of Henry Salmon, and its contents soon became widely divulged and discussed.[34] Mocking rituals, threatening images, and anonymous libels all represented forms of alehouse political culture that were shrewder and more sophisticated political weapons than desperate individual outbursts of people with minimal political awareness.[35]

There was also more to alebench politics than opposition to the injustices meted out by ruling elites. The alehouse was a site where 'topics such as taxation, the royal succession, ecclesiastical policy and the very nature of the relationship between crown and church were the subject of heated debate'.[36] People did not simply rail against authority; they discussed and debated the burning matters of church and state of their time. The Lancashire mercer's apprentice, Roger Lowe, who kept a diary in the 1660s, recorded the details of several such conversations in alehouses. He records that whilst out drinking in February of 1664 'John Pottr and I began to discourse concerning the manner of God's worship he was for Episcopacie and I was for Presbittery. The contention had

[32] For more on this fascinating incident see David Harris Sacks, 'Searching for "Culture" in the English Renaissance', *Shakespeare Quarterly* 39:4 (1988), pp. 484–6.

[33] Andy Wood, 'Subordination, Solidarity and the Limits of Popular Agency in a Yorkshire Valley, c.1596–1615', *Past and Present* 193 (2006), p. 56.

[34] *Read. Boro. Recs*, III, p. 312. The unpopular mayor and burgesses of Reading were commonly the target of 'opprobrious' words uttered in the town's markets and alehouses in the 1620s and 1630s. See Christine Jackson, 'A Town "Governed by a Company of Geese in Furred Gowns": Political and Social Conflict in Reading c.1620–40', *Southern History* 29 (2007), pp. 29–58.

[35] For more on these aspects of popular political culture see Alastair Bellany, 'Libels in Action: Ritual, Subversion and the English Literary Underground, 1603–42', in Harris (ed.), *The Politics of the Excluded*, pp. 99–124; Fox, 'Ballads, Libels and Popular Ridicule'; John Walter '"The pooremans joy and the gentlemans plague": A Lincolnshire Libel and the Politics of Sedition in Early Modern England', *Past and Present* 203 (2009), pp. 29–67.

[36] Shagan, *Popular Politics*, p. 58.

like to have beene hott but the lord prevented [it].' In June of that year Lowe was invited by Thomas Jameson to an alehouse 'to come to drinke with hime and we stayed late in night and we began controversie he a papist began to speak revileingly of Luther and Calvin which I laboured to defend ... We ware in love and peace in our discourse.'[37] That a range of positions on a range of issues might be taken up and debated by alehouse patrons invites us to consider whether, in some sense, the political culture of the alehouse came closer to that of a 'public sphere' – an arena for the public discussion of political and religious issues, and a social space for public criticism of the state. Certainly, a widespread thirst for political discussion – both geographically and socially – did not emerge in England hand in hand with the coffeehouse.[38] It had long been a feature of alehouse culture, something often overlooked in work on the politics of the Restoration coffeehouse.[39] In important respects, though, the political culture of the alehouse does not meet the criteria of the public sphere as laid out in the classic formulation of the sociologist Jürgen Habermas.[40] It was certainly not characterised by open, legal discussion in which a plurality of views could be freely stated and then civilly debated with recourse to reason. Whilst Roger Lowe's discourse with a 'papist' may have ended in 'love and peace', in many instances where rival positions were held by alehouse patrons the conversation ended in a report of seditious words to the authorities. In 1637, at the Lion and Greyhound in Lavenham, Suffolk, Thomas Skinner whispered 'dangerous and treasonable words' against the King to Thomas Dandy. That Skinner deemed it prudent to whisper in itself indicates that such an opinion could not be freely voiced, and Dandy's response was hardly an attempt to talk down his companion with reasoned debate. Instead, he cried out that 'there is one on this room that speaks nothing but treason'. Another patron then instructed that the master of the house

---

37 *Lowe*, pp. 52, 64.

38 For an argument that overstates the degree to which the emergence of the coffeehouse reflected a new thirst for political discussion see Pincus, '"Coffee politicians does create"'.

39 For the deep roots of a plebeian 'public sphere' – which can be traced back to at least the thirteenth century – and its connection with market- and tavern-talk, see David Rollison, *A Commonwealth of the People: Popular Politics and England's Long Social Revolution, 1066–1649* (Cambridge, 2010), pp. 435–43.

40 Jürgen Habermas, *The Structural Transformation of the Public Sphere: An Inquiry into a Category of Bourgeois Society*, trans. Thomas Burger with the assistance of Frederick Lawrence (Cambridge, 1989).

should take charge of Skinner for 'safekeeping' whilst the constable was fetched.[41]

There was then real danger involved in attempting to discourse about political issues in the alehouse. John Cottle, an aleseller from Box, Wiltshire, denied hearing seditious words in his house in 1691 and told the magistrates that he 'usually advises those he keepeth company withall not to talke of ye gouvernment'.[42] Expressing the wrong views in the wrong company could lead to prosecution, and if your words could be construed as seditious – an ill-defined term in law, but covering words that could be interpreted as an attack on the established order of the realm – or worse as treasonous, then you could face punishment ranging from fines, disfigurement and imprisonment, to, for treason, the death penalty.[43] Such draconian laws were only significant, of course, if people were prepared to report such words when spoken. The evidence we have suggests that they were. Not only the case from Lavenham, which provides a particularly detailed account of the dynamics of such reporting, but almost 'every case of seditious words lodged within the archives of the criminal courts . . . speaks not only of some plebeians' capacity to formulate a social critique, but also of the willingness of others to inform against them'.[44] In light of such evidence it becomes hard to sustain the notion that a 'hidden transcript' could have existed in the alehouse, for this was hardly a 'sequestered site' where radical opinions could be freely expressed and where they went unpoliced. One recent exploration of the regulation of alehouses in early modern Southampton has suggested that alehouses there were particular targets of surveillance by the authorities.[45] But even where local officials were not themselves listening closely for dangerous speeches, fellow alehouse patrons such as Thomas Dandy were often prepared to take such policing upon themselves. This suggests that the alehouse was far from being a 'sequestered site', and moreover demonstrates that whilst some alehouse patrons were eager to voice a challenge to authority, others were prepared to act in defence of the same. Once again, then, we see that the political culture of the alehouse was not characterised by a homogenous anti-authoritarianism. Its patrons took up a range of positions, one of which was loyalty to the

[41] Cressy, *Dangerous Talk*, p. 151.

[42] *Wilts. Q.S. Recs*, p. 276.

[43] For more on the legal framework surrounding seditious and treasonous words, see Cressy, *Dangerous Talk*, chs 1–3.

[44] Wood, 'Poore men woll speke one daye', p. 81.

[45] Brown, 'Drinking Houses and the Politics of Surveillance'.

established political order. The result was a heterogeneous and fractured political culture.

The degree of fractiousness varied over time and place, and so too did its nature. Expressions of loyalty and disloyalty to authority can be found across the early modern period, though not necessarily evenly: David Cressy suggests that criticisms of monarchy 'seemed to quiet down or move to a lower register' during the reign of James I compared to those voiced against the Tudors, for instance.[46] There were also periods and places where a degree of factionalism could enter alehouse political culture, creating divisions other than those between the anti-authoritarian and the loyal. Ethan Shagan has argued that Kent – a particularly important county in the early stages of the Protestant Reformation – was in the 1530s and 1540s a hotbed of religious debate and division, where parishioners 'would have had easy access to a variety of points of view, not only from preachers in the pulpit but from neighbours in the alehouse'. This created a 'heightened level of conflict' within the political culture of the county's alehouses, as 'confessional antagonisms often spilled into everyday life'.[47] In Dartford, in 1539, a baker proposed a health to Henry VIII, saying 'God save King Henry, here is good ale', only to be met with the response from a miller and a labourer opposed to the King's religious policies: 'God save the cup of good ale, for King Henry shall be hanged.' In 1543 the parson of Pluckley refused to drink with his parishioner Stephen Giles after the latter casually revealed that he prayed nightly 'in the honour of God and Our Lady and all the company of heaven', a Catholic form of prayer.[48] If such fractiousness was rife in certain parts of the country as the birthpangs of the English Reformation began to be felt, then it was also a marked feature of alehouse political culture during the Civil Wars and Interregnum, when the issue once again became not *whether* dutiful obedience was owed to authority, but rather to *which* source of authority loyalty was owed. The atmosphere was charged in the drinking establishments of Wells, Somerset, in 1649, in the wake of the execution of Charles I. As was so often the case, trouble was sparked by the proposal of a loyal health. Humphry Butler, a seller of sweet powders to barbers, had been drinking in an alehouse when he 'did urge sevrall tymes to drinke the Kings health', and when 'others would not pledge

---

[46] Cressy, *Dangerous Talk*, p. 91.
[47] Shagan, *Popular Politics*, pp. 219–21.
[48] *Ibid.*, pp. 220–1, 223.

the same, quarrelled with them'.[49] Butler was not the only one in Wells loyal to the dead King. A company of tailors taking supper in an inn had fallen to discussing the King's death. When Robert Allen opined 'that the king had a faire tryall for his life', Peter Sandford responded that 'he was tried by a Company of Rogues', and because Allen and others had 'spoke in the behalf of the Parliament the said Sandford replyed that he could find in his hart to throw the jugg in their face'.[50]

If the 1640s and 1650s witnessed a high level of partisan drinking, so too did the years surrounding the various succession crises of the later seventeenth century. The popularity of the Duke of Monmouth – an illegitimate son of Charles II, and seen by many as a potential Protestant alternative to the Catholic heir to the throne, the King's brother James, Duke of York – was one source of tension. In 1683, at 'the Sign of the Angel' in Warminster, Wiltshire, Thomas Morris – an excise officer – proposed to drink a health to the King. William Seare, a clothworker, refused with the kind of scatological flourish so often favoured by early modern dissidents, claiming 'he did not care a turd for the King repeating the same words over two or three times but he would drinke a health to the honest Duke of Monmouth'.[51] Moreover, when Morris reported these words to the magistrates, he related that 'some of the same Company' – which included a tailor, a butcher, and another clothworker – had been 'desirous to drinke the Duke of Monmouths health saying it would come in fashion in a short time'. When James did inherit the throne, in 1685, this too was the cause of alebench divisions. In an alehouse in North Bradley, Wiltshire, in 1685, a brazier William Jennings proposed a health to the new King. John Moore, a labourer, responded by declaring that he would 'drink noe health to any popish Rogue', and then struck Jennings a blow on the head with a stick 'so that he lost much blood by it'.[52]

The 1688 revolution that brought William III to the throne was likewise divisive. In 1689 a Leeds lawyer clashed with the authorities when he and his companions pledged a 'health to the confusion of King William'. An alewife in Carlisle disputed with two Scottish lairds over who was the rightful King to drink a health to, she insisting 'she would pledge King William's health', whilst the laird's insisted they 'knewe no

49 SHC, Q/SR/81/81.
50 SHC, Q/SR/81/87.
51 WSHC, 1683/T/115.
52 Wilts. Q.S. Recs, p. 271.

King but King James'.[53] In the cellar of a Norwich alehouse a grocer exclaimed, 'God Bliss King William King of England. God of the first place saved us, And King William in the next place saved all our Lives', only to be met with the response of a worsted weaver who declared 'that King William was none of the King of England but a Deputy and fitt for no better', and the grocer 'should be hanged for speaking aginst King James'.[54] Whilst this factionalism was most prominent – in the surviving records at least – at times of major religious and political upheaval, it was undoubtedly becoming a more routine feature of alehouse political culture in the late seventeenth and early eighteenth centuries as the positions on these issues began to harden into the 'party' identities of 'Whigs' and 'Tories', and both high and popular politics became increasingly divided and contentious.[55] Indeed, in some towns Whigs and Tories each had their own drinking establishments. In Northampton in the 1680s, for example, the Whigs frequented 'The Swan' and the Tories 'The Goat'.[56] Alebench politics had come to not only revolve around conflicts between those who challenged and those who defended authority, it increasingly reflected divided opinions over who could and should claim ultimate authority over matters of church and state.

Taken together, then, what conclusions can be drawn on the nature of alehouse political culture from the fragments of alebench politics available to the historian? It seems clear that early modern opponents of the alehouse were not as misguided as Peter Clark thought when depicting the institution as a hub of political discussion. There was more to alebench politics than the isolated outbursts of marginal people. In alehouses across England, from major urban centres such as Norwich and Nottingham to small villages in Yorkshire and the West Country, men (and in some cases women) – from Scottish lairds, Leeds lawyers, excise officers, powder sellers, tailors, blacksmiths, weavers, brickmakers, alewives and labourers – discussed theology, the principals of the succession, the administration of justice, and the legitimacy of their rulers. The alehouse hosted an ersatz public sphere, albeit one that was more rough and ready than the bourgeois version more usually sought after by historians. Opinions were as often expressed through a boozy toast or a scatological quip as reasoned oratory, and disagreements were as likely to

53 *York Cast. Deps*, nos. CCLXIII, CCLXXL.

54 Norfolk Record Office, NCR 12 B (1), 1684–9.

55 See McShane Jones, 'Roaring Royalists and Ranting Brewers'; and the changing character of seditious speech as charted in Cressy, *Dangerous Talk*, chs 9–11.

56 Kümin, *Drinking Matters*, p. 130.

end with a jug of beer in the face, or a run-in with the magistrates, as they were in civilised debate. Yet here was an arena of vibrant political expression with greater social depth and geographical breadth than the coffeehouse would ever achieve.

If opponents of the alehouse were right to envisage people 'upon their ale-benches talking of matters of the church or state', they nonetheless overstated the extent to which the resulting opinions expressed tended to the 'trampling underfoot' of all authority. Alebench politics often had a flavour of anti-authoritarianism, and alehouse patrons could actively engage in attempts to destabilise local authority in particular, but this did not amount to a radical plebeian 'hidden transcript'. The political culture of the alehouse was too heterogeneous for Scott's model to apply. It was not a safe place for subordinates to share their levelling desires with fellow travellers, as many of those we would count amongst 'the ruled' in early modern English society were inclined to promptly report seditious mutterings to their 'rulers'. Loyalty, as much as levelling, motivated the political actions of alehouse patrons, though this too could land them in trouble with authority if it was expressed as a health to a deposed monarch during a period of acute political upheaval. Whilst the political culture of the alehouse offered a greater threat to the established order than Clark acknowledged, it was not quite the headquarters of plebeian radicalism that Scott's model of a 'hidden transcript' suggests.

The exercise of authority

To focus exclusively on the threat the alehouse posed to church and state is, though, to miss important aspects of its relationship with authority. The history of the alehouse has more to tell us about the history of power relations in early modern England than the capacity or desire of its patrons to overthrow the political elite. Another of James Scott's concepts that has influenced early modern historians is rather more useful here. Before developing the concept of the 'hidden transcript', Scott had been less interested in the dramatic exclamations of popular opposition to elite authority, instead directing his attention toward more subtle attempts by subordinates to contest authority, those relating to 'the constant, grinding conflict over work, food, autonomy, ritual', what he termed 'everyday forms of resistance'.[57] John Walter, in particular,

[57] James C. Scott, *Weapons of the Weak: Everyday Forms of Peasant Resistance* (New Haven, 1985).

has taken up the pursuit of such forms of resistance in an early modern English context, in an attempt 'to recover something of the quotidian and largely unremarked exchanges by which individuals attempted to blunt the exercise of power in the micro-politics of manor and parish'.[58] Influenced as much by Joan Scott as James Scott, Keith Wrightson has also been key in leading historians of early modern England to expand the range of activities that we consider 'political' beyond those relating to 'the conduct and management of affairs of state'. In particular, Wrightson suggested that we might consider 'the manner in which relationships of power and authority, dominance and subordination are established and maintained, refused and modified'. Like Walter, Wrightson argued that 'one of the best ways to appreciate this is to survey parts of the field from a parochial perspective: to consider the rich variety of political processes which can be observed in the local community', processes that he termed 'the politics of the parish'.[59] Historians of the alehouse have generally sought to identify more dramatic or radical forms of 'political' resistance when assessing the anti-authoritarian credentials of the institution. In consequence, they may have missed some of the more subtle ways in which alehousekeepers and patrons contested authority.[60] It is to the operation of authority at an everyday level – through an analysis of the enforcement of alehouse regulation – that this chapter now turns.

Before considering the ways in which alehousekeepers and patrons sought to 'blunt the exercise of power' in their manor or parish, we need first to consider the manner in which such authority was exercised. Whilst Chapter 1 delineated the framework for alehouse regulation, this section turns its attention to how that system operated in practice. Pivotal here was the role of the magistrates, those members of the county and borough elite appointed by the Crown to administer aspects of law and justice through the regular meetings of the quarter sessions courts – and in between times when required. It was by these men that decisions over alehouse licensing, including orders to suppress unnecessary, unlicensed or disorderly alehouses, were taken. They were afforded considerable scope to use their own discretion: after all, we have seen that the appropriate number of alehouses for a given community was a

---

[58] Walter, 'Public Transcripts, Popular Agency and the Politics of Subsistence', p. 124.

[59] Wrightson, 'The Politics of the Parish', pp. 10–11; See also Joan W. Scott, *Gender and the Politics of History* (New York, 1988).

[60] For a fuller statement of this point see Mark Hailwood, 'Alehouses, Popular Politics and Plebeian Agency in Early Modern England', in Fiona Williamson (ed.), *Locating Agency: Space, Power and Popular Politics* (Newcastle, 2010), pp. 51–76.

matter of interpretation. The result of this discretionary aspect of the licensing system was to create considerable variety across time and space as to the vigour with which the regulatory framework was enforced.

Part of this uneven pattern was a tendency for urban authorities to be more proactive than their rural counterparts. Many larger towns and cities had rights of self-government that allowed them to operate as counties in their own right when it came to holding quarter sessions, and in those that did not the local borough authorities might take advantage of the jurisdictional blurriness characteristic of the early modern English state to nonetheless play an active role in the enforcement of alehouse regulation. In such places the decision makers were usually leading members of the urban elite – men who lived in the settlement they were trying to police, cheek-by-jowl with its alehouses. These borough authorities were often more energetic in regulating the institution than the county magistrates, who were more likely to be residentially segregated from the rural villages and small market towns whose alehouse-licensing disputes they were charged to preside over. The borough authorities in Leicester, for instance, were particularly proactive, and took measures that anticipated later national legislation. Even before the turn of the seventeenth century they were collecting lists of victuallers in the city, appointing members of the corporation to search for abuses in alehouses, and requiring aldermen to make searches of the alehouses in their ward during the time of divine service. The mayoral oath of 1594 explicitly bound the officeholder to the duty of 'the repression and putting downe of ... alehowses'.[61] The corporation at Reading kept close tabs on their alehouses, regularly calling 'all the Victuallers within the Boroughe' to appear before the authorities. Those with 'noe accusations of disorder by the Constables laid against them, and shewinge their licenses, were dismissed and willed to keepe good order in their howses', whereas those without a licence or facing complaints of disorder might be suppressed or fined.[62] The borough authorities also took yearly recognizances of all victuallers not to serve meat during Lent, providing an effective list of all those involved in the drinks trade in the town.[63] The production of systematic lists of licensees was also a part of

[61] For the regulatory efforts in Leicester see *Leic. Boro. Recs*, III, pp. lvi–lix. For the oath see p. 302.

[62] *Read. Boro. Recs*, III, p. 287.

[63] *Read. Boro. Recs*, II, examples can be found at pp. 118–19, 171–5, and *passim*. For more on Reading's proactive corporation see Jackson, 'Political and Social Conflict in Reading'.

the micro-management of the trade in Southampton.[64] However, this close policing was not necessarily a manifestation of a 'militant hostility' to alehouses. Lists of offenders from Reading, for instance, suggest that unlicensed and disorderly keepers were more likely to be fined than to see their house suppressed entirely, a compromise that went against the letter of the law but allowed the authorities both to raise revenue and to ensure that alehouse numbers remained sufficient to meet demand for their services.[65] Likewise, in Southampton, despite the 'state-of-the-art management information' that was collected about the borough's alehouses, no concerted effort was brought to bear on reducing their numbers, perhaps out of recognition for the 'general advantages of an extensive hospitality infrastructure' to the maritime economy of the port.[66] The favoured regulatory approach in such towns seems to have been to marry proactivity with pragmatism.

Such a hands-on approach was not, however, uniform. There were regular complaints from Nottingham's constables in the early part of the seventeenth century that the borough authorities took little interest in alehouse regulation despite the issue being regularly raised: 'ther is noe refformacion conserning the inffinitt nomber of all[e] houses within this towne, considering that the[y] [have] be[e]n continually spoken of both att Assises and Sessions, and yet nothing amended conserning the same'.[67] In the counties, such complaints seem to have been more the norm than the exception. In 1610 the Cheshire magistracy received an angry letter from Whitehall reprimanding them for their neglect of the recent raft of alehouse legislation, complaining that 'there is soe little report and care had by you in that County to the execution of his ma[jes]t[ie]s comandements' that 'it seemith they are altogether neglected and forgotten'. The letter was 'therfore to let you knowe that this yor slacknes, and remisnes (beinge of very ill example) as not any longer to be suffered'. It does not seem to have had the desired effect, as attempts to limit alehouse numbers in the county remained 'half-hearted' before the Civil War.[68] The county bench of south Lancashire was likewise 'passive' when it came to alehouse regulation before the 1640s, with only

64 Brown, 'Alehouse Licensing', pp. 118–19.

65 *Read. Boro. Recs*, III, p. 287.

66 Brown, 'Alehouse Licensing', p. 123.

67 *Nott. Boro. Recs*, IV, pp. 326, 369–70.

68 CRO, QJF/38/4/3; J.S. Morrill, *Cheshire 1630–1660: County Government and Society during the English Revolution* (Oxford, 1974), pp. 243–4.

a 'trickle of cases' dealt with.[69] Petitions from Wiltshire illustrate that the magistrates there were inclined to inactivity, and needed particularly strong goading to get them to join the battle against the alehouse. The minister of Upavon petitioned the county's Justices in 1648 to urge them 'to use your best endeavour against [th]e multiplicity of Alehouses' in the parish, and to overcome their usual leniency:

> Your good natures, I know do incline to Mercie, but tis noe mercie to suffer so greate abuses. As there is a cruell mercie so there is a pious cruelty w[hi]ch tis well if you would be pleased to embrace, especially against this greate corruption of our times.[70]

The Mayor of Salisbury, William Stone, deemed it necessary to employ particularly emotive rhetoric when he petitioned the magistrates to suppress alehouses in the town in 1656:

> You are passing to the grave every day: you dwell uppon the borders of eternity: yor breath is in yor nostreles, herfor duble & treble your resolutions to bee zealous in a good thinge & to doe all that lyes wthin yor power ... how dreadfull will a dieinge bed bee to a negligent magistrate.[71]

This rather bombastic plea to move the magistrates to action suggests that the holders of this office were not always the most enthusiastic standard-bearers of a hostile alliance against the alehouse.

When zeal was forthcoming it was often directed at particular concentrations of alehouses in notoriously unruly 'dark corners' of towns or the countryside. For example, in 1607 the Somerset bench issued an order in response to examinations which had revealed that 'divers notorious misdemeanors and abuses have been committed by such as without or by or under pretence of licences have kept Tippling or Alehouses' in the Mendip hills – a mining area of the sort that early modern authorities deemed virtually ungovernable. The county bench accordingly decided to throw the book at the tipplers of the Mendips, ordering an outright ban on all alehouses on the hills: 'no person or persons whatsoever at or in any place upon the said hill shall be licensed, permitted, or suffered

---

[69] Keith Wrightson, 'Two Concepts of Order: Justices, Constables and Jurymen in Seventeenth-Century England', in Brewer and Styles (eds), *An Ungovernable People*, pp. 33–4.

[70] *Wilts. Q.S. Recs*, p. 204.

[71] WSHC, 1656/H/135.

to keep any Alehouse or Tippling house'.[72] When concern could be roused amongst the Nottingham authorities it was often in relation to their own concentration of alehouses on the 'Backside', a street that ran alongside, and in the shadow of, the town wall.[73] The Leicester authorities had problems with 'disordered alehouses' within the area known as Bishop's Fee – in part because overlapping claims to jurisdiction over the area between the borough and the Countess of Devon had allowed the inhabitants there to avoid close policing.[74] Sir Francis Ashley, when Recorder of Dorchester in the 1610s – a role akin to magistrate – specifically targeted alehouses in the poorly policed suburbs of Fordington and Colleton Row.[75] If regulatory efforts were often focused on particular clusters of alehouses, they were also often concentrated in particular years – representing bursts of activity rather than sustained policing. Justices in Dorchester conducted several 'intensive purges', two of which took place in 1631, one in February and one in October. The first was in response to urgings from Whitehall, the second in response to high food prices – which often led to restrictions on brewing and ale-selling as a means of conserving barley.[76] In fact, the years around 1630 witnessed peaks of activity in a number of counties in response to harvest failure and dearth. The Somerset magistrates ordered 'all alehouses whatsoever within this Countie be suppressed' – barring those deemed absolutely necessary for 'releefe of travellers and poore people'.[77] The Essex magistrates also undertook a regulatory drive in the years 1629–31.[78]

The most significant peaks – and indeed troughs – of regulatory activity came during the period of the Civil War and Interregnum. There were surges in the enforcement of alehouse licensing in previous 'slack' places such as Cheshire, where a vigorous campaign on the part of the Cheshire Justices began from 1648. It stepped up a gear in the Interregnum with the introduction of direct military government under Cromwell in 1655–7. A fresh onslaught under Major General Worsley

---

72 SHC/Q/SR/2/125.

73 *Nott. Boro. Recs*, IV, pp. 237–8, 301; V, pp. 333–4.

74 *Leic. Boro. Recs*, IV, pp. 305–6.

75 David Underdown, *Fire from Heaven: Life in an English Town in the Seventeenth Century* (London, 1992), p. 79.

76 *Ibid.*, p. 104.

77 SHC, Q/SR/65:1/39. It was not unusual for alehouses to be targeted in periods of dearth: see for example John Walter and Keith Wrightson, 'Dearth and The Social Order in Early Modern England', *Past and Present* 71 (1976), p. 32.

78 Wrightson, 'Two Concepts of Order', *passim*.

suppressed two hundred alehouses within a month.[79] Likewise in south Lancashire the years between 1646 and 1658 witnessed the quarter sessions, now under the control of Puritan Justices, develop 'new teeth as courts of aggressive regulation'.[80] Again, though, the pattern was not uniform. If some areas saw new levels of activity result from the Civil Wars, for other areas the mid-century conflict set the regulatory system back. Civil War Somerset saw a breakdown of control over alehouses, amid plentiful evidence of 'tipplers slighting commands and laughing at authority'.[81] In 1648 the Corporation of Reading appears to have had to produce a new list of alehouses and tippling houses in the borough – their pre-war system of keeping an annual list having fallen into abeyance during the wars.[82] After the Restoration in 1660 levels of regulatory activity seem to not only have fallen away from the peaks they experienced in many areas in the 1640s and 1650s, but to decline relative to pre-war levels too. Indeed, there is a widespread consensus amongst historians of the alehouse that concern with the institution subsided to some extent as the aggressive local administrative policy of the early Stuarts was relaxed and the reforming enthusiasm of the church was discredited.[83] The issue is complicated to some extent by the fact that, as both Anthony Fletcher and Susan Amussen have suggested, alehouse licensing and petitions about unruly neighbours became 'almost entirely a matter for petty sessions' in the late seventeenth century – the more informal meetings of magistrates between the quarter sessions, meetings for which few records survive.[84] Alehouse regulation may, therefore, have disappeared from the archive rather than from the priorities of seventeenth-century magistrates. Nonetheless, what evidence we do have of business undertaken in petty sessions seems to confirm the sense that if alehouse regulation had not ceased to be a concern, it was rarely conducted with the same zeal after 1660 that it had been at times and places in the first sixty years of the century.[85]

---

[79] Morrill, *Cheshire 1630–1660*, pp. 244–5.

[80] Wrightson, 'Two Concepts of Order', pp. 34–5.

[81] Clark, *The English Alehouse*, p. 176.

[82] *Read. Boro. Recs*, IV, p. 302.

[83] Wrightson, 'Alehouses, Order and Reformation', p. 21; King, 'Regulation of Alehouses', pp. 35–6; Fletcher, *Reform in the Provinces*, p. 251; Clark, 'The Alehouse and the Alternative Society', p. 71.

[84] Fletcher, *Reform in the Provinces*, p. 236; Amussen, *An Ordered Society*, p. 177. The quote is Fletcher.

[85] J.A. Sharpe (ed.) *William Holcroft His Booke: Local Office Holding in Late Stuart Essex*

What emerges, then, from the role played by those with ultimate responsibility for alehouse regulation is a rather patchy picture. Magistrates did engage in concerted efforts to bring alehouse numbers and disorder under control, but these efforts were neither uniform nor very often sustained, tending instead to be concentrated in particular places and at particular times. There was, therefore, considerable 'slackness' in the operation of alehouse regulation that sits at odds with the degree of anxiety about the institution often expressed in legislation and petitions. How can we account for this? No doubt many magistrates were tempered in their hostility towards the alehouse by a sense of paternalism towards the poor. This is evident in the rhetoric of Sir Richard Grosvenor. Whilst on the one hand, as we have seen, Grosvenor could offer bombast and bluster on the threat posed to civilised society by the alehouse, he also counselled his son to remember his duty as a JP toward the poor and weak: 'When poor men shall bee brought before you … nether triumph over nor trample upon the misery off such … And iff you must punnish by imprisonment etc., doe your duty with sorrow.' In their analysis of Grosvenor's attitudes, Richard Cust and Peter Lake saw in this counsel a recognition on the part of Grosvenor that even 'at the point where the process of social control came closest to simple coercion' (i.e. the enforcement of the law), a tendency to leniency and compassion on the part of magistrates could serve to 'symbolise the paternal nature of social authority' and hence 'cement the ties of loyalty and deference that held the community together and on which Grosvenor's own position was based'.[86] The display of a certain leniency towards the alehouse – an institution that, as demonstrated in Chapter 1, was intimately connected with serving the needs of the poor – might then have been one way in which the magistracy could make good on their duty of care towards the poor. The exercise of patronage may also have served to blunt the exercise of authority. Indeed, Keith Wrightson has suggested that 'the right of a Justice to grant, or of an interested gentleman to procure, a licence [for ale-selling] for a tenant, former servant, or client was a much valued form of local patronage'. Anthony Fletcher has also argued that 'an alehouse licence was one of the most potent weapons in the JP's armoury of patronage'.[87] This exercise of patronage might even lead

---

(Chelmsford, 1986). Holcroft's dealings with alehouses are routine, but usually reactive rather than proactive.

[86] Cust and Lake, 'Sir Richard Grosvenor', pp. 50–1.

[87] Wrightson, 'Alehouses, Order and Reformation', p. 3; Fletcher, *Reform in the Provinces*, pp. 237–8.

to conflicts between Justices when a prospective licensee turned down by one magistrate was able to secure a licence from a neighbouring JP – whose reputation among the poor no doubt benefited by this.[88] The result was that justices 'came to look more and more jealously on the patronage which licensing in the villages around their home involved', and several benches found it necessary to reiterate from time to time that a licence should only be granted with the consent of the JP of the division that the applicant lived in.[89] Both paternalism and patronage served to temper the hostility of magistrates towards the alehouse, and in some areas may even have led to an increase, rather than a diminution, in the number of licences granted.

That said, it should not necessarily be assumed that all the licensing decisions made by the magistrates were based on the exercise of pater-nalism. Less noble 'vested interest' might also play a part – as it no doubt did to some extent in the extension of patronage. Indeed, Fletcher has argued that because Justices' clerks were awarded sixpence for each licence they issued, they 'had a strong incentive to encourage their masters to issue more rather than fewer'.[90] Magistrates, then, were pulled to and fro on the issue of alehouse regulation: they came under intermit-tent pressure from the government; they were implored to act against the alehouse by vitriolic petitions; and they were besieged by requests to grant licenses by patrons of alehouses and would-be alehousekeepers. They were responsible for enforcing legislation that defined alehouses as both necessary and evil, and had to balance this responsibility both with an imperative to demonstrate their 'paternal' care for the needs of the poor, and with the opportunities that alehouse licensing provided for them to pursue their own vested interests. Given these considerations, it is perhaps unsurprising that magistrates seem to have often adopted what has been described as a 'doubly passive' stance.[91] On the one hand, they seem to have rarely taken vigorous action against the alehouse, except in times of crisis, and instead attracted criticism for their 'slackness'. On the

---

[88] For an argument that 'rigorous maintenance of the law conflicted at times with the exercise of patronage' in Cheshire, see Garthine Walker, *Crime, Gender and Social Order in Early Modern England* (Cambridge, 2003), p. 221.

[89] *Ibid.*, p. 238; *Som. Q.S. Recs*, I, p. 241; II, p. 99; IV, p. 150.

[90] Fletcher, *Reform in the Provinces*, p. 236.

[91] See Wrightson, 'Two Concepts of Order', p. 26: Wrightson is here making the point about the attitudes of magistrates towards local government generally, but the conclusion certainly applies specifically to alehouses. Wrightson borrows the phrase from M.G. Davies, *The Enforcement of English Apprenticeship. A Study in Applied Mercantilism* (Cambridge, 1956), p. 220.

other hand, they often passed on the final responsibility for the enforcement of the law, and its associated strains, to humbler local officers.

If magistrates were supposedly the generals of the authorities' campaign
against the alehouse, then constables, tithingmen, churchwardens,
watchmen and overseers of the poor were its 'front-line troops'.[92] Town
and parish constables bore the main responsibility for ensuring that
alehouses conformed to their licensing conditions, but any local officeholder would be expected to support their efforts. In many cases the
village notables that tended to fill these offices were eager, rather than
reluctant, for the magistrates to delegate responsibility over regulation
in their community.[93] The inhabitants of Somerton, for example, petitioned the Somerset bench in 1627 requesting the suppression of an
alehouse that, although recently licensed by the Justices, had not had
the consent of 'the Minister, Constables, Churchwardens or Overseers of
the sayde Towne'.[94] The jurymen of the hundred of Whorlsdown, Wiltshire, similarly petitioned the magistrates in 1646 'to take some course
for the suppressinge of [the] extraordinarie number of alehouses', adding
a request 'that in future here may be none licensed to sell [ale] w[i]thout
the approbacon of the same inhabitants who best knowe theire lives
& conversacons & abilities & fitnes for the undertakeinge theirof'.[95] In
both these cases village notables were explicitly stating their eagerness
to play a more significant role in the regulatory process.

Again though, as with the magistracy, the pattern of activity on the
ground was far from being one of uniformly zealous application. Whilst
there were numerous town and parish officers of John Noyes's ilk who
took their role seriously – performing regular checks of local alehouses
and making presentments to the magistrates – there were also plenty
who attracted the sort of criticisms of 'slackness' we have seen directed
at Justices. In some cases it was incoming officers, who found themselves
faced with a local epidemic of alehouse disorder, who pointed the finger
at their predecessors. In Awliscombe, Devon, in 1662, a new overseer of

[92] King, 'Regulation of Alehouses', p. 32.

[93] An older historiographical tradition argued that these offices were filled not by
parochial elites but by the 'meaner' inhabitants of village society. This has since given
way to a consensus that constables and other village offices 'were usually drawn from
the leading yeomen, husbandmen and craftsmen'. See Joan Kent, 'The English Village
Constable, 1580–1642: The Nature and Dilemmas of the Office', *Journal of British Studies*
20 (1981), esp. pp. 26–9.

[94] SHC, Q/SR/58:1/36.

[95] WSHC, 1646/T/128.

the poor blamed a rising poor relief bill on the fact that 'Remyse Officers' had allowed 'drunkenesse, fornication, unlicensed alehouses' to multiply under their watch. When another Devon parish, Ottery, was faced with a number of disputes about illegal alehousekeepers the following year, the overseer there pointed the finger at the abuses of former officers in previous years.[96] In other cases it was existing officers who were the target of complaints. The minister and chief inhabitants of Stock and Butsbury, Essex, for instance, appealed to the magistrates in 1629 to reverse the recent proliferation of alehouses which they blamed on 'the slackness of inferior officers and other inhabitants of parishes where these evile abound in informing the magistrates of the delinquents'.[97] Frustration could ultimately turn to prosecution. When a constable of Hadleigh, Essex, was asked in 1642 by the rector to 'repair' to an alehouse to bring a halt to excessive drinking there, he instead 'totally neglected and refused to execute his office', and was formally indicted for contempt.[98] The inhabitants of West Monkton, Somerset, petitioned the magistrates in 1654 to complain that the constable and the tithingman 'by their great and grosse neglects of their said offices have occasioned the increase of vice by countenancing drunkennes, multiplicity of alehouses and prophanation of the Sabbath'. They were removed and discharged from office.[99] Clearly then, whilst some village notables were keen to pursue a tough policy against alehouses, there were many occasions when their reforming zeal was frustrated by less enthusiastic local officials.

Such examples illustrate Keith Wrightson's theory that local officials in early modern England found themselves caught between 'two concepts of order'. The first of these he described as 'a positive aspiration towards a national condition of disciplined social harmony' that emanated primarily from moralists, ministers and magistrates and called for assertive action to be taken by authorities to enforce a state of order in society. By contrast, the second concept saw order as 'a negative absence of disruptive conflict locally', an attitude which consequently encouraged local officials to allow 'a larger area of ambivalent permitted behaviour than was compatible with the nice definitions of moralists and legislators'.[100] The petitioners of Stock and Butsbury, or the overseer

---

[96] Pamela Sharpe, *Population and Society in an East Devon Parish: Reproducing Colyton, 1540–1840* (Exeter, 2002), pp. 219–20.

[97] ERO, Q/SR 264/103.

[98] ERO, Q/SR/317/113.

[99] *Som. Q.S. Recs*, III, p. 239.

[100] Wrightson, 'Two Concepts of Order', esp. pp. 22–4.

of Awliscombe, can stand as examples of those village notables who, as Wrightson suggested, were in some areas 'assimilated to the values of their social superiors and religious mentors' during the course of the seventeenth century.[101] The officers they condemned as slack, on the other hand, subscribed to a concept of order that was instead based on tolerating the customary behavioural traditions of their neighbours – even where that included turning an occasional blind eye to alehouse regulation.[102] Wrightson's 'two concepts of order' helps to explain why certain agents of local authority did not fall in line with those advocating a militant hostility towards the alehouse. Such officials were reluctant to embark on a course of action against the alehouse that could potentially disrupt local harmony, and might anger those sections of their local community that patronised the institution.

In many instances, though, there was more to the ambivalence of 'remiss officers' than their turning a blind eye to the alehouse recreation of the local poor. Often they could be counted amongst the patrons of local alehouses themselves. William Alexander, a churchwarden of Lea, Wiltshire, was presented to the quarter sessions in 1634 for spending a Sabbath day in an alehouse 'in the tyme of morning and evening prayer', when he should have been ensuring no parishioners were doing just that.[103] Richard Finch of Upminster, Essex, a yeoman and constable of the parish, was presented in 1623 as he did 'commonly drink and misspend his time' in an alehouse 'many times two or three days and nights together'.[104] Thomas Wilkinson, a wheelwright and constable of Dagenham, Essex, was presented for the double offence of drinking at an unlicensed alehouse in 1674, and failing to report the same alehouse to the magistrates when requested to inform them of unlicensed sellers in the parish.[105] Another example comes from Layer Marney, Essex, in 1604, where several inhabitants of the parish complained to a local

---

[101] *Ibid.*, p. 46.

[102] Joan Kent has offered a similar interpretation of the nature of the office of constable, but whereas Kent argues that the more localised concept of order was more dominant in determining the behaviour of officials, Wrightson argues that such officials came increasingly over time to conform to the dictates of the law. This difference in emphasis may, however, be due to their timescales: Kent's analysis ends in 1642, whereas Wrightson extends his across the seventeenth century, arguing that this change was most evident from the mid century onwards. Kent, 'The English Village Constable', p. 38; Wrightson, 'Two Concepts of Order', esp. pp. 41–4.

[103] *Wilts. Q.S. Recs*, p. 107.

[104] ERO, Q/SR 242/42,43.

[105] ERO, Q/SR 428/109.

magistrate about the misconduct of their constable, John Lufkin. Not only was the constable a regular visitor to local alehouses – often arriving there early in the day and leaving several days later – he was also a notorious trickster who challenged men to drinking contests and had a penchant for practical jokes.[106] John Crosbie, who held the rank of high constable of the hundred of Bucklow, Cheshire, likewise engaged in antics that resulted in complaints to the magistrates in 1609. Two particular instances stand out. On one occasion Crosbie had gone with his sons to drink and 'carouse' at an alehouse in Nether Knutsford, and they had encouraged the publican to join them. When he refused, the sons seized him and began to beat him up. The publican tried to appeal to authority, reminding Crosbie that 'hee beeinge high constable should not suffer him to bee abused in his owne house'. In response, Crosbie merely 'laughed & danced up & downe in the Chamber'. This was not the only time the high constable instigated alehouse disorder in Nether Knutsford. On a separate occasion Crosbie had been drinking in an alehouse when a tinker had entered carrying a trumpet. Crosbie convinced the tinker to sound his trumpet to call for 'all hoore maisters', followed by a second blast to call together 'all drunkerdes'. The disorder caused by the subsequent gathering of a large rowdy drinking company aroused the attention of another local official, the under sheriff, who came into the street outside with a view to quelling the disturbance. Yet, egged on by one of his fellow drinkers to 'forbeare that disorder', Crosbie undermined the authority of his colleague by declaring aloud that 'he cared not for that Crooke backe', and continued to lead the drinking.[107]

Another instance of a constable leading, rather than policing, alehouse disorder, occurred in Chelmsford in 1628, when the constable withdrew his watchmen to go drinking, with the subsequent alehouse session culminating in a drunken affray with the watchmen of neighbouring Moulsham.[108] In a similar case from Fiddington, Somerset, in 1658, a tithingman was presented to the magistrates for twice taking officers from the watch to spend the night drinking in the alehouse instead.[109] There are also instances where local officials took their links with alehouses a step further than simply patronage. William Hart, yeoman and constable of Kelvedon, Essex, was presented in 1625 for

[106] ERO, Q/SR 170/3.
[107] CRO, QJF/38/3/5.
[108] ERO, Q/SR 263/18.
[109] SHC, Q/SR/96:2/100.

'keeping a common alehouse'. Worse than that, he was happy to facilitate recreational drinking there, and 'did suffer divers persons of the parishes adjoining to abide in the house a whole day and night and more'.[110] The constables of Meere, Wilstshire, presented tithingman John Watts for allowing a tenant of his to run an unlicensed alehouse when 'he being an officer and ought by his oath to reforme it'.[111] Watts was certainly not unusual amongst the ranks of officers who 'ought' to have reformed alehouses in playing a role in encouraging them.

As was the case with magistrates, then, the enforcement of the strict letter of alehouse regulation by local officials was patchy. There were, of course, many who took their role in policing the alehouse as a very serious duty. But there were clearly others who were not only prepared to turn a blind eye to aspects of alehouse regulation out of a desire to keep the local peace, or out of a sense of duty to the local poor, but because they themselves patronised alehouses. They even took advantage of the opportunities for recreational drinking on offer, that aspect of the role of the alehouse that aroused the most concern amongst its opponents. Moreover, the evidence here suggests that it was not just the poorest members of local communities who indulged in recreational alehouse sociability. There were those amongst the office-holding ranks of local society who valued this particular alehouse function. Rather than an opposition to recreational drinking motivating their opposition to the alehouse, these local officials exhibited 'slackness' in the application of the law that derived from an attachment to such recreational drinking.

Such a situation may not have been constant across the seventeenth century. For if historians are generally in agreement that legislators, ministers and magistrates all took a more relaxed approach to the alehouse problem after 1660, Keith Wrightson has suggested a different trajectory amongst the ranks of local officials. Wrightson has argued that as central government and county magistrates began to withdraw from attempts to enforce close control over alehouses, the 'chief inhabitants' of local communities increasingly took up the mantle, and that the hostility of village elites 'survived both the administrative and religious changes which had stimulated its development'. Instead they continued to fight a long campaign against the alehouse which resulted, by the early eighteenth century, in the consolidation of the 'cultural hegemony' of parochial elites and a 'control over the labouring population which

---

110 ERO, Q/SR 247/48.
111 *Wilts. Q.S. Recs*, p. 102.

would have been the envy of their innovating predecessors'.[112] Wrightson was careful to concede, however, that such an outcome to the 'battle over the alehouse' was not uniform or universal. Whilst this may have been the result of a sustained regulatory effort on the part of parochial elites in certain Essex parishes closely studied by Wrightson, we can of course find exceptions in other places. The constables of the parish of Kingswood, Wiltshire – another notoriously unruly mining area – were far from bringing the alehouses, and the local labouring population, under their control in the later seventeenth century.[113] In 1673 they petitioned the Wiltshire magistrates to complain that 'the abounding of alehouses' was 'the means of so much drunkenness amongst us that doth beget idleness theevery and whordom and makes it abound amongst us'. If parochial elites in some areas were bringing the alehouse under a tight regulatory hold, in other areas the situation seemed to be as unreformed, if not worse, than ever – even when, as in Kingswood, local officials were proactive.[114] In part, this was because the successful functioning of regulation was never simply down to the level of application shown by magistrates and local officers. Even the most zealous attempts to enforce legislation might founder if met with high levels of resistance from alehousekeepers and their patrons. It is to this aspect of the equation that we now turn.

The experience of authority

Chapter 1 demonstrated that the alehouse regulatory framework was highly proscriptive and prohibitive, and was based to some extent on a class-based critique of the recreational drinking of the poor. It was, in principle at least, a system designed to allow the middling and upper ranks of early modern English society a 'hegemonic' degree of control over the alehouse and its patrons, and Keith Wrightson has argued that, in some areas, such control was indeed achieved by parochial elites. On the whole though, the previous section argued against a 'hegemonic' or

---

[112] Wrightson, 'Alehouses, Order and Reformation', p. 21.

[113] Malcolmson, '"A set of ungovernable people"'.

[114] The constables made regular 'raids' on local alehouses, especially after 9.00p.m. and on Sundays, in attempts to police 'drinking contrary to the statute'. The patrons and keepers did their best to avoid detection, and on one occasion the constable reported that in the alehouse of Alise Robbins he 'founde on the Lords day at night three men tipling that she had shut up in her buttery', WSHC, 1673/E/98.

'social control' interpretation of the relationship between authority and the alehouse, demonstrating that such a view fails to account for a strong current of ambivalence on the part of the individuals responsible for enforcing alehouse legislation. Whilst this line of argument looks to cast doubt on the *enforcement* of the law, it is also possible to question the 'hegemonic' model of the dynamic between authority and the alehouse by reflecting on the *nature* of the law. For, as the recent scholarship on power relations has sought to emphasise, the law was 'not simply a conduit of hegemony and control', or 'an agency of government' that was 'the property of, and in the gift of, the ruling elite'.[115] Garthine Walker has challenged 'hegemonic' models of the law in which 'the people themselves are accorded little agency', as has other recent work that has demonstrated that the law could serve as 'a resource on which the populace might draw'.[116] It has also been argued that, even when the law was mobilised as a regulatory force, 'ordinary people responded to these measures in a number of ways that complicate the view that the law was an effective means of social control'.[117] This section will examine these responses with regard to alehouse regulation. Attempts to evade, reject or resist the application of the law and the exercise of authority will be explored alongside those occasions when notions of lawfulness were evoked or appropriated by those without any formal claim to legal authority – often to legitimate unlawful forms of behaviour.

Perhaps the clearest evidence that alehouse patrons and proprietors actively engaged with the law comes from those cases where 'common people participated in its workings when they asserted their own interpretation of customary rights'.[118] Thanks primarily to the influence of E.P. Thompson and the work of Andy Wood, early modern historians are well aware of the important place of custom in early modern legal culture, and particularly the role it could play in the negotiation of authority on the part of less powerful groups in society.[119] Hitherto such work has tended to focus on customary rights to tenancy, common land or common fuel rights, but claims to customary rights could also be mobi-

---

115 Griffiths, Fox and Hindle, 'Introduction', *The Experience of Authority*, p. 4; Hindle, *The State and Social Change*, pp. ix–x; Walker, *Crime, Gender and Social Order*, p. 211.

116 Walker, *Crime, Gender and Social Order*, p. 212; Hindle, *The State and Social Change*, pp. ix–x.

117 Walker, *Crime, Gender and Social Order*, p. 226.

118 Griffiths, Fox and Hindle, 'Introduction', p. 4.

119 Thompson, *Customs in Common*; Andy Wood, 'The Place of Custom in Plebeian Political Culture: England, 1550–1800', *Social History* 22 (1997), pp. 46–60.

lised by participants in disputes over alehouse regulation. In 1612, John Pearce of Midsomer Norton, Somerset, was suppressed from keeping an alehouse for three years after committing the offence of selling less than a quart of his 'best beer' for a penny – the appropriate measure and price as set down in statute. Pearce denied the veracity of the accusation, and petitioned the magistrates to re-issue his license, adding that 'the house wherein he Dwelleth hath ben a usuall victuallinge house by the space of Thirtie yeres past'.[120] This claim to the longevity of his alehouse was not merely 'window-dressing' for his central complaint that the claims against him were untrue, but was an attempt to render his minor legal offence irrelevant in the face of his customary right to sell ale. William Walton of Brewerton, Cheshire, also made an appeal to the customary nature of his ale-selling when, in 1648, he faced the threat of 'some p[er]son through evill will intendeth to peticion against yor peticioner to have him suppressed'. The main argument of his counter-attack was that he had 'for the space of 34 years and upwards brued and kept ale and beare to sell'.[121] Thomas Shenton of Bickerton, Cheshire, responded to the fact that some of his fellow parishioners did 'endevor to prevent' him being licensed to sell ale out of his newly acquired messuage by claiming that the 'mesuage an Inn hath bin kept for the space of fiftie yeeres nowe last past of thereabouts'.[122] In these cases attempts were being made to rebuff complaints by claiming customary rights to sell ale – despite the fact that licensing legislation placed no formal emphasis on the longevity of such a claim. Such challenges to attempts to suppress alehouses can be interpreted within the context that Keith Wrightson has called the 'politics of custom'.[123] If E.P. Thompson's formulation that custom stood at 'the interface between law and common practice' is accepted, then it certainly seems that these alehousekeepers were invoking the latter to challenge the former.[124]

In many cases, petitions that sought the restoration or continuance of an alehouse licence laid claim to custom not as alternative to official legal guidelines on licensing, but as a supplement to them. When George Miller of Tarporley, Cheshire, had his alehouse suppressed in 1645, he responded with a brief but shrewd petition, claiming not only that his

---

120 SHC, Q/SR/16/73.
121 CRO, QJF/76/3/54.
122 CRO, QJF/74/2/32.
123 Wrightson, 'The Politics of the Parish', pp. 22–5.
124 Thompson, *Customs in Common*, pp. 101–2.

house had 'bene a Inne of soe long continuance that you will be pleased soe farr as to favour yor peticioners as to lett them bee licensed', but also stressing that he and his patrons had a good record for 'demeaning and behaving themselves as they ought to do and as law requires'.[125] Miller was hedging his bets. Instead of asserting that his customary claim to sell ale negated other legal requirements, he emphasised that his record also met the necessary legal requirement of being able to keep good order in his house. A similar approach – appealing to customary rights along-side formal legal requirements – was taken by Somerset alehousekeeper, Lewis Lyninge of Mark. In 1615, Lyninge was presented to the quarter sessions for keeping a tippling house without a licence, an offence he did not deny. Instead, Lyninge claimed that it was unnecessary for him to hold a license because his house was 'an ancient inn'.[126] A year later at the Somerset quarter sessions, Richard Gellicombe likewise responded to an indictment for unlicensed ale-selling by claiming 'his house at Cros-combe to be an ancient inn'.[127] Rather than appealing to general notions of customary rights, these particular appeals represent an impressive degree of popular knowledge of the law, for an 'ancient inn' was, offi-cially, an inn established before the licensing act of 1552. These 'ancient inns' were exempt from licensing under the Edwardian legislation, and it may well be the case that claims to this status were singling out an anomaly in an act passed at least two generations earlier, in an attempt to circumvent punishment for unlicensed, illegal ale-selling.[128] Indeed, a claim by an alehousekeeper to 'ancient' origins for their institution could represent a technically 'legal' challenge to attempts by the authorities to regulate them.

These claims to customary practice and legal exemptions exemplify an agency in the face of authority that extended beyond the indi-vidual alehousekeeper. In response to the petition of Lewis Lyninge, the Somerset bench issued an order sending for 'the ancient men of Mark' to attempt to verify the truth of his claim to run an 'ancient inn'. In the case of Richard Gellicombe, a similar order was made for two officials to 'call before them some parishioners of Croscombe to examine whether the house be an ancient inn or not'.[129] Keith Wrightson has suggested

---

[125]   CRO, QJF/73/3/61.

[126]   *Som. Q.S. Recs*, I, pp. 120–1.

[127]   *Som. Q.S. Recs*, I, pp. 157–8.

[128]   Roberts, 'Alehouses, Brewing and Government', p. 47.

[129]   *Som. Q.S. Recs*, I, pp. 120–1, 157–8.

that defence of custom 'could mobilise whole communities, or sections of them, with a conviction of their rectitude in disputing power'.[130] If the 'ancient men' of Mark or the parishioners of Croscombe united in support of these appeals to 'ancient inn' status, then these communities would potentially have been able to overturn the legal decisions of magistrates through such appeals to customary practice. Indeed, in 1616, Edward Joanes of Burton, Somerset, was able to draw on the collective memory of the community to do just that. Joanes had his licence taken away after information was given against him about disorders that had occurred in his alehouse. In response, he petitioned the quarter sessions to reissue his licence on the grounds that his alehouse had been licensed for 'tyme out of mynde whereof mens memory is not to the contrary'. The plea was successful and it was ordered that 'he shall again be licensed'.[131] What this example demonstrates then is that an appeal to custom, when backed by at least a section of the community (and it should be assumed that Joanes's claim was verified by the 'ancient men' or inhabitants of Burton) could provide a form of collective and effective resistance to power, authority and the law at a local level. That defence of custom could provide a powerful way to 'blunt the exercise of power in the micro-politics of manor and parish' is also hinted at in the language of the order re-issuing Joanes's licence. It stated that the licence was for 'as long as he shall keep himself and his house in good order, *and no longer*'.[132] Clearly the authorities were anxious to downplay the force of custom by reminding Joanes that it was his conduct, rather than custom, upon which his claim to a licence was based. Considering that Joanes had just mobilised a claim to custom to regain a licence that had been taken away from him for keeping a disorderly alehouse, this may have sounded like an empty threat.

Not all were as successful as Edward Joanes in laying claim to customary rights, however, and magistrates were keen to examine such claims rather than to accept them at face value. The authorities may have been suspicious that claims were strategic or instrumental evocations of notions of lawfulness. Indeed, such scepticism appears to have been well founded in a case from 1626, when the Essex magistrates called Jane Holmes of Goldhanger before them to answer for 'pretending' her house

[130] Wrightson, 'The Politics of the Parish', p. 24.
[131] SHC, Q/SR/25/79*.
[132] *Som. Q.S. Recs*, I, p. 180. My italics.

to be an ancient inn.[133] Perhaps the disbelief of the magistrates was reinforced by members of the local community, who did not invariably rally
behind an appeal to custom. That a claim to custom by an unpopular
alehousekeeper could fail to mobilise communal support was discovered
by Edward Miller of Wilton, Norfolk, in the early 1640s. The inhabitants of his parish complained to magistrates that they had granted him
a licence 'upon false suggestions … that the house wherein he nowe
dwelleth hath ben an Alehouse for Fifty years'. The petitioners also went
on to complain that Miller, a blacksmith, was 'a man unfitt to keepe
such a house, beinge a Notorious swearer, a scoffer att Religious duties,
a choloricke hastie moodie man'.[134] Whilst custom could, in cases such
as that of Edward Joanes, trump the more conventional legal requirements for the granting of an alehouse licence, it was not always an effective weapon. There were members of local communities who were – like
the authorities that dealt with Edward Joanes – keen to emphasise that
the qualities of the individual alehousekeeper should be considered at
least as important, if not more so, than a claim to customary rights. The
potential of a claim to customary rights to shape the exercise of the law
in regard to alehouse licensing should not, then, be overstated. That
said, it no doubt constituted one of the 'everyday forms of resistance' or
'weapons of the weak' that could afford some degree of agency to those
without formal power in the local community.

There were other ways, too, in which would-be alehouse licensees
might seek to exploit grey areas within the law. As has been seen above,
an alehousekeeper who was refused a licence by one magistrate might
exploit jurisdictional ambiguities and secure a licence from a Justice of a
neighbouring division within the same county – a practice that appears
to have been common and widespread enough to provoke regular orders
by county benches aimed at preventing this tactic.[135] William Atkins, of
Haselbury Plucknett, Somerset, demonstrated a certain resourcefulness
in defending the legality of his alehouse in 1629 with another strategy.
Called before the quarter sessions court to answer to claims that he kept
a common tippling house without licence, Atkins paid good money to
borrow a licence from a neighbouring innkeeper, George Randall, to
present to the magistrates. Unfortunately for Atkins, the licence he had
borrowed had been granted under the controversial Mompesson patent

---

133 ERO, Q/SR/254/45.
134 Norfolk Record Office, C/S 3/42A(2).
135 See note 88 above.

scheme which had been declared 'void' by the King almost a decade earlier, and the court therefore ordered that the clerk of the peace should 'detain' the licence. Atkins was forced to come clean, and pleaded with the court to allow him to return the document to Randall 'uncancelled and undefaced' or he would have to 'pay him the remaynder of the money for which he contracted with the said Randall for the same' which would 'tend to his utter undoeinge'.[136] The court showed a surprising leniency in allowing this request, but both Randall and Atkins were to be prevented from future ale-selling. Whilst this attempt to mount a 'legal' defence of an unlicensed alehouse was ultimately bungled, it nonetheless provides further evidence that alehousekeepers thought it possible to use legal channels to challenge regulatory efforts. They evidently did not see the legal system as a resource that exclusively served the interests of the authorities.

A rather more successful alehousekeeper who exhibited a degree of legal nouse was James Hayball, keeper of an alehouse in the notoriously disorderly Somerset Mendips. Reports that his house at Green Oar was a centre of drunkenness and blasphemy – it was allegedly 'scandalous and offensive to all well disposed Christians' – and that Hayball harboured criminals and thieves there, had all formed part of the evidence that had led to the decision to suppress all the alehouses on the Mendips in 1607.[137] Twelve years on, however, Hayball surfaces in the quarter sessions records again, still running his alehouse at Green Oar, despite having been suppressed at previous quarter sessions and contrary to numerous orders issued by magistrates. Further orders in 1619 and 1620 sought again to suppress him, but it turned out that Hayball had been letting the house out to tenants to run as a tippling house, in an attempt to dodge the problem that he had personally been forbidden from selling ale.[138] Indeed, the inhabitants of nearby Emborough petitioned the quarter sessions to complain about these tactics:

> noe sooner one is supprest but another stranger shortlye after farmes [i.e. rents] the said housse and tiples being not lycensed in the said housse into w[hi]ch at this instant there is another tenant come into and tiples before the old [tenant] is gon forth.[139]

---

[136] *Som. Q.S. Recs*, II, p. 105.

[137] SHC, Q/SR/2/46.

[138] *Som. Q.S. Recs*, I, pp. 257, 274.

[139] SHC, Q/SR/35/108.

The authorities had taken a strong stance against alehouses in the Mendips, but it appears that James Hayball had exercised an impressive degree of agency in deliberately and tactically evading licensing laws to keep a technically illegal alehouse running for over a decade in the face of official hostility. It is tempting, however, to see Hayball's relationship with the authorities less as an example of shrewd legalism – though it no doubt contained elements of this – and closer to a stance of outright evasion of, and disobedience to, the licensing authorities. This points to another aspect of the limitations on the effectiveness of the law as a conduit for social control and 'hegemony': outright resistance.

Whilst some contemporaries looked to co-opt notions of lawfulness to contest attempts by the authorities to control alehouses, there is also plentiful evidence of what Anthony Fletcher has identified as 'a general disposition in the villages to view regulation uncooperatively'.[140] For all those individuals who saw engagement with the legal system as the most appropriate way to negotiate the exercise of authority, there were always others who simply sought to ignore or defy the law. These forms of resistance could, like James Scott's 'everyday forms of resistance', take many forms. Evasion, wilful ignorance, obstruction, foot-dragging and verbal confrontation were all components of the uncooperative disposition found among some sections of local communities towards attempts at alehouse regulation. Certain alehousekeepers appear to have been completely indifferent to attempts by the authorities to regulate them. Henry Bendell of Westbury, Somerset, who was encountered in Chapter 1, attracted a great deal of hostility from the authorities in 1612. Despite being complained of at the petty sessions, and bound over to the quarter sessions, there was 'no reformacon had' and he 'continued his disorders in his howse'.[141] Honour Bishop, an unlicensed alehousekeeper from Chard, Somerset, proved similarly obstinate in the face of authority in 1657. Not only had she been 'often times convicted' for her unlicensed selling, the local authorities had even attempted to bring patriarchal authority to bear upon her. They had contacted her husband who was 'living from her in the Garrison of Portsmouth' and received word that he 'charged her no longer' to keep an alehouse. Despite their efforts, local officials admitted to the quarter sessions that 'never the lesse shee doth yet constantly to this very day continue to keepe A Comon Alehouse in a

140 Fletcher, *Reform in the Provinces*, p. 236.
141 SHC, Q/SR/16/79.

very disorderly manner'.[142] Some alehousekeepers may even have relished the challenge of frustrating the authorities' attempts at regulation. In 1609, the magistrates of Somerset were becoming increasingly agitated with an alehousekeeper named Walter Withers, a resident of Pilton. A letter was put forward to the quarter sessions explaining that Withers had been presented at a petty session for tippling without a licence, and describing him as 'verie malapert, sawcie and obstinate'. Despite having been 'often suppressed and warned from his unlawful tippling', the authorities could 'find noe conformitie in him'. Indeed, Thomas Hughes, the county magistrate who had written the letter, alleged that Withers 'hath confessed his offence before me, and that he hath no licence but would justify himself by quillets and evasions'.[143] This alehousekeeper was confident enough in the limitations of the authorities that he was happy to confess to giving officials the run-around.

Withers was not entirely exceptional in his boldness in the face of authority, or in his seemingly successful defiance. The inhabitants of the tithing of Monksilver and Bicknoller petitioned the Justices of Somerset in 1631 to take action to suppress the disorderly alehouse of Robert Brewer. The magistrates subsequently ordered that the house be suppressed, but there must be some doubt over the effectiveness of the order as previous attempts had already failed: 'his Ma[jes]t[ie]s officers within the said p[ar]ish of Monksilver who offer to suppresse such disorders dayly committed in his said house' had been consistently rebuffed by Brewer's 'menacing & threatening' responses to their attempts.[144] In 1632, Edward Johnson, a constable in Reading, likewise met with hostility when he tried to stop men from playing the prohibited game 'shovegroat' in the alehouse of Bennett Bailey.[145] Bailey intervened, and inverting the proper functioning of authority proceeded to deliver a reprimand to the official, 'abus[ing] the constable for reprovinge and forbiddinge those poore men for their playeinge'.[146] The constables of Great Coggeshall, Essex, were faced with a similar problem in 1639, in

---

[142] SHC, Q/SR/95:3/217.

[143] SHC, Q/SR/6/5; see also Q/SR/6/48.

[144] SHC, Q/SR/65:2/137.

[145] 'Shovegroat', 'Slide groat' or 'shuffle board', a popular 'pub game' in the early modern period, is a game in which disks are shoved by hand or with an implement so that they come to a stop on, or within, a scoring area marked on a board placed on a table or the floor. It had been forbidden under the Unlawful Games Act of 1541, 33 Henry VIII c. 9. A more recent version, shove-ha'penny, is still played today.

[146] *Read. Boro. Recs*, III, p. 144.

the form of unlicensed alehousekeeper Joseph Clarke. Clarke was known for 'usually abusing officers when they come to his house, by ill language', a form of insubordination made all the more intolerable by his poverty: 'carrying these things with an high hand although a poor man sometimes taking relief'. Clarke was another example of an alehousekeeper willing to defy the authorities in both word and deed, and he did not 'desist his courses although he hath benn admonished, indicted and sometimes convicted'.[147] That said, the authorities may, in this case, have been able to apply additional pressure to Clarke via the overseers of the poor – an additional dimension to the exercise of local authority that may have curtailed the potential for effective resistance.[148]

A decade earlier, in the Essex village of Moulsham, the defiance of the authorities by alehousekeepers had become endemic. A suburb of Chelmsford, Moulsham was another of those areas with a notorious concentration of alehouses – a troublesome 'extra-mural alehouse settlement' – and there was no shortage of alehousekeepers prepared to meet attempts to regulate their alehouses with bold defiance and dismissive insults.[149] Richard Northe and John Boys, who had the unenviable role of constables of Moulsham, entered the alehouse of Peter de Cort in April of 1629 to find two labourers playing 'slide groat', which they subsequently tried to halt. De Cort told the officials that they were 'too busy' and that he 'bad[e] a fart' for them – and later 'skoft' when they came to serve a warrant on him. They encountered a similar response at the alehouse of John Sturgin when attempting to serve him with a warrant for allowing 'misorder' in his house after the legal closing time of nine o'clock in the evening. Sturgin called one officer a 'Knave' and the other a 'hog's che[e]k', and also demonstrated a confidence in the limitations of the local authorities by bidding the officials to 'do their worst' in attempts to suppress his house. Thomas Roule responded to their charge that he had allowed tippling in his alehouse until two in the morning by saying he 'would not be beholden' to the constables. When they requested that William Bouser and his drinking company cease a game of 'slid groat' that was taking place in Bouser's alehouse, he answered that he would not and goaded the constable to 'do what he

147 ERO, Q/SR/308/112.

148 For more on the role of poor relief in local social relations see Steve Hindle, 'Power, Poor Relief and Social Relations in Holland Fen, c.1600–1800', *The Historical Journal* 41 (1998), pp. 67–96; Hindle, *On the Parish?*, passim.

149 Everitt, 'The English Urban Inn', p. 99.

would' to stop it.[150] Moulsham may be far from a typical local community in seventeenth-century England. Nonetheless, it demonstrates that
in certain places – and even when the local officials were prepared to
take action against disorderly alehouses – an 'uncooperative disposition'
on the part of alehousekeepers could act as a serious restraint on any
attempt to establish control over these institutions. Alehousekeepers
were often eager to remind officials of their ineffectiveness, and sometimes even goaded them about their powerlessness.

Resistance to the authorities did not only come from alehousekeepers
determined to defend their livelihood. Patrons too might offer similar
reactions, often in defence of their desire for recreational drinking. In
1652, the watchmen of West Leigh, Lancashire, entered an alehouse to
urge a company of five 'goodfellows' to 'forbear' their 'disorderly courses'
and depart. It was midnight, and the watchmen reminded the company
that 'there is an Acte that none shall continue drinkings after Nyne of
the Clock in the night'. The company did not take the advice kindly,
and replied, 'wee know there is such an Acte but weele not obey it, for
weele drinke as long as wee please', subsequently threatening the officials
'that if they would not goe out of the house they would send them out,
for they had nothing to doe with them'.[151] When, in 1631, two Reading
constables found men drinking in John Hickes's house between midnight
and one o' clock in the morning, one of the 'good fellows' present took
particular exception to their intrusion. John Bagley 'did call them knaves,
rogues', and 'did call for a knife, and used many oathes'. He taunted the
officers to take action against him, claiming he would take any punishment as a badge of honour: he 'urged and dared them to have him to
the Cage, affirming it was his glorye to be out in Cage'.[152] Companies of
drinking companions might defy the regulatory efforts of the authorities
in other ways. As was seen in Chapter 1, an increase in recreational
drinking in the Wiltshire parish of Calne in 1612 was attracting 'all the
great drinkers bothe of the Towne and Countrie to spende theyer tyme
in idleness and theyer monie in excessivie drinkinge', a situation that
local officials were powerless to act against: the constables revealed that
they 'can not punishe them according to the Lawe' because 'all me[n] for

---

150 ERO, Q/SR/267/20.
151 Wrightson, 'Two Concepts of Order', p. 21.
152 *Read. Boro. Recs*, III, p. 144.

the most p[ar]te love these cupp companions so well, that no man will take uppon him to be a sworne witnes against any drunkard'.[153]

Interestingly, the defiance of official attempts to curtail sociability were neither necessarily nor invariably restricted to the poorest members of the local community. Chapter 1 demonstrated that contemporaries were especially concerned that alehouses were providing a forum for that great social evil – recreational drinking by the poor. There is evidence, however, that middling social groups were sometimes prepared to both utilise and defend the role of the alehouse as a site for sociable drinking in the local community. In 1628, the constable of Shenfields, Essex, yeoman Phillip Cragg, found a fellow yeoman, Humphrey Aylett, 'with others in his company drinking in an alehouse'. Cragg singled out Aylett and 'admonished him in friendly manner ... telling him it were more fitting he were in another place than to give such ill example there and desire[d] him to depart home'. Perhaps the constable had chosen to single out Aylett because he saw it as particularly inappropriate for a fellow yeoman to be engaged in recreational alehouse drinking – after all, men of this middling status should be setting a better example to their poorer neighbours. If this was the case, Aylett clearly did not share this view of the appropriate social role of the middling sort, and 'reviled him with very foul language calling him knave and told him he would be there still in despite of him'.[154] Another telling case is that involving Thomas Hanbury, John Tabor and Daniel Wiltshire, who were presented to the Essex quarter sessions in 1630 'for drinking and tippling at Thomas Mayes, one of our alehouses, at an unseasonable time about 10 of the clock at night'. The same men were also found 'tippling' in the same house the following week, 'where they continued so above one whole hour', and when the constable came to ask them to leave they declared that 'if he came again he should come upon his own peril, and they would shut the doors and see if he durst come'. Neither the drinking companions nor the constable were deterred, and two weeks later the company were at Thomas Mayes' alehouse again, 'where they continued an whole hour', which again caused them to be 'admonished by the constable'. Once more, his efforts were unrewarded, and the men affirmed that they 'would be there another hour'.[155] These men were not, however, members of the local poor for whom the provision of alehouse

---

[153] WSHC, 1612/E/177.

[154] ERO, Q/SR/262/80.

[155] ERO, Q/SR, 271/35.

services was deemed a necessity. Rather, they were all examples of the 'ideal type' – established by Wrightson and Levine's classic study – of those emerging middling sorts who supposedly held a hostile disposition towards the alehouse: Terling yeomen.[156] It seems, then, that despite the apparent consensus identified in Chapter 1 that recreational drinking could never be a legitimate function of the alehouse in the local community, patrons of the institution of both poor and middling status were prepared to defend its provision of communal sociability, even when faced with determined official hostility. Indeed, as the preceding section has just shown, sometimes even office-holding village notables might themselves endorse and partake in the 'good fellowship' on offer in their local alehouses.

The preceding discussion of both legalism and resistance has demonstrated a number of ways in which the members of local communities in seventeenth-century England could negotiate the experience of authority as it related to the regulation of alehouses. Far from being an effective tool of 'social control', the law and notions of lawfulness could also act as a resource on which the keepers and patrons of alehouses might themselves draw to contest decisions to suppress them, with the notion of customary rights proving especially forceful within a culture of popular legalism. Furthermore, there were also those who, rather than looking to appropriate notions of lawfulness, opted instead to ignore or defy them, and both alehousekeepers and companies of 'good fellows' often seem to have expressed a confidence that it was local officials, rather than themselves, that were relatively powerless when it came to the control of recreational drinking. Such a conclusion invites us to reflect back on arguments about the changing character of alehouse regulation in the later seventeenth century, and in particular Wrightson's suggestion that whilst monarch and magistrates lost interest in alehouse regulation, parochial elites gained hegemonic control over it. Whilst Wrightson's hypothesis of two concepts of order acknowledged a degree of ambivalence within the attitudes of parochial authorities towards the alehouse, it also argued that this ambivalence gave way over the course of our period. He found evidence that the laws were enforced with increasing effectiveness as the seventeenth century advanced and argued that the 'slow assimilation of the village notables . . . to the values of their social superiors' caused the more proactive pursuit of the disciplinarian 'concept

[156] See Keith Wrightson and David Levine, *Poverty and Piety in an English Village: Terling, 1525–1700* (London, 1979).

of order'.[157] Anthony Fletcher, on the other hand, has posited a radically different explanation for the situation found in the second half of the century. He argued that the relaxation in regulatory zeal occurred among both magistrates and parochial officials, suggesting that at all levels the authorities 'had by and large come to terms with the limitations on the control they could exercise and had abandoned the attempt to execute sections of the alehouse legislation on the statute book that the community most firmly resisted'.[158]

In light of the findings of this section, Fletcher's conclusion appears particularly compelling. Legislation was limited as a tool of social control, and there were numerous ways in which the members of local communities could and did resist attempts at alehouse regulation, even where parochial officials were proactive in pursuit of it. Of course, both Wrightson and Fletcher's conclusions can be reconciled with reference to local and regional variations. Whilst parochial elites may have had firm control over the alehouse in Terling – an important focus of Wrightson's work – it seems less likely they did so in areas such as Moulsham or Kingswood, that have been highlighted here. Nonetheless, even if the attitudes and efforts of local authorities significantly hardened in the later seventeenth century, in some areas it would be difficult to accept that popular legalism and resistance ceased to be effective and buckled in the face of an official hostility that they had successfully contested for much of the period under consideration. A dominant pattern may be difficult to establish, but any attempt to draw general conclusions should not overemphasise the degree of hegemonic control that it was possible to achieve over alehouses and their patrons.

The devil's church

The previous two sections of this chapter have focused primarily on the relationship between the alehouse and those various officers responsible for governance in the early modern English 'state'. As we saw in the opening sections, however, contemporary concerns about the threat the alehouse posed to authority feared the danger to spiritual, as much as political, structures. This section therefore turns the focus onto the relationship between the church and the alehouse in early modern England.

---

157 Wrightson, 'Alehouses, Order and Reformation', p. 15; 'Two Concepts of Order', p. 46.
158 Fletcher, *Reform in the Provinces*, p. 252.

As we saw in the introduction, the late medieval relationship between the two, or at least between the church and communal recreational drinking, was a close and complementary one. In the early years of the Reformation it was not clear that a fissure was coming. Indeed, first-generation Protestants have been described as 'at home' in alehouses, making use of them in the 1530s as sites to discuss scripture. The distinguished Reformation historian A.G. Dickens remarked that 'if the battle of Waterloo was won on the playing fields of Eton, the Reformation was won in the pubs of Colchester'.[159] A second generation of Elizabethan Protestants, however, took a different view, and began to distance themselves from these 'little hells'. The Royal Injunctions of 1559 and the Canons of 1604 both forbade ecclesiastics from resorting to alehouses and taverns, and from the 1580s churchmen 'put out a rising storm of protest which indignantly juxtaposed Church and alehouse as deadly rivals for the affections of the people'.[160] Indeed, in 1617, the writer Thomas Young complained of the average parishioner that 'they goe ten times to an Ale-house, before they goe once to a Church', a perceived rivalry that was reflected in the growing prominence in the conditions of alehouse licences of the prohibition against serving during the time of divine service.[161] Hostile rhetoric reached its apogee in the 1650s, when religious writer Richard Younge denounced alehouses in print in 1655 as 'drinking schools' where drunkards learn the arts of sin; where they 'hear the Devil's lectures read'; 'the shops and markets where Satan drives his trade', where men 'stand on their heads and shake their heals against heaven' and 'God's Name is blasphemed'.[162] Petitioners from Bollington, Cheshire, called for the suppression of an alehouse in 1657, claiming it 'sad to the soules of people fearing God to see prophane persons haste to the Alehouse especially on the Lord's Day'.[163]

Yet we have already seen that the rhetoric espoused by the opponents of the alehouse can conceal a degree of ambivalence in the relationship between the institution and authority, and this can certainly be said of the relationship between the alehouse and the church. Such

---

[159] Quoted in Patrick Collinson, 'From Iconoclasm to Iconophobia: The Cultural Impact of the Second English Reformation', in Peter Marshall (ed.), *The Impact of the English Reformation, 1500–1640* (London, 1997), p. 283.

[160] *Ibid.*; Wrightson, 'Alehouses, Order and Reformation', p. 18.

[161] Young, *Englands Bane*, sig. F.

[162] Richard Younge, *The Blemish of Government, Shame of Religion, Disgrace of Mankinde, or a Charge drawn up against Drunkards* (London, 1655).

[163] *Ches. Q.S. Recs*, p. 165.

ambivalence can be detected, in some cases, on the part of clergymen. In Upwey, Dorset, complaints were voiced in 1617 against an alehouse that facilitated much drunkenness, including the information that Parson Ellis was to be found 'often there adrinkinge', and on one occasion had been so drunk on a Saturday night that 'he could not read devine service on the Saboth day in the morning as he should have done'.[164] Another clergyman inclined to indulge in alehouse sociability was Robert Sharpe of South Cave, in the East Riding of Yorkshire, who had complaints brought against him by his churchwardens in 1682, as he was 'given to excessive or immoderate drinking of strong drinke'. On one Sunday:

> having administered the sacrament to one Mr Sunderland and one Mr Baxter and some other persons you did goe to the alehouse with them and there sate drinking soe immoderately with them all the rest of the day till you were incapable of your duty and neglected to read service in the afternoon, to the danger of your own soule and evil example of others.[165]

The vicar of Ribchester, Lancashire, took his connections with the alehouse further, and was presented in 1614 by his churchwardens as 'an alehouse keeper'. Moreover, his own alehouse had regularly facilitated profanation of the sabbath. On one occasion eleven fiddlers had played there on a Sunday to entertain drinkers; on others he allowed 'tiplying and drinking in his howse in time of divine service'; and on another Sunday he had hosted 'thirty four persons playing on three pairs of cards'.[166]

Some within the church recognised that for parish clergy to attend the alehouse with their parishioners was a way of currying popularity. The preacher Charles Richardson, in a sermon on the duties of a godly minister published in 1616, claimed that 'most men' preferred a minister who 'will sit neighbourly with them, and spend his penny, as they doe theirs in the Ale-house'.[167] In the Derbyshire peak country 'those ministers of the established church who drew the warmest welcome from their humbler parishioners were those who were most willing to join

164 J.H. Bettey (ed.), *The Case Book of Sir Francis Ashley, J.P.: Recorder of Dorchester, 1614–1635* (Dorchester, 1981), pp. 41–2.
165 Diane Carlile, "A comon and sottish drunkard you have been': Prosecutions for Drunkenness in the York Courts c.1660–1725', *York Historian* 16 (1999), pp. 37–8.
166 John Addy, *Sin and Society in the Seventeenth Century* (London, 1989), p. 29.
167 Arnold Hunt, *The Art of Hearing: English Preachers and Their Audiences, 1590–1640* (Cambridge, 2010), p. 249.

actively in the festive, alehouse-frequenting culture which dominated the mining villages'.[168] The parishioners of Castleton, Derbyshire, were loyal to their vicar Thomas Furnace in the late sixteenth century in the face of attempts by a minority to excommunicate him, not despite but *because* he 'loveth good drinke verie well'.[169] When the minister of Old Cleeve, Somerset, faced complaints in 1601 that he was neglecting his duties and spending too much time in alehouses and playing bowls on the village green, a number of parishioners came to his defence, stating that though he did like to often 'make merry' with his parishioners, he only ever kept 'good company' and 'civil order'.[170] There were clearly then clergymen who engaged in alehouse sociability, regardless of the dictates of royal injunctions and canons.

Indeed, Patrick Collinson – drawing on the writings of the 'Tudor anthropologist' George Gifford – identified two contrasting types of clergyman in early modern England: 'the less than professional parson' who 'identified with the community of which he was a part' and 'shared its round of work and leisure', and the 'professional and godly minister' who 'was a strongly contrasted type' opposed to and removed from alehouse recreation.[171] We might draw a parallel here then between the attitudes towards alehouse sociability of the clergy and those of local parish constables. If the latter were motivated, as Keith Wrightson has suggested, by 'two concepts of order', and could be divided into those who sought to tolerate and those who sought to reform parish sociability, the same notion can be applied to the outlook of parish clergy. Was there a hardening of attitudes across the century then to match that which Wrightson suggested was occurring amongst the ranks of parish officials? It is still possible to find members of the clergy engaging in alehouse sociability in the later seventeenth century: in the early 1680s the vicar of East Pennard, Somerset, Mr Alisbury, was known by parishioners as 'Drunken Alisbury' on account of his fondness for visiting alehouses.[172] Yet it may be the case that the attitudes of parishioners towards such behaviour was hardening. In his analysis of the relations between clergy and their

---

[168] Wood, *The Politics of Social Conflict*, p. 193.

[169] *Ibid.*, p. 193–4.

[170] SHC, D/D/Cd/32, Poines v Evans.

[171] Patrick Collinson, *The Religion of Protestants: The Church in English Society, 1559–1625* (Oxford, 1982), pp. 104–5.

[172] SHC, D/D/Cd/97, Office v Alisbury. For other examples see also Donald Spaeth, *The Church in an Age of Danger: Parsons and Parishioners, 1660–1740* (Cambridge, 2001), pp. 123–5.

parishioners in the eighty years following the Restoration, Donald Spaeth detected the prevailing attitude that 'although lay people took a relaxed view of the good fellowship which led most men to "take a cup now & then", they did not extend the same tolerant attitude to the clergy'.[173] Indeed, the parishioners of East Pennard complained that on one occasion, having drunk five or six pots of ale in an alehouse, Alisbury had fallen asleep in the street, causing 'scandal and reproach both to himself and his profession, ill becoming a minister of the gospell'.[174] Again, though, we need to be cautious about suggesting uniform and unilinear patterns of change. In Ashton-in-Makerfield, Lancashire, in the early 1660s, the apprentice Roger Lowe regularly drank in an alehouse with 'Old Mr Woods', a nonconformist preacher who had been deprived of his living in the parish by the 1662 Act of Uniformity, and forced to move away. Woods made regular visits to his former parish to meet with nonconformist parishioners, and the alehouse became the natural venue for such meetings, or 'conventicles'.[175] Indeed, in the religious climate of the Restoration era alehouses may have once more become an important 'home' for those Protestants who found themselves at odds with the established church, as they had been in the early years of the Reformation.[176]

It was certainly the case, therefore, that clergymen and preachers did not always behave as though church and alehouse were rival institutions. Nor did their parishioners, although it is possible to point to some examples of extreme irreligion in alehouses. In Chester, in 1640, one John Edwards allegedly 'upon his knees [did] drink a health to the Divill or to Beelzebub the prince of the Divills' in Hugh Anderson's alehouse in Foregate Street.[177] In 1656 Nottingham feltmaker William Bradshaw was alleged to have said that the story that 'our Savior fed 5000 men with 05 lo[a]ves and 2 fishes' was 'as arrand a lye as ever was spoken'.[178] The Wiltshire miller William Dawkins fell out with an alehouse companion after referring to the Book of Common Prayer as 'Common Turd' in 1665.[179] Far more numerous than such cases of 'scoffing' at religion are exam-

---

[173] Spaeth, *The Church in an Age of Danger*, p. 124.

[174] SHC, D/D/Cd/97, Office v Alisbury.

[175] *Lowe*, pp. 26, 33–4. For More on Woods see p. 124.

[176] For other examples of conventicles being held in alehouses see WSHC, 1646/T/181; CRO, QJF/112/3/66, 71.

[177] Addy, *Sin and Society*, p. 107.

[178] *Nott. Boro. Recs*, V, p. 290.

[179] WSHC, 1665/H/178.

ples of people drinking in alehouses during the time of divine service, but even these should not be taken as evidence that alehouses were the 'nests of Satan' of some preachers' imaginations.[180] Indeed, even the most 'godly' of parishioners could see church and alehouse as compatible institutions of village life. In part this could be logistical. One petition in favour of an alehouse being licensed, sent by the parishioners of Martock to the Somerset bench in 1627, claimed that the alehouse was conveniently located and necessary for parishioners 'sometymes to refreshe them selves in', as they lived 'so farr from the p[ar]ish Church that oftentymes on the Saboth day and other hollydaies they cannot go home & come agane to Church the same day'.[181] The godly apprentice Roger Lowe also relied on alehouses to provide the infrastructure for committed religiosity: he regularly travelled long distances on Sundays to hear preachers, and alehouses provided crucial stopping-off points to take on refreshment.[182] Yet it was not only out of necessity that Lowe frequented alehouses – as we will see in Chapter 4, alehouse recreations sat alongside sermon-gadding as the central activities of his Sundays, and not infrequently this 'godly' apprentice visited the alehouse on other days of the week too.

Instances of those – undoubtedly common – parishioners who combined church-going and alehouse-going in their social round are, of course, relatively rare in the archival record, and are overshadowed by those whose behaviour was deemed more deviant. There is some evidence to confirm their existence, however, with one such source being presentments to the church courts of those who turned up to church drunk. At Winwick, Lancashire, in 1626, John Flitcroft spent the morning in the alehouse before attending church in the afternoon, only to have to rush out to be sick. The following year, in Leeds, Yorkshire, Edmund Saurer was not so quick, and after turning up 'drunk, at morning prayer upon a Sabboath day' he 'did vomite upon the Communion Table'.[183] On one Sunday in Leighes Magna, Essex, in 1630, two men and two women had attended morning service before heading to an alehouse, where they stayed 'eatinge drinkinge and tiplinge' until evening prayer. They had clearly consumed more drink than was necessary for simple refreshment though, as one of the company 'came not at all to eveninge prayer but

---

[180] For the 'nests of Satan' phrase see Clark, 'The Alehouse and the Alternative Society', p. 47.

[181] SHC, Q/SR/58:1/112.

[182] For examples see *Lowe*, pp. 88, 108–9.

[183] Addy, *Sin and Society*, p. 108.

lay asleepe in the fields'. Another, Joane Goodman, made it back to the church but 'went out of the church about the beginning of the sermon and was observed by some of the parishe to goe out reelinge'. Goodman then 'lay downe at the ende of the chancel and there lay asleepe till the later ende of the sermon'.[184]

Whilst the individuals in these examples may not have handled the balance between being a good Christian and being a 'good fellow' particularly well, they nonetheless stand as evidence that it was a balance many parishioners sought to achieve. As Beat Kümin has recently argued, 'for most parishioners, a visit to the public house did not amount to a profanation of the Sabbath; for them, church and tavern belonged together as two sides of the same coin'.[185] Far from being arch rivals, then, we should understand the relationship between the church and the alehouse as one marked – like that between the alehouse and authority more generally – by a degree of ambivalence. There were certainly churchmen who condemned alehouses in the strongest terms, but so too were there clergymen who frequented alehouses, even ran them, and parishioners who patronised both institutions. Once again, then, we see that the rhetoric voiced by opponents of the alehouse to some extent obscures the complexity of the power relations that configured around the 'battle' over the institution in local communities.

Conclusion

Key to understanding the configurations of resistance and authority that centred on the alehouse is the fact that they were localised. The relationship between authority and the alehouse in any given community was dependent on a number of variables, the temporal not least amongst them, and it could take a variety of forms. The character of alebench politics may have been fractured and dissident in West Country alehouses in the wake of the Monmouth Rebellion, but the tone was rather more loyalist in Southampton's closely surveyed drinking estab-

---

[184] W.H. Hale (ed.), A Series of Precedents and Proceedings in Criminal Causes, Extending from the Year 1475 to 1640; Extracted from the Act-Books of Ecclesiastical Courts in the Diocese of London, Illustrative of the Discipline of the Church of England (London, 1847), pp. 253–4.

[185] Beat Kümin, 'Sacred Church and Worldly Tavern: Reassessing an Early Modern Divide', in W. Coster and A. Spicer (eds), Sacred Space in Early Modern Europe (Cambridge, 2005), pp. 17–38; for a similar argument see Paul Griffiths, Youth and Authority: Formative Experiences in England, 1560–1640 (Oxford, 1996), ch. 4.

lishments. Regulatory efforts in Cheshire were zealous under the direction of Major General Worsley in the 1650s, yet they were rather more half-hearted when commanded by the Mayor of Nottingham in the 1610s. Parochial elites were hell-bent on hegemony over the alehouse in Terling, Essex, but other parish constables from the same county – such as John Lufkin of Layer Marney – were hell-bent on trying to drink their fellow parishioners under the alehouse table. An alehousekeeper from Tarporley, Cheshire, could defend himself against complaints by insisting he complied with the requirement to keep 'good order' in his house; others in Moulsham, or on the Mendips, 'scoffed' at attempts to suppress them, and bade officers to 'do their worst'. The Wiltshire minister John Newman exhorted the magistrates to act against alehouses; the Somerset minister Mr Alisbury spent long days occupying them. The relationship between authority and the alehouse needs to be understood, therefore, within the context of 'England's mosaic of parochial diversity'.[186]

That said, this chapter has sought to identify some of the broader contours within which localised peculiarities took shape, and a number of the resulting conclusions call for us to reconsider key aspects of the relationship between authority and the alehouse. The political culture of the alehouse was vibrant, and political awareness was high: all the key matters of church and state were passionately debated on the alebench, albeit in ways that were not always civil. Indeed, opinion was often divided, a fact which mitigated the free expression of plebeian radicalism, and loyalty to established order features as often in the historical record as intentions to overthrow it. If there was more to alebench politics than 'desperate outbursts' of sedition, they were too fractious for the alehouse to serve as the general headquarters of revolution. And if alehouse patrons were ambivalent towards established authority, then the officers of the same were likewise ambivalent about the alehouse. Both magistrates and parochial officials took up the challenges laid down to them by the regulatory framework with efforts ranging from the slack to the zealous, but there is a sense that a more general disposition towards leniency was only occasionally punctuated by bursts of concerted regulation, concentrated in time and space. Opposition to the alehouse, manifested in the regulatory system described in Chapter 1, undoubtedly attracted 'a broad spectrum of support' that went beyond the Crown and the committed godly to embrace 'many moderate Protestants, county land-

---

[186] Wrightson, 'The Politics of the Parish', p. 36.

owners, yeoman farmers and prosperous merchants'.[187] But there were also significant numbers amongst these groups who failed to enforce that regulatory system with any enthusiasm. For those amongst the ranks of village notables, at least, their indifference to strict regulation often had something to do with the fact that they were not prepared to wage war against recreational drinking in alehouses. Indeed, there was a degree of attachment to alehouse good fellowship that extended beyond the ranks of those legitimate alehouse patrons, the local poor, to embrace both office-holding and non-office-holding members of the local middling sort.

Those who did take up arms against local alehouses did not find the licensing system a ready-made tool of hegemony: alehousekeepers and their patrons found a variety of ways to mobilise the law in defence of their institutions. Others simply ignored it, or openly defied it. If the attitudes of parochial elites did harden in certain places as the century progressed, and a degree of social control over local alehouses was achieved, such a feat would have had to overcome widespread and entrenched forms of 'everyday resistance'. It seems unlikely that such victories were common. Even the local minister could not be relied upon as a staunch ally in such battles: many were as likely to line up with their parishioners on the alebench. Perhaps attitudes hardened here too as the seventeenth century progressed, but for many who counted themselves amongst the ranks of the godly the alehouse became an increasingly important pillar of the infrastructure of nonconformity. The idea that church and alehouse were 'polar extremes' was far from universal in the early modern mindset. Historians should not erect a false dichotomy here.[188]

There was considerable friction between authority and the alehouse in early modern England. Most clearly this was articulated through the establishment of a novel and ambitious regulatory system designed to prohibit recreational drinking in alehouses, a system that resonated with the concerns of many amongst the 'better sort', and magistrates, ministers and parish notables across the land threw their full weight behind attempts to implement it. But such application was not uniform, and nor did it go uncontested. There were enough men and women prepared to allow, even to fight for, a more prominent place for the alehouse in their communities than the strict letter of the law permitted. As a conse-

---

187 Clark, *The English Alehouse*, p. 167.
188 For an overly dichotomous view see Martin, *Alcohol, Sex, and Gender*, pp. 62–6.

quence, the alehouse did not languish at the margins of early modern communities; it often assumed a place at their heart. A major reason why it did so was because its patrons – drawn from amongst the ranks of both the local poor and middling sort – valued that alehouse service that so agitated its opponents: the opportunity for recreational drinking. It is to the story of why this activity had such an appeal to many contemporaries that Part Two of this book now turns.

Part Two

The Community in the Alehouse

3

'Good Companions and Fellow Boozers' The Idiom of Good Fellowship

'To be called a good companion and fellow-boozer is to me pure honour and glory.'

François Rabelais, Preface to *Gargantua and Pantagruel*[1]

The French Renaissance writer François Rabelais claimed that recreational drinking was – for its participants at least – a positive socio-cultural activity, one that conferred upon its partakers 'pure honour and glory' derived from the admiration of one's 'fellow-boozers'. In his *Gargantua and Pantagruel*, a chapter entitled 'The Drunkards' Conversation' deployed a celebratory lexicon of alcohol consumption – 'Let's have a song, let's have a drink, let's sing a catch!'; 'fill this up till it spills over'; 'let's knock it all back' – in a tone that revels in liberal drinking and jovial companionship, and highlights that for Rabelais drink was 'the symbol for the uninhibited interchange of affection between man and man'.[2] Part Two of this book argues that a similar celebratory idiom, one that emphasised merriment, liberality, and affectionate social bonds – referred to by contemporaries as 'good fellowship' – lay at the heart of the appeal the alehouse held for early modern English men and women.

Of course, not all alehouse patronage took on the form of good fellowship, and it is important to keep in mind the distinction – so central to the regulatory framework for alehouses – between two broad categories of alehouse visits: those generally acceptable ones in which a moderate amount of alcohol consumption served a 'functional' purpose, and those officially prohibited occasions where patrons were more centrally concerned with consuming larger quantities of drink for recreation. As

1   François Rabelais, *The Histories of Gargantua and Pantagruel*, trans. J.M. Cohen (Harmondsworth, 1955), Preface.
2   Rabelais, *Gargantua and Pantagruel*, pp. 48–51, and Cohen's, 'Introduction' to the same, p. 24.

Chapter 1 showed, visits to the alehouse to obtain essential victuals by those without their own brewing facilities, or by those on the road looking for refreshment, were regarded as wholly legitimate. Sharing a pot of ale as a means to seal a business deal or resolve a neighbourly conflict were also relatively uncontroversial, and drink might often function as a 'mundane marker of accord and good will' and serve to 'oil the wheels of social intercourse'.[3] Provided such visits lasted no longer than an hour and did not descend into drunkenness, they were unlikely to arouse opprobrium from any quarter. That said, many of the occasions on which alcohol was consumed in the alehouse clearly went beyond these routine, functional visits. Several examples have already been discussed in the foregoing chapters – the 'cup companions' of Calne, who sought out the alehouses that sold the strongest ale, and there spent 'theyer tyme in idleness and theyer monie in excessivie drinkinge'; or the Essex constable John Lufkin who often drank for days at a time and participated in drinking contests. The later-seventeenth-century diary of the Lancashire apprentice mercer, Roger Lowe, is also indicative of the fact that trips to the alehouse often took on more than a routine, moderate character. Lowe would often stop off at an alehouse on one of his frequent journeys to hear a preacher in a nearby parish, where he would 'spend 2d' – the cost of one quart, the standard measure for ale – for legitimate refreshment and nourishment. Lowe also conducted business transactions in the alehouse, often consuming 2d worth of ale whilst writing a bond for a fellow parishioner. On other occasions though, Lowe's alehouse visits would take on a more recreational bent, either when a 'functional' visit shaded into a 'recreational' one, or when recreation was the explicit intention from the outset. It was not uncommon for the apprentice to record in his diary spending as much as 10d and staying late into the night, and on such occasions he would often refer to being 'very merry' with his drinking companions.[4] It was precisely these latter, 'merry' visits that elicited condemnation from moral and secular authorities in this period. The following two chapters will be primarily concerned with recovering the underlying logic behind the decisions of many contemporaries to participate in the category of more explicitly recreational drinking in the alehouse, in open defiance of the vitriolic arguments against – and official proscription of – such activity.

---

[3] Shepard, '"Swil-bols and Tos-pots"', p. 120; Wrightson, 'Alehouses, Order and Reformation', p. 6.

[4] *Lowe, passim.*

This chapter will do so through an analysis of a particular type of early modern print – the broadside ballad – that was intimately connected to alehouse sociability. Before embarking on the direct analysis of such sources, however, this argument and approach need to be set in their broader context. The first section of this chapter will explain how such an argument and approach relates to existing scholarly work on the rationale behind alcohol consumption in the early modern period. The second section will introduce the broadside ballad and make the case for its value as a source for the historian of alehouse sociability. The third section will reconstruct the idiom of 'good fellowship' expressed in these sources, and the fourth section will demonstrate that gender is an essential analytical category for understanding the appeal good fellowship held for contemporaries.

Explaining alcohol consumption

'His whole delight was in drinking, not as some drunkards plead, for company's sake, but for the sake of drink.'[5]

In his analysis of the alehouse frequenting of his fellow parishioner Charles Dimock, the late-seventeenth-century resident historian of the Shropshire parish of Myddle, Richard Gough, suggested a more prosaic explanation for heavy drinking in alehouses: it was not good fellowship that underpinned its appeal, but rather something closer to the modern notion of alcoholism.[6] A similar perspective underpins one of the classic narratives about the history of drinking in the early modern period: that drinking and drunkenness became increasingly associated with the pursuit

---

5 Richard Gough, *The History of Myddle*, ed. David Hey (Harmondsworth, 1981), p. 113.
6 The notion of alcoholism as a disease was not, however, fully developed in the early modern worldview. For its development see Roy Porter, 'The Drinking Man's Disease: The Pre-History of Alcoholism in Georgian Britain', *British Journal of Addiction* 80 (1985), pp. 385–96; Virginia Berridge, 'Dependence: Historical Concepts and Constructs', in Griffith Edwards and Malcolm Lader (eds), *The Nature of Drug Dependence* (Oxford, 1990), pp. 1–18; James Nicholls, '*Vinum Britannicum*: The "Drink Question" in Early Modern England', *The Social History of Alcohol and Drugs* 22:2 (2008), pp. 6–25. Jessica Warner, '"Resolv'd to Drink no More": Addiction as a Preindustrial Concept', *Journal of Studies on Alcohol* 55 (1994), pp. 85–91, argues that it can be placed in the 1600s, but her argument is directly disputed in Peter Ferentzy, 'From Sin to Disease: Differences and Similarities between Past and Current Conceptions on "Chronic Drunkenness"', *Contemporary Drug Problems* 28 (2001), pp. 362–90.

of narcotic oblivion on the part of the poor. Indeed, a widely shared attachment to communal 'churchyard' sociability in the late Middle Ages is often thought to have given way as post-Reformation moral zeal and the Renaissance revival of classical doctrine – with its strong emphasis on 'moderation' – created a new sober disposition amongst the upper and middling ranks of English society, marked by a new-found contempt for the excessive and raucous drinking of their poorer neighbours.[7] As elites withdrew their support from communal drinking, the poor were forced to take their drinking out of the churchyard and into the alehouse, an environment often thought to lack the social dimension found in communal festivities. Moreover, life for the lower orders was particularly hard in the century between the Reformation and the Civil War, creating what have been seen as 'conditions [that] were hardly propitious for full-blooded conviviality' on their part.[8] Instead, alehouse-goers in this period have been seen as men simply looking to 'sublimate their miseries in drunkenness', or who 'took to drink to blot out some of the horror in their lives': 'driven on many occasions by adversity to gather in the relative comfort of the alehouse kitchen', but with 'no necessary convergence of interest'.[9] In this well-established view of the relationship between poverty and drinking in this period, it was the drink – and even the warmth – rather than the purposeful pursuit of company, that brought customers through the alehouse door.

Yet recent work on early modern European drinking cultures has questioned whether the straightforward pursuit of 'drunken oblivion' is ever sufficient to explain patterns of heavy drinking. This 'drink-as-despair' approach has come under attack from work that has argued that people

[7] On a growing division between elite and popular culture in the early modern period see Peter Burke, *Popular Culture in Early Modern Europe* (London, 1978; subsequent references are to the 3rd edn, Farnham, 2009); Mikhail Bakhtin, *Rabelais and His World*, trans. Helene Iswolsky (Cambridge, MA, 1968); Norbert Elias, *The Civilizing Process*, trans. Edmund Jephcott (Oxford, 2000). For the English context of these divisions see Wrightson, *English Society*, esp. pp. 228–9; Keith Thomas, 'The Place of Laughter in Tudor and Stuart England', *Times Literary Supplement* (21 January 1977), pp. 77–81; Anna Bryson, *From Courtesy to Civility: Changing Codes of Conduct in Early Modern England* (Oxford, 1998). On the relationship between these narratives and the history of early modern drinking see Wrightson, 'Alehouses, Order and Reformation'; Withington, 'Intoxicants and Society'. On the relationship between drinking and poverty see David Courtwright, *Forces of Habit: Drugs and the Making of the Modern World* (Harvard, MA, 2001).

[8] Clark, *The English Alehouse*, p. 232.

[9] *Ibid.*, p. 341; Keith Thomas, *Religion and the Decline of Magic* (London, 1971), p. 22; Clark, *The English Alehouse*, p. 160.

drank not simply to get drunk, but to participate in a series of meaningful social rituals. As such, historians are beginning to see that 'drinking rituals and their layered meanings' can reveal 'a great deal about how early modern folk defined their lives and relations with one another', and that 'decoding' such rituals could provide a 'key to understanding popular beliefs and values'.[10] This approach of 'decoding' drinking rituals and drunken behaviour owes a debt to anthropologists, who have demonstrated that drunken behaviour varies considerably across cultures. As such, whilst alcohol undoubtedly has a physiological effect on the body, the precise way in which that manifests itself is culturally specific – suggesting that drunken behaviour is to some extent a form of learned social behaviour, and not simply determined by the physical properties of alcohol.[11] The precise form taken by drinking rituals and behaviour can, then, tell us something about the social and cultural values of the host society that helped to shape it.

These insights are increasingly being applied to early modern English drinking cultures, and there have been calls to explore 'the meanings of drinking rituals for the men involved as well as [for] their critics', implying that previous historians had perhaps too readily accepted the dismissive attitudes towards alehouse drinking offered by the likes of Richard Gough.[12] Indeed, Phil Withington has recently argued that it was precisely 'for company's sake' that so many early modern English men and women engaged in recreational and sociable drinking, and that 'keeping company' was understood by contemporaries as a highly significant social activity that was associated with a raft of 'informal conventions' of appropriate ways to behave, and a developed 'politics of participation' shaping decisions about with whom, and whom not, to join in 'company'.[13] In short, all of these historians have called for an acknowledgement that recreational drinking was invariably a form of purposeful and meaningful social interaction, and that greater attention should be paid to the informal etiquette of behaviour that surrounded early modern drinking rituals as a means of gaining greater insight into

---

10 Tlusty, *Bacchus and Civic Order*, pp. 1–6; Brennan, *Public Drinking and Popular Culture*, pp. 11–12; Brennan draws particular inspiration from the work of cultural historians such as Natalie Zemon Davis, *Society and Culture in Early Modern France* (Stanford, 1975).

11 The most influential works of anthropology here are the collection of essays in Mary Douglas (ed.), *Constructive Drinking: Perspectives on Drink from Anthropology* (Cambridge, 1987). See also Shepard, '"Swil-bols and Tos-pots"', p. 120.

12 *Ibid.*

13 Withington, 'Company and Sociability', pp. 292–3, 296, 302.

the wider cultural values of those who engaged in them. Taken together, they represent the emergence of a new 'cultural history of drinking' for the early modern period.

One aspect of this emerging approach has been developed by literary scholars as much as historians, and has focused its analytical gaze upon various forms of printed writing about drinking in the early modern period, in search of 'what kinds of etiquettes and rituals governed different drinking communities'.[14] There is a considerable body of material to draw upon here, for if the rise of the alehouse was one of the characteristically dynamic developments in the early modern period of English history, then so too was the dramatic growth of the market in print. The amount and variety of printed material in circulation expanded significantly between the middle of the sixteenth and the middle of the seventeenth centuries, and as it did so there emerged a variety of works on the subject of drinking – what we might call 'drink literature'.[15] One of the earliest and most enduring positions on drinking to find expression in print were the complaints of moralists and ministers, and sermons and treatises condemning drinking and drunkenness became a staple genre of early modern English literature.[16] This might be taken as a further indication of a growing hostility amongst the middling and upper ranks of early modern English society towards the recreational drinking of the lower orders at this time, of the militant 'battle against the alehouse' manifesting itself in print as an adjunct to its expression on the parchment of petitions, and in the letter of legislation.

Yet much of the recent work on the way drink was dealt with in early modern printed works has cautioned against this established narrative. Instead, literary scholars and cultural historians have pointed to a range of printed genres that demonstrate rather more ambivalent positions amongst the literate and educated on the issue of alcohol consumption, emphasising in particular that the Renaissance humanism that

---

[14] See, for instance, the essays in Smyth (ed.), *A Pleasing Sinne*.

[15] On the expansion of print in early modern England, and the place of drinking literature within this, see Withington, 'Renaissance Drinking Cultures', esp. pp. 142–3. The English genre of seventeenth-century drink literature had precedents in the sixteenth-century German genre of *Trinkliteratur*. See Tlusty, *Bacchus and Civic Order*, pp. 3, 6, 8, 64, 72–4, 79, 90–1; O'Callaghan, 'Tavern Societies', p. 43.

[16] For examples see George Gascoigne, *A Delicate Diet for Dainty-mouthed Drunkards* (London, 1576); Richard Rawlidge, *A Monster Late Found Out and Discovered* (Amsterdam, 1628); Daniel Dent, *A Sermon Against Drunkenness* (London, 1628); William Prynne, *Healthes: Sickness* (London, 1628), and the discussion in Lemon, 'Compulsory Conviviality'.

informed much of this burgeoning 'drink literature' could 'be used to valorise drunkenness' as often as it was used to 'idealize moderation and civility'.[17] Verse and pamphlet compositions that emerged from tavern-based drinking 'societies' in early-seventeenth-century London stressed that wine consumption was an important stimulant to the composition of poetry and to the engagement in competitive wordplay, both of which were becoming central rituals in the expression of a certain educated, urban, male identity.[18] Printed miscellanies – collections of short poems and songs consumed primarily by wealthy, young, urban males – contained drinking songs and poems, some of which served as didactic models of 'civil' etiquette, but others of which were bawdy jests that read more as 'defiant shrieks of misrule'.[19] Even 'prescriptive' advice literature tended to promote a certain carefully controlled level of intoxication as an appropriate lubricant to convivial conversation at dinner parties.[20] Indeed, these various forms of 'drink literature' often articulated 'a volatile yet creative dialogue between civility and licence', and exalted those individuals who had the cherished quality of 'wit' necessary for striking a balance between the two.[21] The celebrated playwright and poet Ben Jonson also promoted the consumption of wine as central to an 'educated, refined, self-controlled conviviality'.[22]

These, largely early-seventeenth-century, works of drink literature promoted a certain level of skilfully controlled intoxication as central to elite identities, but there also existed a more unequivocal and aggressively pro-drink literature. The archetypal writer here is Robert Herrick, who is seen as a central figure in the emergence of a strand of drinking poetry in the 1630s that abandoned the insistence on controlled consumption that was upheld in the verse and plays of Jonson. Such 'cavalier poets' were seen to embrace excess and bacchanalian revelry, and reconfigured heavy drinking as an act of bravado and courage that

17 See Withington, 'Intoxicants and Society', p. 635.

18 O'Callaghan, 'Tavern Societies'; O'Callaghan, *The English Wits*, esp. ch. 3.

19 Adam Smyth, *Profit and Delight: Print Miscellanies in England, 1640–1682* (Detroit, 2004), pp. 3, 154–68.

20 Jennifer Richards, 'Health, Intoxication and Civil Conversation in Renaissance England', *Past and Present* 222, Supplement 9: *Cultures of Intoxication* (2014), pp. 168–86.

21 The quote is from O'Callaghan, *The English Wits*, preface; for more on wit see also Phil Withington, *Society in Early Modern England* (Cambridge, 2010), pp. 186–98.

22 Joshua Scodel, *Excess and the Mean in Early Modern English Literature* (Princeton, 2002), p. 201. For more on Jonson see O'Callaghan, 'Tavern Societies'; O'Callaghan, *The English Wits*, ch. 2; Stella Achilleos, 'The *Anacreontea* and a Tradition of Refined Male Sociability', in Smyth (ed.), *A Pleasing Sinne*, pp. 21–35.

was linked to martial prowess.[23] Their literary expressions are often seen as a form of anti-puritanism, and as an explicit reaction to the treatises and sermons that condemned heavy drinking – condemnations which by no means restricted their opprobrium to the drinking of the lower orders. Indeed, when the prominent puritan William Prynne penned a denunciation of health-drinking in 1628, he identified the root cause of this 'gangrene and leprosy of drunkenness' to be the 'ill-example of some great men, Gentlemen, Clergymen, and others'.[24] If this embrace of excessive drinking in the verse of cavalier poets grew from an aristocratic reaction to puritanism in the 1630s, during the Civil War and Interregnum it took on an added political charge as it became closely associated with Royalists. Supporters of the King came to embrace a culture of heavy drinking – and in particular excessive health-drinking – as a means of expressing their loyalty, and later as a way to drown their sorrows in defeat and to antagonise the puritan regime of the Interregnum.[25] Elements of this aristocratic libertinism persisted after the Restoration, as did the strong association between health-drinking and political loyalty and allegiances.[26] The fulsome embrace of prodigious drunkenness was, then, as characteristic of writing within the genre as Jonson's emphasis on refined and controlled consumption.

The major achievement of the scholars working on these various forms of drink literature has been to demonstrate that the educated and literate classes of early modern England were not uniformly hostile to drinking. If the literature they consumed and produced was any guide, the consumption of alcohol was a central feature of their own recreational activity, was structured around rituals such as health-drinking or competitive wordplay, and was intended to express values such as 'wit', courage or loyalty that were important features of various elite identities. This demonstrates that the sharp dichotomy between an elite culture of sobriety and restraint, and a popular culture of drunkenness, does not capture the complexity of early modern drinking cultures. Yet, whilst

---

[23] Scodel, *Excess and the Mean*, chs 7–8; Lemon, 'Compulsory Conviviality'.

[24] Quoted in Withington, 'Intoxicants and Society', p. 656.

[25] See McShane Jones, 'Roaring Royalists and Ranting Brewers'; Angela McShane, 'The Extraordinary Case of the Flesh Eating and Blood Drinking Cavaliers', in Angela McShane and Garthine Walker (eds), *The Extraordinary and the Everyday in Early Modern England* (Basingstoke, 2010), pp. 192–210; Maria Keblusek, 'Wine for Comfort: Drinking and the Royalist Exile Experience, 1642–1660', in Smyth (ed.), *A Pleasing Sinne*, pp. 55–68.

[26] Scodel, *Excess and the Mean*, ch. 8; McShane Jones, 'Roaring Royalists and Ranting Brewers'.

this significant first wave of a new cultural history of drinking in early modern England has fulfilled its intention of writing the elites back in to the history of intoxication in the period, it has arguably done very little to advance our understanding of the alcohol consumption of the vast majority of men and women who took their drink-based recreation in the local village alehouse. This methodology of approaching literary forms as a means of accessing the values and meanings attached to early modern drinking rituals can, however, be extended to produce a cultural history of the kind sought here; that is, of recreational drinking in alehouses. Whilst much of the early modern drink literature examined by literary scholars was located primarily in the cultural world of the educated and wealthy, the print market in such literature also had a popular dimension. Printed miscellanies, witty pamphlets and dramatic productions may have been targeted first and foremost at young, urban gentlemen, but they were no doubt consumed and appropriated by a broader social clientele.[27] But there were also printed forms of drink literature that were explicitly designed to reach out to the humble alehouse-goer. The main manifestation of this more popular drink literature in early modern England was the broadside ballad.

Broadside ballads

A broadside ballad was a song, printed on a single sheet of paper. The words to the song were usually accompanied by a popular tune title – though rarely musical notation – and woodcut illustrations. This product was sold by 'hawkers' who sang them aloud, in the street or in alehouses, at markets and at fairs, in an attempt to attract customers to purchase them for a penny – the same cost as a pint of ale, or loaf of bread. These ballads were undoubtedly the most prolific genre in the expanding print market of the sixteenth and seventeenth centuries. Between the years of 1557 and 1709 it has been estimated that 18,000 ballad songs were put into print, and with normal print runs for books in this period of 1000 to 1250 copies, it is likely that well over 20 million ballad sheets were put into circulation across this period, without even accounting for the multiple print runs of the most popular ballads.[28] They were ubiquitous

---

[27] See Smyth, *Profit and Delight*, pp. 32–3, 72.

[28] For more on the development of the ballad trade see Tessa Watt, *Cheap Print and Popular Piety, 1550–1640* (Cambridge, 1991), pp. 39–127; Natascha Wurzbach, *The Rise of the English Street Ballad* (Cambridge, 1990), pp. 18–26; Angela McShane Jones, '"Rime

in early modern English society, and historians have seen in their wide circulation and low cost evidence that this form of print had a readership of considerable social depth. This point has been reinforced by the most recent assessment of the market for ballad consumption, which recognises that there were few serious barriers to consumption, and concludes that 'the available evidence encourages considerable optimism regarding the social and geographical reach of balladry'.[29] Those ballad sheets that survive have thus been scoured by historians interested in recovering popular attitudes towards subjects ranging across love, marriage, politics, religion, economic morality, old age, occupational identities, vagrancy and fashion.[30]

They also have considerable potential for revealing attitudes and mores relating to recreational alehouse drinking. Indeed, there was a particular genre of broadside ballads dedicated to that very subject, and Samuel Pepys, whose collection of seventeenth-century ballads is one of the most valuable resources for ballad scholars, designated a specific category of what he labelled 'Drinking/Good Fellowship' ballads. They account for roughly 10% of his collection of over 1700 ballads, and the

and Reason": The Political World of the English Broadside Ballad, 1640–1689' (Ph.D. diss., University of Warwick, 2004), ch. 1. The number of ballad songs (18,000) is taken from Christopher Marsh, *Music and Society in Early Modern England* (Cambridge, 2010), p. 226, whose figures come from Claude Simpson, *The British Broadside Ballad and its Music* (New Brunswick, 1966), p. xi, note 6. The average print run numbers are from Watt, p. 11.

[29] Marsh, *Music and Society*, p. 251; ch. 5 of Marsh's book provides an excellent overview of the issues and evidence relating to the audience for ballads.

[30] James Sharpe, 'Plebeian Marriage in Stuart England: Some Evidence from Popular Literature', *Transactions of the Royal Historical Society*, 5th series 36 (1986), pp. 69–90; Elizabeth Foyster, 'A Laughing Matter? Marital Discord and Gender Control in Seventeenth-Century England', *Rural History* 4 (1993), pp. 5–21; Angela McShane, '"Ne sutor ultra crepidam": Political Cobblers and Broadside Ballads in Late Seventeenth-Century England', in Patricia Fumerton, Anita Guerrini and Kris McAbee (eds), *Ballads and Broadsides, 1500–1800* (Farnham, 2010), pp. 207–28; Watt, *Cheap Print*; Brodie Waddell, *God, Duty and Community in English Economic Life* (Woodbridge, 2012); Mark Hailwood, 'The Honest Tradesman's Honour: Occupational and Social Identity in Early Modern England', forthcoming in *Transactions of the Royal Historical Society*, 6th series 24 (2014); Alice Tobriner, 'Old Age in Tudor-Stuart Broadside Ballads', *Folklore* 102 (1991), pp. 149–74; David Hitchcock, 'The Experience and Construction of the Vagabond in England, 1650–1750 (Ph.D. diss., University of Warwick, 2012); Patricia Fumerton, 'Not Home: Alehouses, Ballads, and the Vagrant Husband in Early Modern England', *Journal of Medieval and Early Modern Studies* 32:3 (2002), pp. 493–518; Angela McShane and Claire Backhouse, 'Top-Knots and Lower Sorts: Popular Print and Promiscuous Consumption in Late Seventeenth-Century England', in Michael Hunter (ed.), *Printed Images in Early Modern Britain: Essays in Interpretation* (London, 2010), pp. 337–57.

genre represents about 5% of the 6000 extant ballads currently available through the digital online resource, the English Broadside Ballad Archive.[31] The genre seems to have flourished in particular in the 1620s and 1630s, and again in the 1670s through the 1690s, in the same periods when the most explicit celebrations of drinking were finding their voice in more elite forms of drink literature.[32] There were, in fact, a number of characteristics the genre of good fellowship ballads shared with elite drink literature – condemnatory as well as celebratory strands; a performative quality; an increasingly political charge; as well as a number of similar attitudes and mores. They no doubt appealed to some of the educated urban men who consumed more highbrow drink literature: Pepys, of course, was a gentleman collector, and Ben Jonson even penned a number of such ballads.[33] But although the sorts of classical motifs and references that abounded in elite drink literature often found their way onto the ballad page too, we should resist seeing good fellowship ballads simply as an expression or extension of elite drink literature. Their production, dissemination and consumption were all intimately connected to the world of the humble alehouse.

Indeed, whilst ballad authors often had one foot in the educated world, they commonly had the other in a more humble environment. Even the most famous of early modern English balladeers were of 'modest social standing', and authors included 'a range of semi-amateur writers, men of other trades who "dabbled a bit" in popular poetry'.[34] If ballad-writing could form part of an 'economy of makeshifts' for men of fairly modest means, then so too could running an alehouse, and the two could sometimes come together. The prolific balladeer John Taylor was known to have kept an alehouse – The Crown in Phoenix Alley, near Covent

---

31 The 10% figure is from Marsh, *Music and Society*, p. 227. A search by genre on the EBBA website for 'Drinking/Good Fellowship' turns up over 300 ballads. See <http://ebba.english.ucsb.edu/> [accessed 1 May 2014].

32 This is based on the estimated publication dates of a sample of 100 good fellowship ballads taken from a range of collections. The most popular decade was the 1630s (21% of the sample), followed by 1680s (18%), 1670s and 1690s (both 15%), and the 1620s (12%). All other decades were between 1%–5%. This sample is discussed in greater depth below.

33 Withington, 'Renaissance Drinking Cultures', p. 146.

34 Bernard Capp, 'Popular Literature', in Barry Reay (ed.), *Popular Culture in Seventeenth-Century England* (London, 1985), pp. 199–200; McShane Jones, '"Rime and Reason"', p. 67; and for an example of one such ballad author see McShane, '"Ne sutor ultra crepidam": Political Cobblers'.

1. An example of a good fellowship ballad, *Heres to thee kind Harry. Or, The plaine dealing Drunkard*, Pepys, 1.432 (1627),

The fecond part to the fame tune.

HEe that is a wenching knaue
  dery dery downe
That for a whore his mony doth fane,
  dery dery downe,
That like a fond
  fantaſticke Aſſe
Will ſpend a crowne
  vpon his Laſſe,
And yet hæ's bnwilling
To ſpend a ſhilling
  with bs in rich Canary,
Let him packe to a wench
That can teach him French,
  come, heres to thee honeſt Harry.

He that is a pilfering thæfe,
  dery dery downe,
That ſteales to giue his corps relæfe,
  dery dery downe,
That though he can
  himſelfe maintaine
By ſome honeſt trade,
  he will take no paine,
I wiſh with my hart,
That the hang man in's cart
  all ſuch to the Galowes may cary.
For if all thæues were gone,
Then we ſhould kæpe our owne,
  and heres to thee braue Harry.

He thats a fawning Sycophant,
  dery dery downe,
And ſæks with tales our eares to inchant
  dery dery downe.
Who giues me
  pleaſant words to my face,
And railes at me
  in another place.
And ſayes right with his tongue,
When his heart meaneth wrong,
  and his thoughts doe poyſon cary,
Let no ſuch ſtay with bs
Who will flatter bs thus,
  heres to thee true hearted Harry.

He that will boaſt without deſert,
  dery dery downe,
And ſækes to applaud his ſtrength or art,
  dery dery downe,
That will brag and daunt
  to ſimple men,
As though he were one
  could fight with ten
Yet being tryde
He will onely but chide,
  his words and his dæds doe vary.
But I like that blade,
Who will doe as he ſaid
  and heres to thee braue Harry.

He that profeſſeth himſelfe a Souldier,
  dery dery downe,
Yet neuer bore armes on his ſhoulder,
  dery dery downe.
That prates of many
  bands he hath ſæne,
But out of the Land
  he hath neuer beene.
He hath learn'd to ſpeak Dutch
And thats as much
  as he deſires to cary.
Some ſay in Bent ſtræt
Many Dutch you may meet,
  but heres to honeſt Harry.

Thus being honeſt iouiall blades,
  dery dery downe,
Let bs be as mery as the maids,
  dery dery downe.
But ſuch as we
  haue nam'd before,
Them and their dealings
  we abhorre.
Now tis time to depart
Let bs drinke bp this quart,
  and then no longer wee'll tary
Each man pay the ſhat,
What falls to his lot.
  but I will pay for Harry.

Printed at London for Henry Goſſon on London bridge.

Garden – during the 1640s.[35] Martin Parker, the best-known seven-teenth-century ballad writer, is also known to have kept an alehouse, and no doubt made use of his position to pick up and try out stories and songs for use in his printed ballads.[36] Contemporary caricatures of ballad writers as 'pot-poets' – who sought inspiration by sitting 'tippling' in the alehouse – were not without a kernel of truth, and it seems likely, as Tessa Watt suggested, that 'stories and tunes may have been picked up in rural alehouses and later disseminated as ballads'.[37] The little we do know about ballad authors – for most were authored anonymously – suggests that they were often intimately connected to the alehouse world that many of their ballads portrayed.

The connection between alehouses and ballads extended beyond their production to their distribution and consumption. Central to the distribution of ballads were the petty traders who carried them amongst their wares along the country's economic networks, and such pedlars would often have stayed overnight at alehouses whilst travelling the country, or stopped off in them during the day for food and refreshment.[38] Whilst there, they could take advantage of the fact that there was a captive market gathered by the alehouse fire to whom they could peddle their ballads. They also persuaded alehousekeepers that a ballad purchase had the potential to increase the drawing power of their houses by providing 'new songs to old tunes for the clientele to roar aloud'.[39] Good fellow-ship ballads undoubtedly played a key role here, and the texts themselves suggest that they were intended to be performed in this context. Indeed, Natascha Wurzbach has demonstrated that evidence from within the text itself can reveal the context in which it was intended to be performed and consumed: ballads – more than most other literary forms – often contain 'a specific concrete speech situation in the text itself, namely the context of performance and sale'.[40] This insight suggests that

---

[35] Bernard Capp, *The World of John Taylor the Water-Poet* (Oxford, 1994), p. 154.

[36] Watt, *Cheap Print*, p. 324.

[37] See John Earle's *Micro-cosmographie* (London, 1628). His caricature of a 'pot-poet' is reprinted in Wurzbach, *The Rise of the English Street Ballad*, p. 275; Watt, *Cheap Print*, p. 6.

[38] See Margaret Spufford, *Small Books and Pleasant Histories: Popular Fiction and its Readership in Seventeenth-Century England* (Cambridge, 1981), ch. 5; Michael Frearson, 'The Distribution and Readership of London Corantos in the 1620s', in Robin Myers and Michael Harris (eds), *Serials and their Readers, 1620–1914* (Winchester, 1993), pp. 1–25.

[39] Spufford, *Small Books and Pleasant Histories*, pp. 65–7.

[40] Wurzbach, *The Rise of the English Street Ballad*, p. 98.

ballads on the subject of sociable drinking were specifically meant to be performed in the *context* of sociable drinking. A clear example of this can be seen in Laurence Price's good fellowship ballad *Good Ale for my money*:

> Thus to conclude my verses rude,
> Would some good fellowes here
> Would joyne together pence a peece,
> To buy the singer beere:
> I trust none of this company
> Will be herewith offended;
> Therefore, call for your Jugs a peece,
> And drink to him that pen'd it.[41]

Ballads such as this were intended to be sung in alehouses and addressed to drinking companies.[42]

It seems clear, then, that sociable drinkers in alehouses were among the intended consumers of drinking and good fellowship ballads, and sociable drinking the intended context for that consumption. Indeed, as is also the case with many of the forms of elite drink literature discussed above, good fellowship ballads were not intended as abstract representations of drinking rituals and practices – they were intended to supplement them. Table philosophies and medical advice books were intended to be read aloud and debated over a jug of wine; the verse poetry of tavern societies was composed and performed during bouts of intoxicated sociability; printed miscellanies were pocket-sized compendia of drinking ditties that could be easily carried about town, and produced to provide material to perform when the situation arose. Good fellowship ballads were part of this practically useful drink literature tradition. They were not to be read at a sober remove from the alehouse, but bellowed aloud from the alebench. This reminds us that much of the drink 'literature' of the period had a more pronounced performative quality than the modern reader often associates with printed works.

It is also important to recognise that ballads were also part of the visual fabric of the alehouse, and commonly performed a decorative function – enhanced by elaborate borders and woodcuts – which has

---

[41] Roxburghe, 1.138 (1645).

[42] For similar examples see Pepys, 1.426 (1617); Wurzbach, *The Rise of the English Street Ballad*, pp. 62–3.

2. John Smith, *Boors Singing at a Window* (1706)

seen them described by scholars as 'the poor man's oil painting'.[43] There is evidence that 'even mean alehouses were expected to provide decoration for their customers', and the fact that ballads often performed this duty is clear from Izaak Walton's 1650s description of 'an honest ale-house where we shall find a cleanly room, lavender in the windows, and twenty ballads stuck about the wall'.[44] Artistic depictions of early modern alehouses invariably depicted broadsides hanging on the walls, or being performed.[45] Even for those who could not read a broadside ballad, then, a visit to the alehouse could involve an optical encounter with a ballad and its woodcut images. Those ballads pasted on alehouse walls no doubt often formed the basis of the singing that took place in these convivial environments too, and this combined audio-visual experience would have created an association between certain ballad themes and particular graphic representations. Seeing a woodcut of a sociable drinking scene, for example, would doubtless have evoked the themes of songs about the same.[46] Broadside ballads played a key role in constituting the sights, sounds, and 'themes' that were encountered, performed and internalised at the alehouse.

Good fellowship ballads therefore have particular potential for revealing the meanings and values that were associated with participation in alehouse recreational drinking. They are not simply abstract 'representations' penned by culturally distant, hostile elites. They were penned by men who often had a foot in the cultural world of the alehouse. Such men were also keen to reflect the attitudes and mores of alehouse-goers so that the latter would purchase their songs – from a pedlar in an alehouse – and perform them on the alebench, paste their wood-cuts on the alehouse wall, and commit their verses to memory to sing

---

[43] Fumerton, 'Not Home', p. 499.

[44] Watt, *Cheap Print*, p. 194; Wurzbach, *The Rise of the English Street Ballad*, p. 279. For further evidence that ballads were often pasted on alehouse walls see Capp, *The World of John Taylor*, p. 139, esp. note 129.

[45] See, for instance, the cover of this book. Whilst this is a Dutch work, in depictions of English alehouses ballads also conventionally form part of the alehouse furniture. See for example, Egbert Van Heemskerck the Elder's 'London tavern scene' (c.1690–1700) (used as the cover for Marsh, *Music and Society*), and Figure 2 here, which is an engraving of a scene also by Van Heemskerck that was reproduced for an English audience. See also Mark Hailwood, 'Everyday Life and the Art of the Dutch Masters: A Social Historian's Perspective' (Lincoln, 2013), reproduced at <http://manyheadedmonster.wordpress.com/2013/06/28/everyday-life-and-the-art-of-the-dutch-masters-a-social-historians-perspective/> [accessed 1 May 2014].

[46] For examples of woodcuts depicting such scenes see Pepys, 4.239; Pepys, 4.130; Pepys, 4.432, and Figure 3 below.

during future bouts of alehouse merriment. These ballads were intended to be consumed alongside ale, in the alehouse: they were embedded in alehouse sociability. What, then, do they reveal about the attitudes and mores associated with recreational drinking in alehouses? The following analysis draws upon a sample of just over one hundred ballads, taken primarily from the Pepys and Roxburghe collections and a number of ballads from other collections – consulted through the English Broadside Ballad Archive (EBBA), Early English Books Online (EEBO), or in printed editions.[47] The ballads were selected on the grounds that the recreational drinking of alcohol was either the primary or a prominent motif. With only a handful of exceptions, ballads relating to recreational drinking fall into one of two broad thematic categories. On the one hand, there are those ballads which serve as a warning about the negative effects of excessive drinking, and set out to appeal against participation in good fellowship. On the other, there are ballads which celebrate sociable drinking, and which stress the positive qualities of good fellows and the benefits of good fellowship.

A good representative of the first type is a ballad from the 1630s entitled *I tell you, John Jarret, you'l breake*.[48] The narrative voice is provided by John Jarret's long-suffering wife, who rehearses a list of her husband's drinking practices and warns him about their negative consequences, urging him to reform. Jarret is guilty of spending both considerable time and money in the alehouse:

> You rise in the morning before break of day,
> and unto the alehouse you straight make your way,
> where you in a base manner at shuffle-board play,
> until you have wasted your money away.

This leads him not only to neglect his family ('You into ill company daily doe rome,/ whilst I and your children sit sighing at home'), but also his work ('When you in shop should be plying your work,/ in some

---

[47] All subsequent ballad references are to the EBBA versions (freely accessible online) unless otherwise stated. Dates cited are those provided by EBBA (or, where applicable, EEBO/the editors of a printed collection) and represent (sometimes estimated) dates of publication rather than dates of composition.

[48] Pepys, 1.170 (1630). The suitability of this ballad as a representative example is reinforced by the fact that it appears to have been particularly well known. John Taylor was certainly aware of it, and his reference to it in his own work suggests that he thought his readers would be familiar with it: see Capp, *The World of John Taylor*, p. 182, esp. note 129.

scurvy blind alehouse you all day do lurke'). Jarret is accused of spending money on 'wenches', and one of his illicit relationships is alleged to have produced a bastard child that he has to maintain. The ballad concludes with a warning from his wife that this behaviour – in which drinking, illicit sexual activity and the wasting of resources are inextricably linked – will lead Jarret and his charges into poverty.

The appeal to consumers of a ballad such as this was primarily didactic, and ballad writers and publishers thought that moralising advice could sell. A similar condemnation of alehouse-haunting, *A Groatsworth of Good Counsel for a Penny*, ended with the following sales pitch:

> Now in the Conclusion I have a word more to say,
> Take every one one, and make no delay,
> The price is but a penny and that is not dear,
> The best penny worth of wit that you bought this 2 year:
> And be sure to observe it when you have it at home,
> It may chance do you good when I am dead and gone.[49]

The seeming popularity of these didactic ballads serves as an important reminder that condemnations of heavy drinking circulated *within* popular culture, and were not just hostile attacks 'from above'. Again, we should not assume that pro-drink and anti-drink sentiments lay neatly either side of a line between 'popular' or 'elite' culture, and broadside ballads provide considerable scope for analysing the character of antipathy toward the recreational function of the alehouse that was no doubt felt by many humble men, and especially married women – a point we will return to below. The principal concern of this chapter is, however, the motivations of those who did see fit to endorse recreational drinking in the alehouse. It seems improbable that such ballads would have been hawked at, or indeed recited by, companies of good fellows in the alehouse. They may well have had an appeal to their wives though, or to guilt-ridden and hungover husbands passing through the market place, who on the morning after an expensive bout of alehouse sociability were resolved not to drink so excessively again. That said, ballads that condemn drinking often provide indirect evidence of the appeal of alehouse sociability, occasionally rehearsing arguments in favour of good fellowship before attempting to overturn them. As a result, such ballads still prove useful in the recovery of the positive meanings of alehouse sociability for those involved.

---

[49] Pepys, 4.78 (1684–96).

Of greater value, and representing a larger proportion of the sample, are those ballads that celebrated good fellowship, a good example of which is *Roaring Dick of Dover: Or, The Jovial good fellow of Kent*.[50] Also a 1630s ballad, the narrative voice here is provided by 'Roaring Dick', and from the outset strikes a very different tone to John Jarret's wife:

> Here's a health to all good fellows
> that intend with me to joyne
> At the taverne, or the alehouse
> And will freely spend theyre coyne
> But for such as hate strong liquor
> Are not for my company
> O it makes my wits the quicker
> When I taste it thoroughly.

Roaring Dick makes it clear that to qualify as a good fellow requires both drinking and spending liberally: a desire to taste strong liquor 'thoroughly' and a willingness to 'freely spend' one's 'coyne'. The ballad elaborates that the intention of such prodigality is to maximise the enjoyment of the present:

> Then let's take some part of pleasure,
> drinke and sing and freely pay.
> Whilst our time and money lasteth,
> Let's not prove Curmudgeon boores.

This celebration of sociable and heavy drinking is underpinned by a carefree, present-centred attitude, one which refuses to dwell on current miseries or longer-term financial considerations. As Roaring Dick proclaims:

> Hang up sorrow, I can borrow,
> money for to buy two pots
> Who can say to live tomorrow
> Then lets never sit like sots.

---

[50] Pepys, 1.434 (1632). For a more detailed analysis of these two particular ballad characters – John Jarret and Roaring Dick of Dover – see Mark Hailwood, 'John Jarret and Roaring Dick of Dover: Popular Attitudes toward Drinking in Seventeenth-Century England', in Karen Christianson (ed.), *Intersecting Disciplines: Approaching Medieval and Early Modern Cultures* (Chicago, 2010); available online at <http://www.newberry.org/sites/default/files/textpage-attachments/2010Proceedings.pdf> [accessed 1 May 2014].

What this ballad seems to offer us then is a celebration of sociable drinking which appealed to consumers by invoking what we might call an idiom of liberating prodigality.

Yet we need to be cautious about taking the seemingly apparent messages of these ballads at face value: any given ballad might present a 'multiplicity of interpretative possibilities'.[51] Whilst Roaring Dick may have been taken by some ballad consumers as a flattering portrayal of their own self-image, a champion of the positive virtues of good fellowship, other consumers might instead see this ballad as a parody of the idea that those of limited means should spend their resources in excessive drinking. Is Roaring Dick actually just the butt of a joke, rather than a spokesman for the benefits of good fellowship? The tune of a ballad could play a role here, and whilst some ballads may appear to celebrate a set of values when simply read, when performed to the stipulated tune a satiric reading becomes unavoidable – when, for instance, a good fellowship ballad championing prodigality on the part of the poor is set to a funereal dirge.[52] It is also possible to imagine John Jarret's story being recited for comic effect in certain contexts: a group of good fellows in an alehouse could have performed the ballad as a dismissive satire on nagging wives. The context in which a ballad was performed could, then, have altered its meaning in ways forever lost to the historian.[53]

Nonetheless, ballads tended to operate around binaries, articulating the attitudes of those on both sides of contemporaries' favourite issues and debates: bachelorhood and marriage; the battle of the sexes; age and youth. Authors might willingly adopt a variety of different, even antagonistic, subject positions within a given ballad, or in a series of ballads, a playfulness that amounts to what Chris Marsh has usefully termed 'broadside banter'.[54] So, whilst meanings and messages were fluid, and two different consumers might take the same ballad as flattery or satire – or draw meaning selectively from a ballad – they did so within a

---

[51] Marsh, *Music and Society*, p. 277.

[52] Christopher Marsh, 'The Sound of Print in Early Modern England: The Broadside Ballad as Song', in Julia Crick and Alexandra Walsham (eds), *The Uses of Script and Print, 1300–1700* (Cambridge, 2004), pp. 171–90.

[53] For more on the relationship between performative context and meaning see Mark Hailwood, '"Come hear this ditty": Seventeenth-Century Drinking Songs and the Challenge of Hearing the Past', *The Appendix: A New Journal of Narrative and Experimental History* 1:3 (August 2013), pp. 31–5; available online at <http://theappendix.net/issues/2013/7/come-hear-this-ditty-seventeenth-century-drinking-songs-and-hearing-the-past> [accessed 1 May 2014].

[54] Marsh, *Music and Society*, pp. 231, 281.

framework that tended to construct two fairly clear positions on a given subject. In other words, ballads offer a relatively stable construction of the idiom of alehouse good fellowship – as one side of a ballad 'debate' about the pros and cons of recreational drinking – even if consumers' appropriation of that idiom to give meaning to their own recreational drinking was a more fluid and varied process. What follows, then, will reconstruct the main contours of the idiom of good fellowship as articulated in ballads, and analyse how that idiom appealed in different ways to different ballad consumers. It will be suggested here that the idiom of good fellowship had a broad appeal that helps us to make sense of those bouts of recreational drinking so regularly facilitated by early modern England's alehouses.

A good fellow's name

> I trust none of this company,
> Will with this song offended bee,
> therefore let some kind Creature heare
> give hansell for to buy me beere.[55]

Laurence Price, the author of *Round boyes indeed. Or, The Shoomakers Holy-day*, clearly hoped that the depiction of sociable drinking in his ballad would appeal to the 'company' to which it was sung by its seller. What sentiments did Price, and others ballad writers like him, hope would go down well with groups of alehouse good fellows? Recent literary analysis of good fellowship ballads by Patricia Fumerton has argued that they portrayed the alehouse as 'a liberating space situated in opposition to the domestic home', erecting a dichotomy between the home as a 'constricting female space' and the alehouse as an alternative environment in which 'the man/husband could be powerfully unobligated and free'. Ballads are seen in Fumerton's analysis as depicting the alehouse environment as a 'simulation of community and home: an ungrounded likeness without constraining ground rules'. Particularly appealing to the poor and to vagrants, the alehouse presented an opportunity to access a community that 'made few demands on its frequenters', and 'required no obligations other than financial ones'. Consequently, she argued, alehouse relationships were in fact 'ephemeral and ungrounded'.[56] The

---

[55] Pepys, 1.442 (1637).
[56] Fumerton, 'Not Home', pp. 494, 509, 497.

analysis of good fellowship ballads that follows here draws a rather different conclusion. It argues that whilst good fellowship *could* have some of the appeal suggested by Fumerton – as a refuge from patriarchal demands, as an attractive activity for poorer men – it was by no means necessarily defined by the exclusion of women, or wives, and had the potential to appeal to a much wider clientele than just poor men and vagrants. Most significantly, good fellowship *was* an activity hedged about with demands, rules and expectations.

Perhaps the most prominent of these, acknowledged by Fumerton, were practical financial obligations. Critics of good fellowship complained that the financial demands of participation were not insignificant. A *Caveat for Young Men. Or, The Bad Husband turn'd Thrifty* was a ballad with many similar themes to *I tell you, John Jarret, you'l breake*, though in this instance the narrative voice was provided by a former good fellow who had since reformed his ways and turned his back on recreational drinking. On the brink of bankruptcy, he calculated the cumulative cost of his drinking:

> I went into an Ale-house,
> where all my Coyn I had drown'd;
> In company with good fellows,
> I had spent an hundred pound.

The former alehouse-goer was forced to concede that 'a Good Fellow's a costly name'.[57] *No body loves mee* was a ballad with a similar complaint, warning that 'Company asketh cost/ Company wasteth gain', and advising that those who hoped to 'thrive' should from 'much company refrain'.[58]

Ballads that celebrated good fellowship did little to disavow the notion that sociable drinking could be an expensive pursuit that consumed resources. The ballad *Heres to thee kind Harry. Or, The plaine dealing Drunkard*, set out the positive characteristics that were expected of the 'ideal type' drinking companion: he that 'Will spend what he gets,/ And drinke more then he eates' could expect to have his health drunk by his companions. In part such expense arose because the ideal good fellow was expected to adopt a liberal approach to ordering drinks, and at the same time was required to pay his share of the 'score' or 'shot'. A good fellow was one who 'will freely call for drinke,/ And never repine to part

---

[57] Pepys, 2.22 (1668–78).
[58] Pepys, 1.430 (c.1615).

with his chinke'.[59] In a ballad entitled *It is bad Jesting with a Halter*, one member of a drinking company makes a case for allowing a shoemaker to join their group, emphasising that 'he is good company', 'will sing and be merry', but above all will 'pay his share'. Such an individual clearly met the 'entry requirements' for good fellowship, and was welcomed into their subsequent liberal-spending merrymaking.[60] *In Praise of Lancashire Men* implied that the sociable drinking of Lancastrians was also predicated on the understanding that they would drink plenty of beer – enough to become 'merry' – without making a fuss about paying their share of the subsequent cost:

> They will be merry great and small,
> when they do meet together,
> and freely pay for what they call,
> a figg for wind and weather.[61]

The centrality of a willingness to spend to notions of good fellowship is also evident in a particularly interesting ballad entitled *Nick and Froth*. The ballad takes the form of a petition to alehousekeepers to stop selling short measures of ale, in which the petitioners are self-styled as the 'Society of Good Fellowship'. Part of their appeal to alehousekeepers drew on this idea that a characteristic of good fellows was their willingness to liberally spend. The argument was that sociable drinkers would send plenty of 'chink' the way of ale-sellers – providing they sold full measures – so that there was no need to try to squeeze these consumers to make a profit:

> Freely their money will spend,
> but fill them good drink,
> they value not chink,
> where ever they meet with a friend.[62]

Other ballads made it clear that those who refused to subscribe to the mantra of free spending were not welcome drinking companions. 'Roaring Dick of Dover' expressed his disdain for the reluctant spender, condemning he who would 'not freely spend his chinke' as 'no right

---

[59] Pepys, 1.432 (1627).
[60] Pepys, 1.440 (1632).
[61] J.W. Ebsworth, *The Bagford Ballads*, Vol. II (Hertford, 1878), no. 136 (1685–88).
[62] Roxburghe, 2.376 (1665).

true-hearted fellow'.[63] The same ballad also implies that this willingness to spend operated as a form of 'entry requirement' for participation in instances of company and good fellowship:

> Let such sharking base companions,
> be kickt out of company,
> For they be but beastly hang on's;
> and will call, but we must pay.

The 1630s ballad *Hang pinching, or The good fellowes observation*, laid out the necessary criteria for 'all those which lay clame,/ To a good fellows name', and similarly poured scorn on those who refused to pay their way. Those drinking companions who 'when that the Reckning's to pay,/ Away they will sneake,/ And not a word speake' could not claim to be an 'honest good fellow', and their behaviour, claimed the balladeer, 'doth draw me with spleene': 'His Company I,/ Detest and defie'.[64] It seems clear from these ballads that being willing and able to pay liberally for drink was a crucial obligation for those wishing to participate in good fellowship.

Of course, this went hand in hand with the expectation that considerable quantities of drink would be consumed by any good fellow worthy of the name. A 1670s condemnation of good fellowship, *Looking-Glass for Drunkards. Or, The Good-Fellows Folly*, began with great indignation: 'Drunkards how dare ye boast of your hard drinking?'[65] It was not an ungrounded criticism, for many ballads championing good fellowship did indeed boast about feats of 'hard drinking'. In an echo of the exploits of the 'cup companions' of Calne, another 1670s ballad *The Good Fellows Frolick* described the policy of its characters as one of trying 'each house throughout the town/ to find out drink that's strongest'.[66] If it was important to search out strong beer or ale, it was just as vital that any good fellow worth the name would not fail to drain their cup. Indeed, Price's *Good Ale for my money* suggests that the convention that 'weele leave no drinke behinde us' had proverbial status: 'A proverbe old I have heard told,/ by my deere dad and grandsire,/ he was hang'd that left his drinke behinde.'[67]

---

[63] Pepys, 1.434 (1632).
[64] Roxburghe, 1.518 (1633).
[65] Pepys, 4.258 (1674–79).
[66] Pepys, 4.242 (1665–74).
[67] Roxburghe, 1.138 (1645).

If those who failed to match the drinking capacity of their companions were vulnerable to censure or exclusion, those who set the pace stood to enhance their status. Ballads that urged good fellows to reform their prodigal ways often accepted that this aspect of sociable drinking could have a particularly strong appeal to alehouse-goers. A 1630s ballad detailing the recantation of former good fellow Charles Rickets revealed that a widespread reputation as a 'stout' drinker had seduced Rickets into the world of recreational drinking. Rickets revealed that he was formerly 'for a rorer knowne', and boasted that even when drinking with groups of gipsies:

> the stoutest there
> for wine and beere,
> Me in expence could not outgoe,
> for all the day.[68]

A similar ballad from the 1620s lamented that Rickets was not the only one to be drawn in by the opportunity to build a reputation on the basis of heavy drinking, with bravery in particular associated with such feats. The ballad revealed that good fellows that could hold their drink laid claim to the title of 'Bacchus brave soldiers'.[69] The opportunity to seize the 'honour and glory' that went along with being a 'brave soldier' of Bacchus was, then, a key part of the positive appeal of excessive drinking for both alehouse-goers and heavy drinking aristocratic Royalists alike.

Certain ballads were themselves intended to provide a framework that could put these drinking capacities to the test. *A Health to all Good-Fellows* carries the subtitle *The good Companions Arithmaticke*, and begins with the lines 'Be merry my hearts, and call for your quarts,/ and let no liquor be lacking.' The opening verse ends with the line 'for he that made one, made two', with each subsequent verse ending with a similar line but counting up to the final verse, which ends with 'for he that made twelve, made thirteen'.[70] This type of counting in drinking songs may be related to the pastime called 'drinking for a muggle', whereby each person in a circle had to drink a pint – or perhaps a quart – more than his predecessor.[71] This ballad was not only then a drinking song about drinking, it was also a song to drink to, once more emphasising the

---

[68] Pepys, 1.172 (1633).

[69] Pepys, 1.446 (1622).

[70] Roxburghe, 1.150 (1637).

[71] Vic Gammon, *Desire, Drink and Death in English Folk and Vernacular Song, 1600–1900*

3. 'Drinking for a muggle'? A woodcut image of a drinking
ritual, detail from *Heres to thee kind Harry. Or, The plaine
dealing Drunkard*, Pepys, 1.432 (1627)

performative quality of drink 'literature' forms that were often embedded
in social practice.[72]

The level of alcohol consumption such a song would have entailed
implies that they were intended to seriously challenge the prodigious
drinking capabilities of their singers. Other ballads also make reference
to feats of heavy drinking being central to good fellowship. One example,
for which there is evidence of circulation from the 1590s to the 1680s,
details the drinking exploits of a number of different tradesmen keeping
company together. Heavy drinking and bravery were among the defining
features of the company: 'Thus like to men of courage stout,/ Coura-
giously they drank about,/ Till such time all the ale was out'. Access to
this positive collective identity of the group was regulated by individual
feats of prodigous drinking. A successful example was a hatter:

> He scorned to drink cold water,
> amongst that Jovial crew,
> And like a man of courage stout,
> He took the quart-pot by the snout,
> And never left till all was out.

Others, however, were less successful, a notable example being a
Dutchman, who 'took too much':

(Aldershot, 2008), pp. 120–1. For the pastime of 'drinking for a muggle' see also Young,
England's Bane, sig. E4v.

[72] For similar examples see Euing Ballad Collection (accessed via EBBA) *A jolly company
of jovial blades*, Euing, 152 (1663–74); Gammon, *Desire, Drink and Death*, pp. 120–1.

He drank so long as I suppose,
Till grease drops fell from his nose,
And like a beast befoul'd his hose.[73]

There was clearly no 'honour and glory' derived from this instance of excessive drinking.

This points to a further aspect of the part played by heavy drinking in the idiom of good fellowship. Whilst hard drinking could provide a source of positive identity and a focus for celebration, those who failed to maintain control of their physical and mental capacities when heavily intoxicated did not qualify as good fellows. There was a crucial distinction between heavy drinking and excessive drinking. A 1690s ballad praising porters declared that an ideal drinking companion would be able to drink his share but without overstepping the limits of physical control: for 'a right honest Man' only 'tipples as long as he's able to stand' – 'like a Porter'.[74] A ballad in praise of 'St Monday' – a workers' tradition of routinely taking Monday as a 'holiday' – entitled *Mondayes Worke*, also emphasised the importance of drinking soundly whilst remaining vertical:

Let's take off our Liquor roundly,
And though we doe drinke soundly,
Our humour is such,
Weele not drinke so much,
untill we both on the ground lye.[75]

These ballads suggest that heavy drinking was not practised in the pursuit of drunken stupor. Instead, it seems to have represented a far more positive socio-cultural activity from which participants could derive a degree of status or honour. And yet, if the ability to consume large quantities of alcohol could provide a gateway to 'honour and glory' this was conditional upon the ability to push the limits of intoxication without overstepping them: a sentiment, as we have seen, that was often central to elite drink literature. If feats of heavy drinking may have appealed to soldiers or young men as acts of bravado and courage, they might also

---

[73] Pepys, 4.245 (1594, 1680).

[74] Pepys, 4.292 (1690–96).

[75] Roxburghe, 1.262 (1632). For a fuller discussion of St Monday see Thompson, 'Time, Work-Discipline and Industrial Capitalism', pp. 73–6.

then have appealed to patriarchs and married men keen to display their capacity for self-control and mastery.

Indeed, this interpretation is reinforced when we look at the ways in which ballads deal with the physical effects of alcohol. In an echo of the elite drink literature that heralded the creative enhancement that could be derived from wine consumption, ballads more often than not portrayed drink as a stimulant that enhanced the senses, rather than a narcotic that dulled them. The 1630s good fellowship celebration *A Health to All Good-Fellows* suggested that alcohol served as an antidote to sorrow by making its consumers 'merry', rather than oblivious.[76] A group of seamen's wives in one ballad were transformed by consuming bowls of punch into 'jolly dames' who 'merrily danc'd', and a company of 'courageous gallants' in another took to drink 'resolving to be merry' and declaring that it would make them 'jolly'.[77] If drinking lifted the spirits, it could also enhance mental faculties. 'Roaring Dick of Dover' declared of 'strong liquor': 'O it makes my wits the quicker, when I taste it thorowly', and *The Careless Drunkards* of a late-seventeenth-century ballad expressed a similar belief that liquor 'elevates' the mind, and 'puts good reason into brains'.[78] The seamen's wives claimed that punch served to make their 'Noddles the quicker', whilst *The Couragious Gallant* put it more effusively in the lines:

> Let me enjoy the charming bowl,
> Of liquor when in season
> It quickens every noble soul
> And ripens all our reason.[79]

In each of these cases alcohol was celebrated as a substance that lifted the mood, and sharpened the mind: qualities best understood as complementary to the *sociable* character of recreational alehouse drinking, rather than as a means to achieve narcotic stupor. The aim of good fellows was, therefore, to capitalise on the stimulating effects of alcohol *without*

76 Roxburghe, 1.150 (1637).

77 Pepys, 4.184 (1690–1702); Houghton Library Ballad Collection, consulted via EEBO, *The Couragious Gallant, or Cupid Degraded*, Wing C6579 (1685–88).

78 Pepys, 1.434 (1632); Pepys, 4.238 (1680–1702).

79 Pepys, 4.184 (1690–1702); Houghton Library Ballad Collection, consulted via EEBO, *The Couragious Gallant, or Cupid Degraded*, Wing C6579 (1685–88).

succumbing to a state of drunken oblivion that resulted from an inability to control the effects of intoxication.[80]

That such heavy drinking was first and foremost a sociable, rather than escapist, act, can also be seen in the way good fellowship ballads played on the metaphor of the drunkard as a 'beast', a motif favoured in condemnatory drink literature. A favourite theme of moralists and condemnatory ballads alike was the idea of drunkards inverting the 'gendered chain of being' which placed men above women and women above beasts, on the grounds of the capacity to reason.[81] Drunkenness seriously impinged upon this capacity to reason and thus reduced men to the level of beasts, an inversion explicitly acknowledged in the ballad, *A Statute for Swearers and Drunkards*: 'You that by guzzling transforme your best features,/ changing your selves from men into swinish creatures.'[82] It was a complaint also directed at John Jarret, with his wife declaring that 'Men being drunkards are worse than base swines'.[83] Yet this metaphor could be turned upside down in good fellowship ballads: as has been shown above, Roaring Dick described those that refused to liberally spend in alehouse company as 'beastly hang on's'.[84] Here it is the frugal drinker, rather than the excessive one, who is described as beastly. Similarly, the good fellows in *Heres to thee kind Harry* referred to he who was 'unwilling/ To spend a shilling/ with us in rich Canary', as 'like a fond fantasticke Asse'.[85] The intention here was to suggest that it was only the capacity to be sociable that really set man apart from beast, and it was thus the reluctant socialiser rather than the good fellow who was in fact the least humane.

This logic erected a sharp dichotomy between the sociable and unsociable, which extended to an attack on the unsociable as miserly money-hoarders. Roaring Dick, for example, condemned misers who prefer to

---

[80] I develop this particular point about the stimulating qualities of alcohol in Mark Hailwood, '"It puts good reason into brains": Popular Understandings of the Effects of Alcohol in Seventeenth-Century England', *Brewery History* 150 (January, 2013), pp. 39–53.

[81] For more on the idea of drunkards as beasts see Shepard, '"Swil-bots and Tos-pots"', p. 111; Cathy Shrank, 'Beastly Metamorphoses: Losing Control in Early Modern Literary Culture', in Herring *et al.* (eds), *Intoxicants and Society*, pp. 193–209.

[82] Pepys, 1.214 (1624).

[83] Pepys, 1.170 (1630).

[84] Pepys, 1.434 (1632).

[85] Pepys, 1.432 (1627).

save their money than to spend it in the alehouse, suggesting that no happiness will come to them:

> There's many men get store of treasure,
> yet they live like very slaves,
> In this world they have no pleasure
> The more they have the more they crave.[86]

A 1690s ballad entitled *The Careless Drunkards* took up the same theme, ridiculing those who refuse to spend their wealth on worldly pleasures:

> The Miser that doth hoard his Coin,
> and dotes upon his Pelf,
> His life's a plague to thine and mine,
> and he's a silly Elf
> That won't allow himself good things,
> his Misers heart to chear.

This critique centred not only on the fact that such misers were missing out on pleasurable activities, but also that saving was ultimately futile: 'For Coin will in the Coffer rust,/ if long you let it lye.'[87] Another late-seventeenth-century ballad, *The Distruction of Care*, took this argument further, suggesting that liberal spending was actually healthier for trade than miserly hoarding:

> Boys, Money was made to fly like the dust,
> yet Misers will hoard it we understand,
> Until it is almost consumed with rust,
> but we'l keep it moving from hand to hand:
> Creating a trade from morning till night.[88]

Whilst a preference on the part of these ballad good fellows for liberal spending over long-term saving might at first appear tongue-in-cheek, or self-satirising, a more serious logic begins to emerge here. Indeed, for Roaring Dick an unwillingness to spend on alehouse sociability reflected a broader reluctance on the part of misers to contribute to the common wealth:

---

86 Pepys, 1.434 (1632).
87 Pepys, 4.238 (1690–1702).
88 Pepys, 5.97 (1684–96).

I can fuddle, roare and swagger,
    sing and dance in severall sort,
And give six pence to a begger,
    in all this there's little hurt.
Whilst some churle thats worth a million,
    will give nought in charity,
But to himselfe he proves a villaine:
    judge who's better he or I.[89]

The tone here is one of genuine moral indignation, rather than of self-satire, and it suggests that contemporaries could take seriously the philosophy espoused in Martin Parker's A Mess of Good Fellows: 'The Userer with all his bags, is not so content in mind,/ As honest good fellows in rags,/ that are to each other kind.'[90] In a sense, then, good fellowship ballads depicted alehouse recreation not as an extreme to be opposed to moderate and functional drinking, but rather as a form of moderation – or 'mean' – in itself. Good fellowship, for its participants, was positioned between the unsociable poles of the reckless excess of the drunkard who could not hold his drink, and the miser who refused to ever join in company with friends or neighbours. Engagement in alehouse recreation was an expression of the liberality that sat as a 'golden mean' between profligacy and miserliness.[91]

It could also be an expression of a certain form of 'conspicuous consumption'. Indeed, those who were unwilling or unable to meet the requirement of drinking and spending liberally were often accused of idleness. The ballad Heres to thee kind Harry suggested that those who looked to avoid paying their share of the shot were synonymous with individuals who were unwilling to work:

He that is an idle Shark,
That lives by shifts, and will not worke,
That like a rascall, base and rude
Into any company, will intrude
That though he have mony,

---

[89] Pepys, 1.434 (1632).

[90] Roxburghe, 1.260 (1634).

[91] For liberality as the 'mean' between miserliness and prodigality in printed advice literature see Muldrew, The Economy of Obligation, p. 159. For the importance of the mean in early modern society and culture in general see Ethan Shagan, The Rule of Moderation: Violence, Religion and the Politics of Restraint in Early Modern England (Cambridge, 2011); Scodel, Excess and the Mean.

Will scant spend a peny,
At home let such a one tarry.[92]

Evidence of this relationship between attitudes to work and access to sociability occurs regularly in the ballad literature. Laurence Price's *Round boyes indeed* specified quite clearly that to be considered a good fellow required subscription to a certain mantra: 'Since we are here good fellows all,/ drinke we must and worke we shall.'[93] The necessity of drinking, and of work as the appropriate means to acquire the necessary funds, was also touted by other fictional good fellows, such as the three merry cobblers who were the subject of a Martin Parker ballad. The cobblers do not fret 'When all our money is spent', as they are able to 'worke for more' to 'pay off the score'.[94] What emerges from the ballads is the notion that the often considerable financial obligations of participation in good fellowship were expected to be met by recourse to hard work. Indeed, it may be the case that the liberal spending associated with good fellowship functioned to some extent as a form of conspicuous consumption that allowed those in work to distinguish themselves from vagrants, beggars, and others often grouped together as the 'idle poor' by contemporaries.[95]

Such a conclusion is further supported by the ballads' firm association of forms of good fellowship with workers in skilled trades. *No body loves mee* described prodigal spending on sociable drinking as a common characteristic of tradesmen: a particular 'folly' of 'such as live by their trade'.[96] Celebrations of good fellowship on the other hand insisted on the strong links between alehouse sociability and a positive sense of occupational identity. *A merry new ballad ... In praise of the Blacksmith* set out to flatter the heroic self-image of members of this trade, and ended with a call to drink a health to smiths, again suggesting that such ballads were intended for consumption with alcohol.[97] *Round boyes indeed. Or, The Shoomakers Holy-day* exalted members of that 'gentle craft', and made much of their attachment to excessive drinking as a positive quality. The ballad also reinforces the idea that the practise of

---

92 Pepys, 1.432 (1627).

93 Pepys, 1.442 (1637).

94 Roxburghe, 1.408 (1634).

95 For contemporary distinctions between the 'labouring poor' and the 'idle poor' see Slack, *Poverty and Policy*, pp. 17–18.

96 Pepys, 1.430 (c.1615).

97 Roxburghe, 1.250 (1635).

4. A ballad woodcut highlighting the connection between tradesmen and the alehouse: *The bonny Black-smiths delight. Or, A Noble Song in praise of the Black-smiths*, Pepys, 4.264 (1663–74)

skilled work conferred on a good fellow both the means and the right to engage in sociable drinking: 'We get our livings by our hands,/ then fill us beer at our commands.'[98] Being a good fellow and being a tradesman were closely entwined.[99]

Here, though, we might again be sensitive to the ways in which good fellowship could appeal in different ways to different groups or individuals. To a relatively prosperous tradesman, it might be an expression of a certain degree of affluence. For a poor labourer, liberality and prodigality could be a defiant gesture aimed at providing a temporary release from worldly cares. Again, though, it was not a *narcotic* release these individuals sought, but rather a moment of temporary joy and festivity. Such a belief is reflected in the fact that a desirable drinking companion was someone who brought a jovial disposition with them to the alehouse regardless of material concerns, whereas an individual with a downcast outlook who dwelt on life's difficulties was not welcome. Indeed, *Heres to thee kind Harry* described the ideal-type drinking companion as someone

---

[98] Pepys, 1.442 (1637).

[99] For a more developed argument on the relationship between alehouse sociability and occupational identity see Mark Hailwood, 'Sociability, Work and Labouring Identity in Seventeenth-Century England', *Cultural and Social History* 8:1 (2011), pp. 9–29; Hailwood, 'The Honest Tradesman's Honour'.

That will laugh and sing in the midst of care,
Though sorrow force him to despayre,
That scornes to brawle for trifles small,
But himself doth quietly cary.[100]

The clearest indication that good fellows were expected to adopt a defiantly cheerful outlook and leave their worldly worries behind when they stepped through the alehouse door can be found in constant calls in these ballads to 'hang' sorrow, care or 'pinching'. In the ballad *It is Bad Jesting with a Halter*, a participant in a drinking company strikes a defiant tone in his declarations: 'Hang money it is but an Asse' and 'Let sorrow and care go pack', which precede his calling for a round of drinks for his twelve companions. The potentially liberating effect of this consumption is also evident when he breaks into song: 'I sing, A Flye, a figge for care.'[101] Martin Parker's *A Mess of Good Fellows* describes a group of 'merry Comrades' who 'laugh and make good sport', and 'cry a fig for care'.[102] The ballad *The Good Fellows Frolick* also demonstrates a preference for a tone of merriment over one of melancholy in its call to 'hang pinching [and] let us frolick'.[103] Even ballads condemning good fellowship reaffirm the centrality of this attitude to sociable drinking, identifying excessive drinkers as those that cry 'hang up all sorrowe'.[104] Both critics and champions of alcohol-fuelled sociability recognised that the idiom of good fellowship configured it as a joyous and defiant response to difficult material realities, rather than as a means of simply blotting them out.

Taken together, these various features of good fellowship again highlight the present-centred prodigality that was central to the mentality that underpinned recreational drinking in alehouses. Some ballads linked this philosophy to an egalitarian notion of death. Indeed, *The Careless Drunkards* declared that both rich and poor would ultimately endure the same fate as money and turn to dust, rendering any accumulated wealth irrelevant.[105] A 1670s celebration of good fellowship, *The Careless Gallant*, based its argument for enjoying sociability on similar grounds: 'In frolicks dispose your pounds, shillings, and pence,/ For we

---

100 Pepys, 1.432 (1627).
101 Pepys, 1.440 (1632).
102 Roxburghe, 1.260 (1634).
103 Pepys, 4.242 (1665–74).
104 Pepys, 1.214 (1624).
105 Pepys, 4.238 (1690–1702).

shall be nothing a hundred years hence.'[106] *The Good Fellows Frolick* likewise explicitly articulated the belief in death as the great leveller – coming for 'both the beggar and the king' – as a justification for alehouse recreation: 'let us always merry be/ until that death do find us'. Within this ballad, death would not only strip those misers who spurned sociable merriment of their hoarded wealth, it would also serve to wipe clean the debts of the prodigal drinker: 'The Sexton shall lay, our bodies in Clay/ Where our Creditors ne're shall find us.'[107] These examples suggest that an egalitarian notion of death was one broader cultural assumption that informed positive attitudes toward heavy drinking. This general short-term outlook within the idiom of good fellowship is also captured in the ballad *The Jolly Porters*: 'Whose kind Advice to their Fellow-Brethren is, That they should love Mirth better than Money, and prize Strong Beer before Small.'[108]

Ballads condemning good fellowship often focused their warnings on the recklessness of a short-term approach to resource management, and a common method for doing so was to utilise a seasonal metaphor. An example can be found in the 1690s didactic ballad, *A Groatsworth of Good Counsel for a Penny*, which warned good fellows to save their money because 'Foul Winters are long, and cold weather is hard/ And a man without money no one will regard.'[109] Another warning ballad, *The carefull wife's good counsel*, made similar pleas, ending each verse with an appeal to the prodigal husband to 'save something for a rainy day'.[110] The central character of *No body loves mee* lamented learning this lesson too late, and when he sought out his kin to help him in his poverty, 'Nought but old proverbs on me they venter,/ Save nought in summer and starve in winter.'[111] Celebrations of good fellowship on the other hand looked to turn this proverb on its head, suggesting that a bout of sociable drinking was the best antidote to bad weather. *The Good Fellows Frolick* declared that 'We'l quench our thirst in liquor till/ we fear no Wind nor Weather.'[112] *It is bad Jesting with a Halter* made the same case, suggesting that a visit to the alehouse to sit beside its fire could mitigate

---

[106] Roxburghe, 2.44 (1674–79).

[107] Pepys, 4.242 (1665–74).

[108] Pepys, 4.292 (1690–96).

[109] Pepys, 4.78 (1684–96).

[110] British Library Ballad Collection, accessed via EEBO (hereafter BL), *The carefull wife's good counsel*, Wing C539 (1688–92).

[111] Pepys, 1.430 (c.1615).

[112] Pepys, 4.242 (1665–74).

the worst effects of winter: 'The coldnesse of the weather,/ made them their liquor take/ ... / Sayes he here is cold weather,/ lets have a better fire.'[113] The 1630s drinking contest song, *A Health to all Good-Fellows*, was set to the tune of 'To drive the cold Winter away'.[114] If critics of good fellowship used the metaphorical threat of winter to deter a prodigal approach to alehouse spending, then champions of the idiom were just as eager to establish counter-proverbs that posited alehouse sociability as the most effective strategy against both literal and metaphorical rainy days.

The appeal of such a present-centred mentality could be manifold. Most obviously, it could appeal as an antidote to the uncertainty of life in early modern society. In work on plebeian culture in the eighteenth century, E.P. Thompson argued that the unpredictability of life for pre-industrial plebeians meant that 'fluctuations in the incidence of mortality, of prices, of employment, are experienced as external accidents beyond any control', and therefore 'the populace has little predictive notation of time – they do not plan "careers", or see their lives in a given shape before them, or salt away weeks of high earnings in savings, or plan to buy cottages'. As a result, he suggested, 'experience or opportunity is grabbed as occasion arises, with little thought of the consequences'.[115] For the young, presented-centred prodigality might appeal as a remit to enjoy life before it was impinged by the serious responsibilities of marriage, and running and maintaining a household. It could represent a defiant reaction to the highly prescriptive moralising of the period, for both poor men and aristocrats alike, or a bout of temporary defiance for the middling householder against the constant and considerable demands of patriarchy. For others, a willingness to seize the moment may have grown from a confidence that their trade, or their family fortune, had assured their prospects in the longer term. They could afford it. At specific historical moments, such a short-term mentality may have been a reaction to the seeming bleakness of the political future: we have seen, for instance, that Royalists took to prodigal drinking in the 1640s and 1650s. The idiom of good fellowship, with its emphasis on liberality, was a call to enjoy the present, in good company, in a convivial and jovial atmosphere, stimulated by alcohol. These characteristics may have

---

113 Pepys, 1.440 (1632).

114 Roxburghe, 1.150 (1637).

115 E.P. Thompson, 'Eighteenth-Century English Society: Class Struggle without Class?', *Social History* 3 (1978), pp. 157–8.

carried different significance for different drinkers, but their appeal was wide.

Printed expressions and portrayals of alehouse sociability therefore disclose some of the core values that were associated with the name of a good fellow. These were not unchanging. Previous chapters have alluded to the notion that the political culture of the alehouse was becoming increasingly charged and fragmented in the later seventeenth century, with political *allegiance* coming to play a greater role in the character of alehouse culture. This transformation is also evident in good fellowship ballads. From the 1640s onwards, some ballads began to incorporate appropriate political allegiances into the credentials for obtaining a good fellow's name.[116] *The Distruction of Care*, a ballad dating from the 1680s or 1690s, made reference to many of the standard conventions of good fellowship: liberal spending, heavy drinking, merriment, an attack on misers, the dismissal of worldly care. Tellingly though, the ballad ended with a behavioural requirement of a good fellow that was not evident in earlier good fellowship ballads: 'And always will drink a good Health to the King/ out of my beloved the Mug, the Mug.'[117] Often statements such as this were designed to disavow any subversive link between drinking and politics, suggesting that the idiom of good fellowship was one of unquestioning loyalty to the monarch. *The Good Fellows Frolick* suggested that ideal-type good fellows were those that took no interest in matters of state at all: 'Affairs of S[t]ates, loads not our pates/ such troubles shall not find us.'[118] Another post-Restoration ballad, *The Loyal Subject (as it is reason)/ Drinks good Sack and is free from Treason*, took this message much further, as is clear from its title and the following assertion:

> Sack's the Princes surest Guard,
> if he would but try it,
> No Rebellion e'r was heard,
> where the Subjects soundly ply it.[119]

Indeed, Angela McShane has identified in many broadside ballads 'an "anti-political" argument which brings to mind the soma of Huxley's *Brave New World*', whereby a large number of ballads 'pointed out that

---

116 For an early example see Roxburghe, 3.395 (1648).

117 Pepys, 5.97 (1684–96).

118 Pepys, 4.242 (1665–74).

119 Pepys, 4.243 (1665–74).

a major benefit of drinking was that those who drank made themselves incapable of political designs and plotting'.[120]

Yet this ostensible disavowal of politics in good fellowship ballads was often accompanied by sentiments that were decidedly political. A 1690s ballad entitled *The Pot-Companions: Or, Drinking and Smoaking prefer'd before Caballing and Plotting*, again claimed that the convention for good fellows was to avoid politics: 'And here let us sit like honest brave Fellows,/ That neither are Tories nor Whigs in an Alehouse.' As the ballad reaches its crescendo, however, it becomes apparent that the protagonists were far from neutral in the religious and political debates of the time:

> We raise no Disputes that belong to the Pulpit,
> Nor start from our Text, but profoundly we gulp it;
> We have not amongst us a Canting Presbiter,
> But all honest Souls that will stand by the Miter:
> The Crown and the Miter we all will defend,
> Here's a Health to them both, and so let us end.[121]

It seems unlikely that such a ballad would have been sung in Northampton's Whig drinking establishment 'The Swan'.[122] Certain ballads seem to reflect, then, the emergence of a political dimension to the credentials of a good fellow, and even where this took the very simple form of an unequivocal statement of unquestioning loyalty to the King, this too could carry a political message.

Other ballads were much more overtly political. *The couragious loyalists, or, A health to the royal family* was not particularly subtle in its anti-Whig message:

> Let the Whigs lament,
> and whiningly complain,
> We with one consent,
> drink to the Royal Train.

The opening verse was dedicated to praise of good fellowship in fairly conventional terms, making reference to calling for more drink and 'letting misers pine', but the remainder of the ballad focuses far more

---

120 McShane Jones, 'Roaring Royalists and Ranting Brewers', p. 79.

121 Pepys, 5.98 (1682).

122 See p. 73 above.

on political messages than the celebration of good fellowship.[123] Ballads such as *The Oxford health or, The jovial loyalist* and *The couragious seamens loyal health* followed a similar pattern, with political messages relegating the celebration of sociability to a secondary concern.[124] Whilst some examples suggest a creeping politicisation of the drinking and good fellowship ballad genre, these cases demonstrate that in some instances the very character of the genre itself had been radically transformed by the end of the seventeenth century.[125] Indeed, such evidence reinforces the conclusion of recent work that has argued that 'from the mid-seventeenth century onwards, in a substantial number of these ballads the perennial duo of drink and song became a threesome – with politics or "state affairs" making the third member of the "jovial crew"'.[126] As with the elite drink literature of the seventeenth century, the genre of good fellowship ballads began to develop an increasingly explicit political charge from the middle of the century. Alehouse culture, as we have seen, had always been politicised, but this changed in both character and degree as politics – and in particular political allegiances – were becoming an increasingly defining feature of who qualified as a good fellow in the late seventeenth century. As we will see in Chapter 4, this was not just a development that took place in print.

Gendering good fellowship

The foregoing discussion has outlined a number of the key characteristics of good fellowship as it was expressed in broadside ballad drinking songs, and sought to demonstrate that its central features and values could have a broad appeal in early modern English society. Did that appeal extend to women? And to what extent did it appeal to *different types* of men? It might be assumed that the answer to the first of these two questions would

---

[123] BL, *The couragious loyalists*, Wing C6581 (1683).

[124] BL, *The Oxford health*, Wing O855 (1678–81); Bodleian Library Ballad Collection, accessed via EEBO (hereafter Bodleian), *The couragious seamens loyal health*, Wing C6583 (1688).

[125] For a much fuller discussion of the politicisation of drinking ballads see McShane Jones, 'Roaring Royalists and Ranting Brewers'. For more on the politicisation of other forms of sociability in the later seventeenth century see also Newton Key, '"High feeding and smart drinking": Associating Hedge-Lane Lords in Exclusion Crisis London', in Jason McElligott (ed.), *Exclusion and Revolution: The Worlds of Roger Morrice, 1675–1700* (Aldershot, 2006), pp. 154–73.

[126] McShane Jones, 'Roaring Royalists and Ranting Brewers', p. 70.

be relatively short, for there is a strong and continuing historical orthodoxy that sees alehouses as 'males spaces', with little place for women
except as alewives and serving maids. The archival evidence for women's
involvement in recreational drinking in alehouses will be explored in
the following chapter. Those who have confined their discussion to the
printed evidence have differed over its significance and meaning. Arguments that ballads 'celebrated the gendered co-opting of the alehouse
by lowly housed men', and that jest books defined alehouses as 'male-
dominated micro-sites', contrast sharply with arguments that ballads,
jests and woodcuts often show the alehouse as a fairly benign 'mixed-
gender space'.[127] There is, therefore, clearly scope for further analysis of
the relationship between women and alehouse sociability in print.

Ballads are again a particularly propitious source here. Recent work
emphasising the considerable reach of balladry has shown that despite
much lower average levels of literacy among women than among men,
ballads were 'sung by and for men and women of all ages', and their
oral dimension therefore meant that even illiterate women 'were often
familiar with their words and tunes'.[128] The strong presence of a female
voice in ballad literature has been taken as evidence that this was a
genre that articulated ideas and values designed to appeal to female
ballad consumers as much as male ones.[129] Furthermore, those women
who were patronising alehouses – as we will see in the following chapter,
they were not an insignificant category of alehouse patrons – would
doubtless have been familiar with the drinking and good fellowship
ballads that were being sold, sung and displayed at these sites. It is less
clear what messages and meanings those ballads would have carried
for such women. Historians have often tended to see the relationship
between ballads and female audiences as 'serving the function of rein-
forcing gender control', depicting negative female stereotypes which
were designed to elicit mocking laughter by both men and women. Such
a view assumes, for instance, that 'wives listened to ballads in which the

---

[127] Fumerton, 'Not Home', 494; Tim Reinke-Williams, 'Misogyny, Jest-Books and
Male Youth Culture in Seventeenth-Century England', *Gender and History* 21 (2009),
p. 329. Reinke-Williams revises his own position to some extent in his 'Women, Ale and
Company in Early Modern London', *Brewery History* 135 (2010), pp. 88–106; Pamela
Allen Brown, *Better a Shrew than a Sheep: Women, Drama, and the Culture of Jest in Early
Modern England* (Ithaca, NY, 2003), p. 73.

[128] Marsh, *Music and Society*, p. 270; Foyster, 'A Laughing Matter?', p. 6.

[129] See Sandra Clark, 'The Broadside Ballad and the Woman's Voice', in Cristina
Malcolmson and Mihoko Suzuki (eds), *Debating Gender in Early Modern England, 1500–
1700* (Basingstoke, 2002), pp. 103–20.

uncomeliness of scolding women was emphasised and learnt how they might be regarded if they adopted such behaviour', and that women were therefore more likely to draw on ballads for encouragement to conform to dominant gender norms, rather than for 'models for rebellion'. [130]

The dominant gender norms of the period naturally provided little scope for female recreational drinking. If attitudes towards male drinking and drunkenness were at best ambivalent, those towards female drinking were more unequivocally condemnatory, and early modern historians have emphasised the existence of a 'drinking double standard' that was intimately connected to the sexual double standard, because of 'the widespread opinion that a sober woman was a chaste woman while a drunk woman was promiscuous'.[131] Yet close analysis of drinking and good fellowship ballads questions the idea that encouragement to gender conformity was the only message these ballads carried for women. *The Catalogue of Contented Cuckolds* is one such ballad that has been cited to demonstrate the gender control function of ballads. The ballad describes a tavern meeting between ten men from different trades who discuss the adulterous activities of their wives. The men are all resigned to their cuckold status, confessing that little can be done to control such women and declaring that 'he's a fool that will weep for the sins of his wife'.[132] On one reading, the ballad message relies on 'age-old misogynist humour' in its suggestion that 'as women are sexually voracious men should not despair if they cannot control their wives'.[133] A 1630s ballad entitled *The Cuckolds Haven* seemed to carry a similar message, but associates women's sexual voracity specifically with their drinking. A disgruntled married man complained that:

> A woman that will be drunk,
> will easily play the punck,
> for when her wits are sunk,
> all keyes will fit her trunk.[134]

The intention of these ballads may well have been to appeal to misogynist sentiments held by male consumers – and to chastise female listeners – but there are arguably other messages at play. As we have

---

[130] Foyster, 'A Laughing Matter?', pp. 6, 18; Sharpe, 'Plebeian Marriage', p. 88.

[131] Martin, *Alcohol, Sex and Gender*, p. 134.

[132] Pepys, 4.130 (c.1651–86).

[133] Foyster, 'A Laughing Matter?', p. 7.

[134] BL, STC 6101 (1638).

seen, ballads were open to 'multiple interpretative possibilities', and these could no doubt be gendered. It is entirely plausible that whilst the message patriarchs gained from such ballads 'was that women needed to be kept in their place lest female dominance led to cuckoldry', it is possible that 'women may have delighted in seeing wives get the better of their husbands'.[135] For female consumers of such ballads the impotence of husbands to control their wives, and the fact that female drinking compounded men's sense of powerlessness in this regard, may well have had an alluring and empowering appeal.

Of particular relevance here is the image of the 'woman on top' in early modern culture, a phenomenon famously conceptualised by Natalie Zemon Davis.[136] Anthropologists and historians have found plenty of evidence of the ritual inversion of gender roles in pre-industrial cultures – most commonly associated with periods of festival or carnival – in which women could be portrayed as dominant and men as subservient.[137] Yet scholars have generally argued that such images and rituals of sexual inversion, like other rites and ceremonies of reversal, 'are ultimately sources of order and stability in a hierarchical society', serving to 'clarify the structure by the process of reversing it' and acting as a 'safety valve for conflicts within the system'. Davis challenged this conclusion, arguing instead that such inversion 'could *undermine* as well as reinforce' existing hierarchies through its connections with 'everyday circumstances outside the privileged time of carnival'. Through its spillover into more everyday contexts – such as alehouse sociability – Davis argued that 'the image of the disorderly woman did not always function to keep women in their place', and speculated instead that 'the ambiguous woman-on-top of the world of play made the unruly option a more conceivable one' to the 'majority of unexceptional women living within their families'.[138] Ballads detailing dominant drinking women may well have appealed to female alehouse-goers in precisely this way: as 'models of rebellion' rather than as warnings against deviant behaviour.

Ballads such as *The Cuckolds Haven* and *The Catalogue of Contented Cuckolds* not only reveal something of the appeal of alehouse sociability to women, they also contain more complex messages for their male consumers. Ballads like these did not simply pander to the misogynistic

---

135 Reinke-Williams, 'Misogyny, Jest-Books and Male Youth Culture', p. 335.

136 Davis, *Society and Culture*, ch. 5.

137 For the importance of inversion in early modern culture see Peter Burke, *Popular Culture*, ch. 7.

138 Davis, *Society and Culture*, pp. 130, 145.

leanings of male drinkers. Indeed, *The Catalogue of Contented Cuckolds* could be read as an indictment of male sociability as much as of female promiscuity. The tavern setting for the ballad implies that it was those men who regularly indulged in sociable drinking who were most likely to end up as cuckolds. The fact that the drinking companions drink a toast to themselves as 'cuckolds in grain' may suggest precisely this.[139] There is therefore evidence here to suggest a problematic relationship between male involvement in alehouse sociability and the assertion of patriarchal masculinity, a theme that has been developed by Alexandra Shepard's recent work in particular. Shepard has demonstrated that the conceptual framework developed by sociologists and historians of masculinity is useful for understanding early modern drinking culture.[140] In particular, she has suggested that drinking culture appealed to certain types of men: especially young men, but also an increasingly wide age range of poorer men, who were unable to set up a household, and were thus prevented from laying claim to the dominant masculine identity of a patriarchal head of household. As a consequence, Shepard argued, these young men 'adopted what might be labelled "anti-patriarchal" stances in direct opposition to normative codes of manhood'. Drinking rituals were central to the articulation of these 'counter codes of manhood', which 'replaced the normative virtues of manhood – such as thrift, moderation, sobriety and self-government – with the competing attributes of prodigality, bravado, raucousness and excess'.[141] In this analysis, recreational alehouse drinking had a particular appeal to young and unmarried men and was characterised by an antagonistic relationship to patriarchal values. These conclusions imply that the idiom of good fellowship was likely to appeal primarily to these same men, and may have been intimately connected with counter-codes of manhood – a feature of the idiom that may have circumscribed its breadth of appeal. In what remains of this chapter, then, these important questions of the gendered appeal of the ballad idiom of good fellowship will be explored by first

---

[139] Pepys, 4.130 (c.1651–86).

[140] Particularly influential has been the work of R.W. Connell and John Tosh: R.W. Connell, *Masculinities* (Cambridge, 1995); John Tosh, 'What Should Historians do with Masculinity?', *History Workshop Journal* 38 (1994), pp. 179–202.

[141] Shepard, '"Swil-bots and Tos-pots"', pp. 122–3. Tim Reinke-Williams draws on Shepard's work to forward a similar conclusion that 'some men never attempted to become patriarchs and defined their manhood through alternative codes of gender behaviour in which power and credit was based on sexual prowess and drinking, promoted in all-male environments at life-cycle stages when heterosexual relationships played little part': 'Misogyny, Jest-Books and Male Youth Culture', p. 326.

considering ballad portrayals of all-female alehouse sociability, second by examining mixed-gender depictions, and finally by turning to the relationship between good fellowship and various codes of manhood.

Writing in 1617, the Jacobean pamphleteer Ester Sowernam regretted that female drinking could not take on the positive connotations of male good fellowship. She complained that contemporaries considered it 'an hatefull thing … to see a woman overcome with drinke, when in men it is noted a signe of good fellowship'.[142] There was undoubtedly a great deal of truth in Sowernam's analysis, for broadside ballads only rarely offered a positive discourse on female drinking to match that of male good fellowship. That said, there are a number of ballads that do represent female drinking companies in ways similar to groups of male good fellows. A 1630s ballad depicting an instance of all-female sociability, entitled *Fowre wittie Gossips disposed to be merry*, noted that the women called for liquor with the claim that 'bravely we will drinke it'. The drinkers also cried 'Let every woman have her cup,/ of sacke and drinke it roundly', and then spent the whole day 'in merriment and laughing', only concluding their song in the 'morning very early'.[143] The female drinking company that was the subject of the 1680 ballad *Five merry wives of Lambeth* were described as 'lusty lively lasses' who 'took of their glasses round', and the 1690s ballad *The Seamens Wives Frolick Over A Bowl of Punch* was another based on an instance of all-female sociable drinking, in which the seamen's wives declare: 'We love our Liquor to drink it all up,/ None of us but love a full Glass or a Cup.' The consumption in this ballad also took on a dimension of ritualised heavy drinking, with the women ordering the drawer to 'fill us a Bowl, and Rouzing Bowl,/ As large as our Capacious Soul'. There is an echo here of those rituals of male good fellowship based around heavy drinking games and songs: 'To e'ry good Bowl they told it it's doom,/ And Merrily Danc'd it about the Room;/ With many a pleasant New Song and Catch.'[144] Although Alexandra Shepard has suggested that rituals of heavy drinking 'were closely tied to assertions of specifically male forms of prowess', these ballads

---

[142] E. Sowernam (almost certainly a pseudonym), *Ester hath hang'd Haman: Or An Answere to a lewd Pamphlet, entituled, The Arraignment of Women* (London, 1617), p. 24, cited in Tim Reinke-Williams, 'Women, Ale and Company', p. 93.

[143] Pepys, 1.436 (1632).

[144] Bodleian, *Five merry wives of Lambeth*, Wing F1113 (1680); Pepys, 4.184 (1690–1702).

suggest that female drinking might have involved elements of ritualised heavy consumption.[145]

Another aspect of overlap between all-female sociability and good fellowship in the ballads relates to the politics of payment. The *Fowre wittie Gossips disposed to be merry*, for instance, requested of the women drinkers 'blithly let us spend our coine', and the seamen's wives indulged in bowls of punch that they knew would 'empt[y] their Pock[e]ts of their Coin'.[146] Here too then was a prodigal attitude to spending, but as with respect to male good fellowship the ballads also emphasised the importance of each woman being able to pay her share of the score. The witty gossips were faced with a score of twelve shillings, and 'each one lay downe their store'. They could, however, only muster ten shillings between them, so each one pawned an item of their clothing to ensure their credit remained good, and the burden was equally shared.[147] That female drinkers too were governed by a politics of payment in similar ways to men is also suggested in Samuel Rowlands's 1602 pamphlet, *Tis Merry When Gossips Meet*, when a widow buys a round with evident pride in her ability to pay for it.[148] Politicisation may be another feature of sociability that crossed gender boundaries. In 1692, *An Excellent New Song call'd the Female Duel* described how a 'Williamite lady' of Yorkshire challenged to a duel another lady (a Jacobite) who refused to drink a loyal health to the King.[149]

If drinking ballads situated in instances of all-female sociability contained some similarities with those situated in all-male sociability there were also, however, some notable differences. One is that all-female sociability is often depicted as more occasional than its male equivalent. In *Fowre wittie Gossips disposed to be merry* the women come together on a market day, and declare that 'wee seldome meet together'. Indeed their meeting is opportunistic, seizing the occasion as their husbands are all in bed nursing hangovers from their own more regular alehouse sociability the previous night. *The Seamens Wives Frolick Over A Bowl of Punch* takes place shortly after their husbands left shore – implying that their sociable drinking also only took place when their husbands were out of the way. Unlike depictions of male good fellowship – which

---

145 Shepard, '"Swil-bots and Tos-pots"', pp. 121–2.
146 Pepys, 1.436 (1632); Pepys, 4.184 (1690–1702).
147 Pepys, 1.436 (1632).
148 See Brown, *Better a Shrew than a Sheep*, p. 63.
149 McShane Jones, 'Roaring Royalists and Ranting Brewers', p. 87.

are invariably geographically neutral – female sociability is, moreover, usually described as a metropolitan affair: the seamen's wives met at 'an Ale-house near London'; a 1690s ballad described the meeting of *The Seven Merry Wives of London*; another focused on *Five merry wives of Lambeth*.[150]

Ballad depictions of female drinkers 'bravely' and 'roundly' drinking large quantities, and insisting on and taking pride in paying their own way, may well have been intended to suggest that women could match up to men when it came to exhibiting the positive qualities associated with good fellowship. Of course, female reactions to such messages would not have been uniform, as *Fowre wittie Gossips disposed to be merry* implies. As the drinking session of the wives wore on throughout the day, some of the younger wives began to panic about their husbands' likely reactions to their heavy drinking: 'The younger wives did weep for feare/ their husbands would abuse them.' No doubt similar concerns about any involvement in alehouse sociability would have been shared by many of the women who heard this ballad. Yet the positive messages about participation in instances of all-female sociable drinking were reinforced when one of the more senior wives, the 'somewhat stout' Mother Joan, reassured her younger companions to be of 'good cheere', as she would 'excuse them' of any blame if their husbands discovered them.[151] Within the ballad itself, then, the dominant 'woman on top' figure of Mother Joan was seen to trump the inclinations to gender conformity of her more timid companions – sending a very clear message to female audiences or performers about which behavioural option offered female empowerment.

Whilst female reactions to these ballads may have been mixed, there is evidence to suggest that men's attitudes may have varied too. Some ballads suggest that male drinkers had a degree of respect for stout female drinkers. The 1660s ballad *Nick and Froth* included women who 'drink for pleasure' within an imagined – and primarily male – 'Society of Good Fellowship', praising 'Billings-gate Nan, and all her whole gang' as 'True Topers they are, as e[v]er scor[e]d at the bar'.[152] The good fellows in the ballad *Heres to thee kind Harry* also seemed to celebrate a culture of

---

150 Pepys, 1.436 (1632); Pepys, 4.184 (1690–1702); Pepys, 5.413 (1690–1700); Bodleian, Wing F1113 (1680). That all-female sociability may have been a largely metropolitan phenomenon has been suggested by Bernard Capp in *When Gossips Meet: Women, Family, and Neighbourhood in Early Modern England* (Oxford, 2003), pp. 331–2.

151 Pepys, 1.436 (1632).

152 Roxburghe, 1.376 (c.1665).

jovial female sociability, encouraging their drinking companions to be as 'merry as the maids'.[153] More characteristically, however, these ballads imply male anxiety about instances of all-female sociability. A primary concern for men, and especially husbands, was that the topic of conversation would inevitably turn to their own (lack of) sexual prowess.[154] This theme was taken up in the 1690s ballad entitled *The Seven Merry Wives of London*, in which the wives of a range of tradesmen meet for a sociable drink, with each woman proceeding to bemoan her husband's sexual failings using metaphors relating to the husband's trade. A metal worker's wife complained that although she took him to be 'A Man of much mettle', his sexual performance was ultimately disappointing: 'he'll seldom cast into the mould that he should'. Another woman who had been married to a surgeon for a year revealed how 'he never had enter'd nor found the right Vein,/ Therefore surely, said she, I have cause to complain'. The exception was the wife of the blacksmith, who boasted that 'she had no kind of cause to complain of these wrongs,/ For he follow'd his labor with hammer and tongs'.[155] Although this ballad clearly played on male anxieties about female sociability and gossip, it was again far from a straightforward condemnation of female drinking – its humour would no doubt have appealed to many women and perhaps even to some men. Blacksmiths perhaps.

Men's greater source of unease over female sociability was that an all-female drinking company might morph into an instance of mixed-gender sociability involving illicit sexual activity. Indeed, both *The Seamens Wives Frolick Over A Bowl of Punch* and the sociability of the *Five merry wives of Lambeth* ended with the women inviting men into their company, and cuckoldry onto their husbands.[156] Even ballads such as these, which might contain some positive sentiments towards female sociability, often ended with a warning about what might happen when male and female drinkers mixed. As was the case with all-female sociability, though, ballads reveal that ambivalent meanings were associated with mixed-gender sociability. On the one hand, there was a fear that the mixture of men, women and intoxication could lead to sexual misadventure, spawning cuckolds and bastards – an anxiety heightened by a strand of jest-book humour that implied that women were occa-

---

153 Pepys, 1.432 (1627).
154 Capp, *When Gossips Meet*, p. 62.
155 Pepys, 5.413 (1690–1700).
156 Pepys, 4.184 (1690–1702); Bodleian, Wing F1113 (1680).

sionally accepted and integrated into alehouse sociability primarily for the sexual gratification of male customers.[157] On the other hand, it is possible to locate within the cultural media of the period more positive images of men and women drinking together. There are certainly examples of ballads which make reference to mixed-gender sociability without implying an illicit sexual dimension. A ballad subtitled *The Good Fellows Frolick*, a celebration of good fellowship, called for 'Peg and Sue, and Frances' to join the drinkers for music and celebration, and the 1670s ballad *The Careless Gallant* encouraged good fellows to 'sport and be free, with Frank, Betty, and Dolly'.[158] Roaring Dick of Dover listed his drinking companions as a mixed-gender set of 'Lads and honest Lasses,/ that to each others are kinde', and concludes his verses with a toast that made a point of including both male and female drinkers:

> Thus for to conclude my Ditty,
> heeres a health to all true blades,
> Remembring, Kate, Nell, Sis, and Betty,
> and all other kinde true Maides.

Yet Roaring Dick's attitude to the involvement of women in his company may not necessarily be so innocent. The jovial good fellow of Kent explains that when 'I have spent away my money ... I have a kinde sweet hony/ that sometimes will pay my score.'[159] It could be argued that Dick is merely suggesting that female drinking companions were expected to share their burden of the bill just like men, but his enthusiasm for female drinking companions could potentially be read as a tongue-in-cheek cover for his real purpose – the financial, or perhaps even sexual, exploitation of the women with whom he drinks. That said, if this was the intended message of the ballad it seems just as plausible to imagine a mixed-gender company performing the song and laughing at the tensions over who was meant to pay, as it is to imagine an all-male company aiming mocking laughter at unsuspecting female victims of such deceit.

What about those ballads that did portray mixed-gender sociability in more explicitly sexualised terms? Can they be read as misogynistic attempts either to discourage women from alehouse sociability or to promote their exploitation? Ballads that do depict sexual activity in the

---

157 Reinke-Williams, 'Misogyny, Jest-Books and Male Youth Culture', p. 329.
158 Pepys, 4.242 (1665–74); BL, Wing J1021 (1674–9).
159 Pepys, 1.434 (1632).

alehouse often cast alewives and alehouse workers – rather than female sociable drinkers – in the lead female roles, but there are examples of the latter becoming involved in carnal misbehaviour. Whilst the former type of ballad often implies the sexual commodification of female alehouse workers, those ballads that detail the participation of female customers in sexual activity tend to portray their henpecked husbands – rather than the women themselves – as the victims of exploitation. *Cuckolds Haven* told the story of an alehouse-going wife whose drinking led to sexual promiscuity and the 'hornifying' of her husband, but the ballad focuses rather more on the incapacity of the husband to control his domineering wife than on the woman herself falling victim to predatory alehouse-going men.[160] The 1640 ballad *The discontented married man* told of another alehouse-frequenting wife, who 'cannot keepe her lips' together – a rather crude double entendre. The husband here is portrayed as a victim, and the female participant in alehouse sexual activity is depicted as consenting.[161] There was, of course, a certain misogynistic logic at work in these themes, but their intention was as much to pour scorn on weak men as it was to discourage female drinking, and as we saw in *The Catalogue of Contented Cuckolds* the involvement of a husband in alehouse sociability was often cited as likely to increase the prospect of his being cuckolded.[162] Davis' perspective on inversion, especially her suggestion that patriarchy accorded a 'complex license' to the unruly women, is once again useful here: 'on the one hand she was not accountable for what she did. Given over to the sway of her lower passions, she was not responsible for her actions; her husband was responsible, for she was subject to him.'[163] Ballad depictions of sexualised mixed-gender sociability seem therefore to offer as much of a warning to men about enforcing dominant gender roles as they do to women about transgressing them.

Broadside ballads dealing with mixed-gender sociability seem then to offer a two-fold appeal of such activity for women. On the one hand, they suggest that women could be involved in non-sexual alehouse sociability with, and perhaps even on the same terms as, men, and that the positive idiom of good fellowship may have also been accessible to women. On the other hand, they suggest that women who participated in sexualised

---

160 BL, STC 6101 (1638).
161 BL, STC 17232 (1640).
162 Pepys, 4.130 (c.1651–86); See also Pepys, 1.436 (1632).
163 Davis, *Society and Culture*, p. 146.

mixed-gender sociability were likely to develop an ambivalent reputation – promiscuous yes, but also subversive, dominant and empowered, with responsibility for such actions to some extent deflected, at least for married women, onto their husbands. Furthermore, the ballads suggest that there was as much anxiety about the relationship between alehouse sociability and male gender norms as there was about women's drinking and appropriate female behaviour. Indeed, a favourite theme of many of the didactic ballads that dealt with drinking was the incompatibility of good fellowship and patriarchy. The 1615 ballad *No body loues mee* warned that men who regularly spent time and money in the alehouse were unlikely to invest sufficient of either in their family. A good fellow was, by definition, not a good domestic provider, and his wife and children would find that 'Their stomack seldome shall be fild.' Instead, the appropriate behaviour for a patriarchal male was to spend his days:

> Among thy familie,
> at thy worke merrilie.
> Then happily shalt thou speed,
> having coine at thy need.

A stark but straightforward decision therefore faced any men who wished to be considered good patriarchs and to lay claim to the dominant masculine identity. They must 'Cease their Ale-house songs' and join their 'true wedded wives' at home.[164]

Interestingly, the discourse surrounding appropriate forms of masculine behaviour was not, in ballads at least, rehearsed solely between men. Jennifer Jordan has criticised historians of early modern masculinity for tending to assume that 'manhood was constructed and negotiated between men, sometimes to the exclusion of some men according to age or status, and always to the exclusion of women'. Jordan argues that such a view serves to 'diminish women's active participation in male gender construction. It cannot be the case that women were impartial witnesses to the construction and enforcement of manhood'.[165] The ballads provide some tentative evidence of women's active participation in male gender construction, not least because the opinion that alehouse sociability undermined patriarchy was voiced as often by female as by male characters. A classic example is that of John Jarret's wife, who urged her

---

164 Pepys, 1.430 (c.1615).

165 Jennifer Jordan, 'Her-story Untold: The Absence of Women's Agency in Constructing Concepts of Early Modern Manhood', *Cultural and Social History* 4:4 (2007), pp. 575–83.

Husbâd, beware the Stocks

5. Ballad wives often took the lead in reminding husbands of the tensions between good fellowship and the performance of patriarchal masculinity: *A Statute for Swearers and Drunkards*, Pepys, 1.214 (1624)

husband that his drinking was interfering with the performance of his patriarchal duties such as work and provisioning. Furthermore, Jarret's wife encouraged her miscreant husband to 'Be rul'd by my counsell, good husband, I pray', a sentiment that was repeated in many other ballad appeals to alehouse-frequenting husbands to 'be ruled by your wife' – providing, of course, that their wife was a spokeswoman for patriarchal values.[166] Paradoxically, then, whether a man should be ruler of, or ruled by, his wife was dependent upon which one was the greater champion of patriarchal values.

Not all women were such champions, and other ballads suggested that alewives in particular were more likely to try to entice men into counter-codes of masculinity. *A Caveat for Young Men* narrates the tale of a former good fellow whose wife had entreated him to cease his alehouse-going

[166] Pepys, 1.170 (1630).

as she and her children were left sitting at home starving. Yet the lure of good fellowship was too strong and he ignored his wife's counsel – not least because the alewife, 'as Venus drew Adonis in', always lured him to stay longer and spend more, occasionally throwing in kisses to encourage a prodigal masculinity that eventually resulted in his financial ruin. A valuable lesson learnt, the husband reformed his ways, and advised all other men to 'be ruled by your wives' and never to trust alewives.[167] In these ballads then, women could be central to – rather than excluded from – the promotion and enforcement of the different codes of manhood available to seventeenth-century men. In fact, what emerges from drinking and good fellowship ballads is a debate which seems to situate the alehouse not at the centre of a divide between men and women, but between the upholders of patriarchal values on the one hand and participants in a counter-code of prodigal masculinity on the other – with some men and some women standing on either side of the battle lines.

Further evidence attesting to the close relationship between the alehouse and anti-patriarchal codes of manhood can be seen in the 'fear of, antagonism toward, and exclusion of wives' found in many good fellowship ballads.[168] The late-seventeenth-century ballad *The Distruction of Care* advised men that if 'thy Wife proves not one of the best', then diversion could be found in drink, and Laurence Price's 1645 ballad *Good Ale for my money* depicted a man who was so enamoured with alehouse sociability that he refused to go home to his wife despite being newly wed.[169] If some men were keen to avoid their wives and exclude them from their sociable drinking companies, other ballad good fellows were eager to stress that this was not intended to pave the way for illicit sexual activities. In the ballad *Robin and Kate* the alehouse-going husband responded to his wife's accusation that he kept a lover at the alehouse by assuring her:

> I seek not for wenches, but honest good fellowes:
> A pipe of Tobacco,
> A Pot, or a Jugg,
> These are the sweet honies
> That I kisse and hugg.[170]

---

167 Pepys, 2.22 (1666–78).

168 Fumerton, 'Not Home', pp. 507–8.

169 Pepys, 5.97 (1684–96); Roxburghe, 1.138 (1645).

170 Fumerton, 'Not Home', p. 511.

The protagonists of the ballad *Mondayes Worke* knew that their alehouse visit would provoke a scolding from their wives, but whilst they were prepared to renege on their patriarchal duties they were also keen to emphasise that they scorned alehouse-going 'whorers' who wasted means on 'wooing'.[171] *Heres to thee kind Harry* suggested that an ideal-type drinking companion would not be a 'wenching knave' who spent money on 'whores' and 'lasses' instead of on drink for his male companions. Another celebration of good fellowship, *A Mess of Good Fellows*, declared that 'we scorn to spend money on queanes ... For he that so wasteth his means,/ at last will be paid with a p[ox]'.[172] These ballads insisted on a distinction between good fellowship and illicit sexual activity. If good fellowship was anti-patriarchal in its attitudes towards wives, it did not necessarily promote a culture of sexual profligacy.

In fact, there is evidence in the ballads to suggest that in principle good fellowship was neither antagonistic towards wives nor at odds with a well-ordered family life. Although 'Roaring Dick of Dover' condemned wives that 'brawl and wrangle', he was not opposed to men's wives joining drinking companies, and in fact advised the wives of alehouse-going men: 'In your minds be not tormented:/ but take part as well as he.'[173] It was not wives *per se* to whom good fellows were hostile, but rather those wives who were in turn hostile to good fellowship. Those wives who were well disposed to alehouse sociability appear to have been welcome participants. Other good fellowship ballads sought to emphasise that being a good fellow and being a good husband were not incompatible. *The Careless Drunkards* claimed that

> Drink is the thing supports our lives,
> and fills our hearts with ease,
> This makes us kind unto our Wives
> while them we strive to please.[174]

Some ballads, such as *A Mess of Good Fellows*, even concluded by proposing that good fellows should drink toasts to their wives.[175] The 1637 ballad *A Health to all Good-Fellows* likewise ended with a 'health to our wives', and went further in its attempts to defuse associations between

---

171 Roxburghe, 1.262 (1632).
172 Pepys, 1.432 (1627); Roxburghe, 1.260 (1634).
173 Pepys, 1.434 (1632).
174 Pepys, 4.238 (1690–1702).
175 Roxburghe, 1.260 (1634).

good fellows and bad patriarchs, claiming that 'at home I confesse, with my honest Besse,/ I practice good husbandry well'. This ballad husband stated that his neighbours 'will praise me at large, for maintaining my charge', and that this reputation for good husbandry was not incompatible with one as a hard-drinking good fellow: 'but when I to drinking incline,/ I scorne for to shrinke, go fetch us more drinke'.[176] In these ballads, then, good fellowship and good husbandry could be reconciled.

Indeed, alehouse culture, and in particular the idiom of good fellowship, was not necessarily marked by a positive embrace of an anti-patriarchal manhood that appealed primarily to young and unmarried men. Whilst good fellowship undoubtedly did attract such men through its rejection of many of the values associated with patriarchy – thrift, moderation, sobriety – it does not appear to have invariably exalted sexual conquests and prowess, or offered uniform hostility to marriage, in the ways that might be expected of a youth or bachelor counter-culture. Instead, these ballads suggest that the idiom could also be configured to appeal to married men, disassociating itself from sexual promiscuity and attempting to reconcile good fellowship with effective patriarchy. That it might appeal to both bachelors and married men is implied by the fact that ballads condemning good fellowship addressed themselves as often to 'bad husbands' as they did to 'young men', or sometimes to both.

This analysis of good fellowship ballads therefore suggests a more complex set of relationships between drinking and gender identities than is implied by the received historiographical wisdom that alehouse sociability reaffirmed dominant gender norms through the exclusion of women. Female involvement in alehouse sociability was a common theme, and although it was often seen as problematic, its implications were ambivalent. It is possible to see why alehouse sociability may have appealed to women on several different levels, both in ways analogous to the appeal of good fellowship to men, and through its associations with the notion of the 'woman on top'. This analysis has also demonstrated that alehouse sociability had an antagonistic relationship with dominant male gender norms, which it tended to undermine as often as reinforce. Yet this antipathy should not be read as confirmation that good fellowship was synonymous with anti-patriarchal codes of manhood. Instead, good fellowship could appeal to counter-codes of manhood conventionally associated with young men and bachelors, but might also appeal to notions of good husbandry that were important to patriarchal heads

---

[176] Roxburghe, 1.150 (1637).

of households. Once more, then, we can see the considerable potential appeal of the idiom of good fellowship.

Conclusion

This chapter has reconstructed the rationale behind the recreational drinking that was practised in early modern English alehouses. Drawing inspiration from an emergent 'cultural history of drinking', and in particular its analysis of forms of printed drink literature, the focus has been on what drinking ballads – a form of print intimately connected to the *practice* of alehouse sociability – reveal about the rituals, conventions and meanings that contemporaries attached to their recreational alcohol consumption. These ballads reveal that alehouse culture was informed by an idiom of good fellowship – a characteristic mode and set of conventions – that configured sociable and recreational drinking as a positive activity.

Good fellowship was characterised by certain rituals – the drinking of toasts, competitive drinking games, the performance of songs – and governed by a set of behavioural expectations and conventions. Good fellows were expected to be able to drink heavily, spend liberally, pay their share of the shot, and express a jovial, 'merry' disposition. These expectations functioned as a series of 'entry requirements', and underpinned a 'politics of participation' that determined who should be included in, and excluded from, a drinking company. These conventions also reflect on the way contemporaries understood the effects of alcohol: as a stimulant rather than a narcotic, to be consumed to an appropriate level to optimise sociability, but not to induce a drunken stupor. The more a good fellow could consume without losing control, the greater the level of respect they drew from their fellow boozers. Drunken oblivion, however, brought shame. Though it no doubt occurred often enough, and doubtless motivated at least some of those who stepped through the alehouse door, it should not be seen as the principal goal of the heavy drinkers who gathered in the early modern English alehouse. This accolade, as far as good fellowship ballads expressed it, was the opportunity to engage in bonds of fellowship based on a shared ethos – values of hard work, political loyalty, self-control, courage, patriarchal prowess, even defiance of patriarchal values.

Indeed, it has been argued here that although all of these meanings could be expressed through bouts of good fellowship, they were not always all present at all times for all participants. There was a common stock of cultural codes and meanings associated with good fellowship, but they could be appropriated in a number of different ways by different groups.[177] Tradesmen might engage in a bout of liberal imbibing as an expression of their industriousness; a group of apprentices as an attack on the values of their patriarchal masters; a company of soldiers as an expression of their courage; a company of married women as a claim to subversive empow- erment; a mixed-gender group of servants and maids as an expression of platonic amity. All of these meanings of good fellowship are possible from readings of the ballad literature, and each coalesced around the core characteristics of liberal drinking, equal spending, joviality and sociable interaction, all of it stimulated by alcohol. Good fellowship, then, enjoyed a broad appeal, one that could transcend gender bounda- ries and class boundaries, and good fellowship ballads were consumed across the social scale. That it was this idiom, rather than the pursuit of drunkenness, that motivated recreational drinking in alehouses helps us to account for the fact that the alehouse was able to claim such a central place in early modern communities. It therefore becomes less surprising that many amongst the ranks of the middling-sort office-holders of towns and villages were prepared to defend the alehouse, and even patronise it. They, too, could find positive values in good fellowship that they would have struggled to see in narcotic oblivion.

This chapter contributes to the new cultural history of drinking, and has shown that there was a popular dimension to the emerging seventeenth-century genre of 'drink literature'. Like that aimed at the educated and urbane, it portrayed recreational drinking as an impor- tant socio-cultural activity that was integral to the formation of posi- tive identities. It was not just elite, urban, male wine-drinkers for whom drinking was hedged about with rituals, conventions and meanings – the drinking of the alehouse crowd was equally ritualised. That there were a number of similarities and connections between the two should not, however, be taken to mean that either educated and literary elites necessarily saw it this way, or even that they accepted the legitimacy of alehouse sociability. Whilst some amongst the ranks of the middling sort may have joined their poorer neighbours in the local alehouse, there were undoubtedly others who refused to recognise any affinity between alehouse sociability and more elite forms of drinking culture. Ben Jonson,

---

177   This reading comes close to Roger Chartier's 'appropriation' model. See, for instance, his 'Culture as Appropriation: Popular Cultural Uses in Early Modern France', in Steven L. Kaplan (ed.), *Understanding Popular Culture: Europe from the Middle Ages to the Nine- teenth Century* (Berlin, 1984), pp. 229–54.

for all his love of conviviality and tavern-going, condemned the 'brutish and ignorant excesses of low-rank beer-and-ale drinkers' as the 'wild anarchy of drink'.[178] If we can now recognise Jonson's position as one of class-based prejudice, rather than a dispassionate guide to understanding alehouse culture, his vitriol nonetheless reminds us that the legitimacy of recreational drinking in alehouses had many enemies in high places, even if it won some friends amongst the middling and upper ranks of society.

Of course, it might be objected that the insights offered by good fellowship ballads provide nothing more than a window onto printed prescriptions that say little about the actual practice and performance of alehouse sociability. Too sharp a dichotomy between print and practice should, however, be avoided: good fellowship ballads, like many forms of drink literature, were not abstract 'representations' of drinking rituals, but performative genres of print intended to be embedded in drinking practices. And yet, whilst they reveal a great deal about the meanings associated with recreational drinking in alehouses they do not provide a direct window onto practice. No source can offer this, but there is other evidence that presents further insights into early modern English alehouse sociability – and it is to legal records, diaries and depositions, that the final chapter will now turn.

---

[178] Scodel, *Excess and the Mean*, p. 201; Lemon, 'Compulsory Conviviality'.

4

'Joining and Fastening Together'
The Practice and Bonds of Good Fellowship

On a Wednesday evening in October 1604, in the Essex parish of Layer Marney, at around 6.00p.m. John Oultings entered a drinking establishment known locally as Turner's alehouse. Oultings was in search of refreshment and accommodation, and in the course of his overnight stay witnessed some rather intriguing drinking antics. On his arrival he found John Lufkin, Thomas Marsh, and other unnamed men drinking together. It's not entirely clear whether Oultings joined these men or watched them from across the room, but at around 9.00p.m. he witnessed John Lufkin call for 'a huge great stone pot' – 'conteyneinge by his estemacon very nere two gallons' of beer – a vessel that was apparently known to the drinkers by the name of 'Fowler', a rather odd nickname for a drinking vessel, the provenance of which will become clear. Oultings was not interested in participating in whatever drinking ritual was about to ensue, and retired to his bed chamber. He rose the next morning between 4.00 and 5.00a.m., only to find Lufkin and his fellow drinkers still 'playing', as he put it, with the great stone pot. But one of the company had apparently been defeated in the attempt to drain this mighty vessel, for Thomas Marsh was, as Oultings observed, 'so drunk he fell fast asleep at the table, hanging down his head, foaming, slavering, and pissing as he sat'. He had, in short, got so drunk he had befouled himself. That was not the end of his indignity. One of the company fetched a sack, and placed it over Marsh's head, whereupon John Lufkin, the ringleader of the drinking company, bellowed in Marsh's ears that he too would forever after bear the nickname 'Fowler'. Just to top off the shaming ritual, Lufkin undid Marsh's codpiece, and left him sitting there, unconscious, soiled, and with what contemporaries would have referred to as his 'carnal instrument' publicly exposed. By 7.00a.m. Oultings was on his way, leaving the company to breakfast, but this was not the end of their bout of good fellowship: Oultings later

171

heard reports that they had not left Turner's alehouse until the following morning.[1]

Oultings' deposition provides us with a remarkable glimpse inside the early modern English alehouse, and offers a particularly rich and detailed account of the acting out of a drinking ritual. The historian of everyday non-elite drinking cultures in the early modern period might reasonably assume that an account of this kind would be the privilege of the anthropologist or ethnographer. Indeed, it is generally thought that the prescription of drinking rituals in the past is considerably easier to recover than their actual practice.[2] That said, the previous chapter argued that too sharp a distinction should not be drawn between the two, and whilst 'drink literature' may have greatest value as an indicator of drinking's prescriptive conventions it was also intimately connected to its quotidian practice. Moreover, as Oultings's testimony suggests, other sources also survive that allow us to glimpse what took place behind the doors of early modern English alehouses. Legal records represent a treasure trove for the historian of good fellowship, and drinking rituals and practices regularly feature in testimony from all sorts of cases ranging across defamation, assault, sedition, adultery, theft, or as in this case, neglect of office. Oultings was, in fact, one of a series of deponents giving evidence about John Lufkin's failure to fulfil his duties as parish constable. The man who called for 'Fowler' was none other than the very man charged with ensuring that the alehouses in his community did not facilitate recreational drinking and drunkenness. As we saw in Chapter 2, Lufkin was not unusual in neglecting that aspect of his office.

But this case, and others like it, have the potential to illuminate much more than just the relationship between the alehouse and the authorities. The attempt to drain a two gallon pot of beer in an all-night drinking session resonates with the emphasis placed in ballads on ritualised feats of heavy drinking as a central component of alehouse culture. That Marsh was elaborately shamed for his failure to keep control of mind and body – and bladder – reinforces the point that good fellows gained honour for holding their drink, but dishonour for succumbing to a state of drunken stupor. Oblivion was not the goal, even if it was occasionally the outcome, of alehouse-going. This case also sheds further

---

[1] ERO, Q/SR 170/3. The quote in the title of this chapter, 'joining and fastening together', is the meaning of the Latin word 'compages', from which the word 'company' – of which 'good fellowship' is the alehouse-based variety – is derived. See Withington, 'Company and Society', p. 297.

[2] *Ibid.*, p. 303.

light on the breadth of the appeal of good fellowship. Lufkin was not a representative of the ranks of the local poor, but an office-holding 'chief inhabitant'. In a neat twist on those cases where alehousekeepers showed a distinct lack of deference to such officials, Henry Pannell – who ran an alehouse at nearby Layer Breton – gave testimony that Lufkin 'tarried' in his establishment from noon until midnight, but 'he being this examinate's better [I] would not presume to bid him go away'.[3] If Lufkin was not a poor man in pursuit of drunken oblivion, neither was he a young bachelor involved in rituals of excess aimed at defying patriarchal values that were beyond his own reach. He was a married man, and on occasion his wife would join him in both company and in his high-spirited antics, as we will see below. The ritual witnessed by Oultings undoubtedly had something to do with the expression of masculinity – laying bare Marsh's 'carnal instrument' was surely a symbolic flourish intended to 'expose' his manhood, or rather lack thereof – but Lufkin's expression of a positive male identity through heavy drinking cannot be neatly labelled as 'anti-patriarchal' behaviour, and nor can the participation of his wife be explained in such terms. The complex operation of gender norms and values in relation to alehouse sociability, the social profile of those who participated in it, and the character and meaning of rituals of heavy drinking, are just some of the key themes that this type of material will allow us to pursue further in this chapter.

This material has its limitations, of course. Few cases are quite as richly detailed as John Lufkin's antics, and references to the behaviour and practices of good fellows are usually more fleeting – though the seam of sources we can mine for such incidental references extends beyond depositions to include various other legal records such as presentments and indictments. There is, then, no shortage of material, but what follows represents the piecing together of many fragments of evidence buttressed by a handful of nuggets such as Oultings's testimony. All of which, it could be objected, are hardly propitious for revealing 'everyday' or 'routine' drinking practices. Behaviour recorded in legal records is usually taken to represent transgressive or exceptional activity, and it is undoubtedly the case that the vast majority of the incalculable instances of everyday alehouse sociability that took place left no imprint on the historical record. The 'dark figure' of unrecorded instances of good fellowship is immense, and what evidence we do have may over represent those instances characterised by violence, illicit sex, or extreme

3   ERO, Q/SR 170/3.

drunkenness. Deponents in legal cases were not, of course, ethnographers, and their observations could be vexatious, exaggerated, evasive, or simply misremembered, and it is not uncommon to find rather different versions of events in cases where multiple witnesses testified.

Historians have learnt, however, not to be too quick to dismiss the value of such testimony.[4] Even in instances where the relationship of a deposition to 'what really happened' can be questioned, witnesses tended to construct their stories in accordance with cultural conventions and expectations. If the events in Turner's alehouse did not play out exactly as Oultings described them, he needed to tell a tale that was plausible if his testimony against Lufkin was to be believed. Contemporaries needed to recognise the forms of behaviour attributed to these good fellows, and as such the testimony can be taken as a reasonable guide to the character of early modern drinking rituals, even if it was not entirely accurate in relaying the particulars of any given instance. Moreover, gleaning evidence of drinking practices from such sources may be less hazardous than trying to recover the exact details and circumstances of a murder, theft or defamation. In many of the instances discussed below drinking is not itself the crime under the spotlight, but is described by deponents in the process of providing details about the backdrop or build-up to a more serious offence such as an assault or theft. Descriptions of drinking practices in depositions are often tangential and incidental, rather than carrying significant weight, and are perhaps less likely to have been constructed 'fictions'. This also makes depositions a better guide to more routine and everyday drinking practices, for deponents commonly offered a narrative in which it was 'just another day' of going about their ordinary routine – which often included a visit to the alehouse – when they witnessed something out of the ordinary.

Furthermore, the analysis offered here will be supplemented by another genre of source material that sheds light on routine drinking practices – diaries. The diary of Samuel Pepys famously records his regular visits to the inns, taverns and alehouses of Restoration London, and provides a fascinating insight into the practice of recreational drinking in our

[4] For more on what historians can learn from potentially 'unreliable' testimony see Natalie Zemon Davis, *Fiction in Archives: Pardon Tales and their Tellers in Sixteenth-Century France* (Stanford, 1987). For the application of these ideas to the English context see Malcolm Gaskill, 'Reporting Murder: Fiction in the Archives in Early Modern England', *Social History* 23 (1998), pp. 1–30; Tim Stretton, *Women Waging Law in Elizabethan England* (Cambridge, 1998), pp. 1–20; Laura Gowing, *Domestic Dangers: Women, Words and Sex in Early Modern London* (Oxford, 1999).

period.[5] Pepys's metropolitan world – and his regular if not exclusive movement in elite social circles – places his diary at somewhat of a remove from the relatively lowly and provincial alehouses that have been at the centre of this book, but whilst no diary can be taken to be broadly representative there are some 'village Pepyses' whose diaries provide valuable additional fragments of evidence about the social round in such institutions. A contemporary of Pepys, the Lancashire mercer's apprentice Roger Lowe, who we have met already, kept a diligent record of his alehouse visits in the 1660s, and the Yorkshire yeoman Adam Eyre kept a 'dyurnall' covering the years 1647–49 that likewise represents a valuable account of his routine alehouse recreation, and both will be drawn upon in what follows.[6] These various sources do not constitute an undistorted lens onto the 'reality' of alehouse sociability in practice, but taken in conjunction with each other and the good fellowship ballads explored in the previous chapter they allow us to sketch out, in a level of detail that is often thought beyond reach in the study of the cultural lives of non-elite men and women in this period, some of the key contours of an activity that was of central importance to many of those lives.

Many of the particular contours traced in this chapter have already been noted and explored in the previous chapter. The nature of the drinking rituals that took place in early modern English alehouses, and the meanings, values and appeal they held for a range of contemporaries, will continue to be central to the analysis. One particular, and highly significant, additional question will also, however, come increasingly into focus: what was the nature of the bonds that were forged through good fellowship? Were they significant social bonds that historians have

---

5   See Earnshaw, *The Pub in Literature*, ch. 5; Bernard Capp, 'Gender and the Culture of the Alehouse in Late Stuart England', in Anu Korhonen and Kate Lowe (eds), *The Trouble with Ribs: Women, Men and Gender in Early Modern Europe*, Collegium: Studies across Disciplines in the Humanities and Social Sciences 2 (Helsinki, 2007), pp. 103–27; Karl E. Westhauser, 'Friendship and Family in Early Modern England: The Sociability of Adam Eyre and Samuel Pepys', *Journal of Social History* 27 (1994), pp. 517–36; Ian Archer, 'Social Networks in Restoration London: The Evidence of Samuel Pepys's Diary', in Alexandra Shepard and Phil Withington (eds), *Communities in Early Modern England* (Manchester, 2000), pp. 76–94.

6   *Lowe*; Adam Eyre, 'A dyurnall, or catalogue of all my accions and expences from the 1st of January, 1646–[7]', ed. H.J. Morehouse, in *Yorkshire Diaries and Autobiographies in the Seventeenth and Eighteenth Centuries* (Durham, 1877) (hereafter *Eyre*). The value of these particular diaries for the study of alehouse sociability has been highlighted by Westhauser, 'Friendship and Family in Early Modern England', and A.L. Martin, 'Drinking and Alehouses in the Diary of an English Mercer's Apprentice, 1663–1674', in Holt (ed.), *Alcohol: A Social and Cultural History*, pp. 93–105.

injudiciously overlooked, or were they fleeting, frivolous and tangential, adding little meaning to contemporaries' lives? The previous chapter sought to uncover the appeal of alehouse sociability for the ordinary alehouse-goer, and argued that 'drink-as-despair' explanations fail to do justice to the positive appeal of the alehouse, which instead rested on a distinct idiom of good fellowship. Whilst this idiom was underpinned by a liberating logic, it does not suggest an alehouse culture that was unconstrained and free from ground rules. Instead instances of alehouse sociability were governed by a set of informal conventions and a politics of participation. These were focused on the politics of payment, a jovial disposition and liberal consumption, and these behavioural expectations were in turn shaped by more general cultural values relating to the pursuit of short-term contentment, attitudes to work, the expression of a range of masculine and feminine identities, and – increasingly as the seventeenth century passed – political allegiances. The implication here then is that alehouse sociability was emphatically not characterised by the absence of any convergence of interest between the parties involved. Nor was it an activity whose appeal lay ultimately in the fact that its relationships were ungrounded and ephemeral. Instead, it offered the opportunity to enter into meaningful bonds of what ballads termed good fellowship – to partake in a collective sociable activity that was based on agreed behavioural conventions and a shared cultural outlook. If alehouse sociability was based on the existence – rather than the absence – of shared values between fellow drinkers, this raises the question of the relative strength of the resulting bonds. How did ties between good fellows compare to, or overlap with, those between friends, families, kinsfolk and neighbours upon which this society put such emphasis?

The early modern period saw many debates about the nature of such relationships, with a crucial axis being that between 'instrumental' and 'affectionate' bonds.[7] Ballad evidence suggests that champions of good fellowship saw it essentially as an affectionate bond. The narrative voice of *A Health to all Good-Fellows* certainly suggested that genuine affection was felt between drinking companions: 'To those my good friends, my love so extends,/ I cannot truely expresse it.' If words were inadequate for demonstrating affection, the ballad suggested that another potent gesture could suffice: 'if neede be Ile pay for my friend'.[8] Considering the importance of paying one's share of the shot, a gesture such as this would

---

[7] Keith Thomas, *The Ends of Life: Roads to Fulfilment in Early Modern England* (Oxford, 2009), ch. 6.

[8] Roxburghe, 1.150 (1637).

no doubt have been significant. The message of *Heres to thee kind Harry* was not dissimilar. After delineating the many qualities that Harry, the ideal-type drinking companion, possessed, the ballad concluded with the lines, 'Each man pay the shot,/ What falls to his lot/ but I will pay for Harry.'[9] The implication was that a *bona fide* good fellow might expect to have the requirement to pay his own share waived to symbolise that his bonds with his fellow drinkers went beyond the instrumental.

Other ballads, though, were far more sceptical. A 1630 ballad entitled *A goodfellowes complaint against strong beere* warned against this very message. The narrator claimed that when he had money: 'Then would good fellowes to me say,/ Heere honest Jacke ile drinke to thee.' But when poverty ensued from his prodigal drinking, such friends did not last long:

> Now all is gone and nothing left,
> It is not as it was wont to be,
> Of all my friends I am bereft,
> O thus strong beere has undon me.[10]

A Laurence Price ballad, *Oh Gramercy Penny*, was narrated by a reformed good fellow, who warned that good fellowship was at its core a mercenary and duplicitous form of 'instrumental' relationship:

> I lite in a company lately by Fate,
> who scornfully me disdained,
> And that they were vext with a monylesse Mate,
> unto my face they complained:
> But when they thought I had money by'th pound,
> To make me most welcome, each of them was bound,
> Entreating me kindly to pledge them one round.[11]

These ballads suggest a widespread scepticism about the strength of bonds between good fellows in early modern England. Keith Thomas has argued that contemporaries generally believed that 'common familiarity and good fellowship' were not to be confused with proper friendship, and that the 'sharing of talk, news, drink, mixed together' was seen as mere

9   Pepys, 1.432 (1627).
10 Pepys, 1.438 (c.1630).
11 Pepys, 1.218 (c.1628).

acquaintance.[12] Thomas Young also cautioned that 'pot friendship, is no friendship'.[13]

Alexandra Shepard, on the other hand, has suggested that the fact that moralists worked so hard to characterise good fellowship as 'involving false bonds suggests that the opposite may well have been true for participants'. Shepard offers an alternative conceptualisation of the bonds between drinking companions that falls between mere acquaintance and fully-fledged friendship. She argues that bonds underpinning rituals of male drinking 'were often fleeting and transitory rather than deeply rooted in long-term relationships' and 'rather than offering opportunities for self-exploration and self-disclosure, the ties of what might be labelled "comradeship" in contrast to "friendship" were instead based on collective activity and the subordination of individual identities to the expectations of the group'. Ultimately 'comradeship' appealed to alehouse-going men 'not because it was an especially meaningful form of male subjectivity, but precisely because (albeit in carefully studied ways) it was not'.[14] This chapter will offer a rather different conclusion, arguing that good fellowship was more often than not both instrumental *and* affectionate – a combination that was not uncommon in early modern friendship – and that the resulting bonds between drinking companions should, in fact, be understood as a form of meaningful friendship.

The first section of what follows considers the social and gender profile of the participants in alehouse sociability. The second section examines evidence of the character of alehouse sociability and its rituals in practice, and considers areas of resonance and dissonance with the evidence derived from the ballad literature. The third section returns to the nature of the ties between drinking companions, arguing that these should be seen as a particularly meaningful form of social bond in early modern English society.

The profile of drinking companies

Historians have shown a great deal of interest in the social profile of alehouse patrons in early modern England. The best-known view on the subject is undoubtedly Peter Clark's assertion that the alehouse was

[12] Thomas, *The Ends of Life*, p. 196.
[13] See Shepard, '"Swil-bots and Tos-pots"', p. 119.
[14] *Ibid.*, pp. 120, 113, 126.

'run by the poor for the poor', and elements of this conclusion persist in recent work on the link between the vagrant poor and the alehouse.[15] This emphasis on poverty being the defining characteristic of the average alehouse-goer was also – as shown in Chapter 1 – a contemporary trope, but it has nonetheless been recently subject to revision. Scholars working in the European context have been prominent in questioning the long-standing emphasis on poverty, and recent work by Amanda Flather in particular has now provided a fresh perspective on the English context.[16] Flather counted and analysed every reference to individuals recorded as present in drinking establishments in depositions from the ecclesiastical, quarter sessions and borough courts of Essex between 1580 and 1640. Her breakdown of drinkers in alehouses – as opposed to inns and taverns – by social status is particularly interesting: of those men for whom a social status is provided 3% were gentry, 4% professionals, 12% yeomen, 20% husbandmen, 5% artisans, 26% servants, 19% labourers, and 10% victuallers.[17] If, following Flather, we take yeomen, husbandmen and artisans to represent the 'middling ranks of local society', they represent as much as 37% of the sample, with a further 7% of more 'elite' social status. Even if, following Peter Clark, we classify husbandmen as a group on the edge of poverty rather than as well established and prosperous householders, we can still point to a figure of close to 25% of the sample as individuals from the middling and upper ranks of society.[18] These suggestive figures resonate with the findings of previous chapters that there was a significant section of the middling ranks of many local communities who were more likely to patronise the alehouse than join a militant campaign against it.

This broadening out of the profile of the alehouse crowd can also be seen in recent work on the gender composition of its patrons. The early

---

15 Clark, 'The Alehouse and the Alternative Society', p. 53; Fumerton, 'Not Home'.

16 Amanda Flather, *Gender and Space in Early Modern England* (Woodbridge, 2007), pp. 110–21. For a summary of work on the profile of alehouse patrons that takes a European-wide focus see Beat Kümin, 'Public Houses and their Patrons in Early Modern Europe', in Kümin and Tlusty (eds), *The World of the Tavern*, pp. 44–62.

17 I have left out those of unknown social status from my percentages, so they are higher than Flather's calculations, which include them.

18 Clark, *The English Alehouse*, p. 125. Flather also provides figures for the social status of women in alehouses, based on information about their own or their husband's social status. Again, leaving out those of unknown status, and including husbandmen in the middling sort, the figures are 0% elite and 33% middling sort. There are also figures for those found in the joint category of 'Taverns/Inns': for men, 25% elite and 49% middling sort; for women, 28% elite and 38% middling sort.

social history of the alehouse tended to portray the institution as a 'male dominated milieu' which only featured a small minority of women at its margins.[19] Women working in alehouses have long been recognised as a key constituent of that minority, but female patrons were thought to be rare, and only ever present in a highly restricted set of circumstances which invariably involved accompaniment by an appropriate male chaperone – usually their husband. Women who were either unaccompanied, unmarried, or especially women who were both, are thought to have been 'vulnerable to defamatory attacks on their credit, accusations of adultery or even physical assault'.[20] This emphasis on the active exclusion of female patrons has been reasserted in some recent work on literary sources – as we saw in Chapter 3 – and in work on archival records. Shepard has suggested that one of the functions of the bonds of male 'camaraderie' was 'undoubtedly to exclude women'.[21] Others, though, have emphasised the broad range of uncontroversial contexts in which women could patronise alehouses, arguing that rites of passage celebrations, courtship activities for younger women, involvement in mixed companies of young friends, or even participation in a large all-female company of married women, were all circumstances in which women might legitimately make a visit to the alehouse without fear of reprisal, abuse or exclusion.[22] Beat Kümin has argued that women could and did go to alehouses more freely than even such conventions suggest, and without sanction: 'women did not need an excuse to visit public houses. Court records suggest that many simply enjoyed a sociable drink, behaving just as merrily and at times reprehensibly as male patrons.' Crucially, Kümin also argued that 'women did not get cited simply for attending, but for overindulgence and moral offences'.[23] This interpretation of alehouses as rather more open spaces for women to patronise helps to make sense of Flather's figures on the gender composition of the alehouse crowd in Essex: her sample suggested 36% of social visits to the

[19] Clark, The English Alehouse; Wrightson, 'Alehouses, Order and Reformation'. The quote is Barry Reay, 'Introduction: Popular Culture in Early Modern England', in Barry Reay (ed.), Popular Culture in Seventeenth-Century England (London, 1985), p. 11.
[20] On the 'select range of marital and vocational contexts' in which women attended alehouses see Brown, 'The Landscape of Drink', p. 208; Tlusty, Bacchus and Civic Order, pp. 138–45; Clark, The English Alehouse, pp. 131–2. The quotes are from Brown, p. 208.
[21] Shepard, '"Swil-bots and Tos-pots"', p. 126.
[22] Capp, 'Gender and the Culture of the Alehouse'.
[23] Kümin, Drinking Matters, p. 72.

alehouse were made by women and 62% by men.[24] If women made up a minority of the crowd that engaged in alehouse sociability, they were a significant and far from marginal one.

Taken together then there seems to be an increasingly compelling argument in recent work that the alehouse entertained 'a broad range of customers' of varying rank and gender.[25] There is an important caveat to this conclusion, however, for it should not be taken to mean that the alehouse was a space where distinctions of rank and gender were collapsed, and where a broad-based community of drinkers were united by bonds of good fellowship. Evidence suggests that in practice it was rare for all the patrons that were co-present in an alehouse to drink collectively. Instead, it was more usual for an alehouse crowd to be compartmentalised into smaller 'companies' of drinkers, and arguably it is more significant for understanding the sociology of alehouse-going to ask not who drank in alehouses, but rather who drank in alehouses *with whom*. A 'company' by 'company' approach – conducted below – may be the more appropriate way to approach the social profiling of alehouse patrons, and it demonstrates that whilst the alehouse crowd *as a whole* may have had a fairly extensive social profile, the profile of a given company was generally more restricted.

First, though, it is worth considering the average size of such a company. Clearly solitary drinking was not sociable drinking, and it should be noted that it appears to have been rare – except, perhaps, during more functional alehouse visits for refreshment or when travelling. That said, Roger Lowe only once mentioned going to the alehouse alone, and even then he made a joke of it by referring to himself in the third person, perhaps demonstrating that this represented unusual behaviour: 'att evening payr I went to the Alehouse with one Rogr Lowe and spent 4d'.[26] That extended visits to the alehouse and participating in company were virtually synonymous is also demonstrated in the fact that references to 'alehouse haunting' and 'company keeping' could be conflated in legal depositions. In 1656, John Salter, a parishioner of Wraxall, Somerset, disrupted divine service by making 'strange, ugly, mimicall faces and gestures' and pointing at the minister. Salter was suspected to have been drunk at the time and a fellow parishioner confirmed that 'the said Salter is a keeper of Company and haunt[er]

---

24 Flather, *Gender and Space*, pp. 112–13.

25 *Ibid.*, p. 110.

26 *Lowe*, pp. 51–2.

of alehouses'.[27] From the experiences of Roger Lowe and Adam Eyre it would seem that sociable alehouse drinking most commonly took place in groups of between two and four people. On roughly 70% of the occasions that Lowe recorded the numbers of his alehouse companions, he appears to have been drinking with just one or two others. Adam Eyre drank with one or two others on 50% of occasions, and with three companions on roughly 25% of occasions. The particularly active constables of the Wiltshire parish of Kingswood found a similar pattern in 1673. They made regular visitations to several local alehouses in attempts to catch men tippling at inappropriate times, and not without success, for they often found groups of drinkers that usually numbered two or three. On one Sunday they found three 'tipplers' whom the alewife had tried to conceal by shutting them up in her buttery, and on another they discovered 'two men a bed in time of divine service that had been there in her house all night'.[28]

It is also not unusual to find evidence of slightly larger drinking companies numbering five or six. On one August evening in 1663, Roger Lowe and three fellow parishioners were 'altogether in [an] Alehouse very merry' with 'Old Mr Woods', the nonconformist preacher who had 'come to town'.[29] In 1652, the constables of West Leigh, Lancashire, encountered a company of five 'good fellows' drinking in an alehouse after the cut-off time of 9.00p.m.[30] Less common were companies larger than this. At the 'Blackboy' in Ashcott, Somerset, in 1656, a deposition reveals that a company consisting of four named men – 'and severall other persons' – 'were there drinking'. This instance of alehouse sociability took place on 23 December though, and it may be that this was a festive occasion that had swelled the size of the company.[31] Eyre recorded in his diary a day of drinking in February of 1648 with a company that was unusually large by his standards, including at least five others – 'I met Mr Greaves of Tankersley, Mr Foljamb, Capt. Barber, my coz. Joseph, and Capt. Rich. I spent 7s, and so came home at night late' – but this meeting was for an 'ale' (a parish festival) and here too perhaps the occasion enlarged the size of the company.[32] In April 1654, Lowe went to an alehouse at 'Goose Greene' in a company comprising five named

27 SHC, Q/SR/93:2/171, 172.
28 WSHC, 1673/E/98.
29 Lowe, p. 26.
30 Wrightson, 'Two Concepts of Order', p. 21.
31 SHC, Q/SR/95:3/253.
32 Eyre, p. 97.

individuals 'and others'. On this occasion though several of the company were female, and it may be that instances of mixed-gender sociability also inflated the size of an average all-male drinking company.[33] Indeed, Eyre's largest-recorded alehouse company numbered eleven individuals, but this included five married couples.[34]

No doubt the total number of patrons in a given alehouse at one time often exceeded these numbers, but the crowd was usually subdivided. The dynamics of division can sometimes be glimpsed in diaries and depositions. On one November Sunday in 1666 Roger Lowe and his friend John Potter had travelled to hear a preacher, and afterwards sought refreshment in an alehouse. Yet, Lowe recalled, it 'was so thronged that we could not attain a fire to sit by but we sacrificed ourselves our twopenny flagon in a cold chamber'.[35] Clearly on this occasion the 'thronging' alehouse crowd was split into multiple companies huddling around separate fires or sitting in discrete chambers. This compartmentalising of the alehouse crowd may have been determined by the physical layout of the alehouse, with the limited amount of space beside each fire and in each chamber forcing Lowe and Potter into a cold corner.[36] It is also plausible that Lowe and Potter chose to set up their own distinct drinking company in their own cold chamber of their own accord, in preference to attempting to enter an existing company. Indeed, some drinking companies evidently chose to associate in a discrete chamber of their own. The Somerset men who, in 1620, met in an alehouse chamber to discuss their secret plot to travel to Tickenham to dig up a pot containing £500 in coin – rumoured to be buried on a hill there – wanted a suitably private environment to discuss their lucrative secret.[37]

If some companies had very practical reasons for separating their drinking off from the rest of the alehouse crowd, there is evidence that others formed distinct companies out of a desire to avoid drinking with certain individuals. In an incident in Fyfett, Somerset, in 1609, a minister was in company with 'diverse honest men', detailing how he had recently been the victim of several acts of poultry theft. Unexpectedly, the clergyman was met with a response by one Robert Parker and his associate William Burrell – who were according to the minister not

---

[33] *Lowe*, p. 58.

[34] *Eyre*, pp. 12–13.

[35] *Lowe*, pp. 108–9.

[36] For more on the ways in which the physical and material properties of drinking spaces could shape sociability see Brown, 'The Landscape of Drink', ch. 5.

[37] SHC, Q/SR/33/3, 4.

'of our company' – 'That it was no offence to take awaye a little needed preists cocke.' The ensuing dispute ended with Parker assaulting the minister and being bound over to keep the peace.[38] Here then there were two discrete companies in an alehouse, but they were in close enough proximity for one group to overhear the other and for insults to be exchanged between them. There was obviously enmity between Parker and the minister, and it seems plausible that the reason the two companies had not conflated into one was rather more to do with personal choices than with any spatial constraints. A similar incident occurred in Donyatt, another Somerset parish, in 1687. Edward Wilcox, a taylor, was 'drinking in company' with one Thomas Woodward, when one John Bond – 'being in the same roome drinking with some other company' – unexpectedly assaulted him: 'without any provocation ... [Bond] came up to him took him by the arme threw him on the ground and gave him severall violent blowes with his fist on his face'.[39] That Bond had been unprovoked at the time suggests that his animosity to Wilcox pre-dated this incident, and again it seems plausible that the two men had been drinking in distinct companies out of a conscious choice to avoid each other.

A similar dynamic was at work in the formation of company in a case from Bowdon, Cheshire, in 1626. James Berech and Philip Ashton entered the alehouse of Widow Barrington, where William Cottrell was drinking. Cottrell later deposed that upon entering 'Ashton asked the said Widow Barrington whether she had noe better Companie to be with her then [Cottrell] and comanded [tha]t she should putt [Cottrell] out of her house for he could not endure the sight of him, calling [Cottrell] pockie rogue and offering many other disgracefull speaches against him.' Ashton then struck Cottrell and drew a knife on him, which prompted Cottrell to remove himself from Ashton's company and to set up in a separate chamber. Here too the depositions surrounding the case reveal pre-existing animosity between the two men.[40] A defamation case from Eastbourne, Sussex, from 1613, reveals a company of women who had gone into an alehouse one Sunday 'to drink after evening prayer' and to 'make merry'. When Mercy Locke sought to join them she was challenged by an existing member of the company, Margaret Grovett, who demanded, 'Thou wilt not sit down, wilt thou?' Mercy Locke retorted,

38 SHC, Q/SR/6/95.
39 SHC, Q/SR/171/9.
40 CRO, QJF/55/1/39.

'Indeed, I have forsaken much company for your sake, but I will do so no more.' Grovett had railed at Locke on previous occasions, and had apparently succeeded in excluding her from company before. Locke was not, however, going to be deterred on this occasion. But neither was Grovett, who proceeded to denounce Mercy Locke as a brazen whore for seducing her husband, revealing once again the personal animosity that often underpinned the creation of distinct drinking companies with forcefully policed boundaries of participation.[41] These cases provide us then with a vision of the alehouse crowd divided into small subsets of company, sometimes in separate rooms and chambers, and at others cheek-by-jowl but nonetheless in discrete groups within the same room. Co-presence in the alehouse did not, then, equate directly with co-presence in company. Instead, decisions about entering into the latter appear highly charged and personalised, and resulted in the often uneasy fragmentation of the alehouse crowd into relatively small groups.

Such groups were, more often than not, comprised of individuals of similar social status, though there is some evidence of mixing between social groups. As we saw in Chapter 2, a yeoman of Shenfields, Essex, was reprimanded by a fellow yeoman for keeping company with his social inferiors in an alehouse in 1628.[42] At the 'Sign of the Angel' in Warminster in 1683, a drinking company consisted of Thomas Morris, described as a gentleman, John Kerlye, a tailor, Richard Horler, a cloth worker, Nicolas Bolton, a butcher, and John Hawkins, an innkeeper.[43] The presence of a gentleman amongst a group of tradesmen – a more conventional alehouse type – may perhaps be explained by the fact that this was likely an inn rather than a humble alehouse (given that an innkeeper was present), and examples of gentlemen drinking in inns and taverns, as Flather's figures would suggest, are fairly common.[44] We do catch glimpses of them mixing with other classes in more humble establishments too. In June 1629, at Rayleigh, Essex, three gentlemen, Edward Bury, Thomas Pynson and Thomas Roone, spent the evening getting 'excessively drunk' with William Tylford, a labourer, at the

---

[41] Capp, *When Gossips Meet*, p. 212.

[42] ERO, Q/SR/262/80, and p. 000 above.

[43] WSHC, 1683/T/115.

[44] For examples see SHC, Q/SR/10/27–29; *Read. Boro. Recs*, III, pp. 464–5. The first of these involves a gun-and-sword fight outside a Yeovil inn in 1610, and the latter instance involved a riot over a dog at the George Inn, Reading, in 1639. Not only, then, did the gentry engage in recreational drinking, they often did so in ways that were just as unruly as those that they criticised their poorer countrymen and women for.

latter's alehouse, before the company went on to assault another local man William Terry.[45] In Carlisle, in 1689, two Scottish lairds drinking in an alehouse 'desired' the alewife, Jane Wallas, to 'sit downe and drinke with them'.[46] In both of these instances it was lower-status victuallers, rather than other patrons, who were able to participate in company with their superiors, and it seems likely that even this occurrence was fairly unusual. When Jane Wallas offered testimony that the lairds had proposed a health to the recently deposed King James, she recalled that the proposal had come from 'the person who had a laced coat, and who is called Laird of Stableton'. That the gentleman's fine coat had stuck vividly in her memory suggests such close encounters with social elites were particularly noteworthy. Alice Ballson, who was patronising a Dorset alehouse on New Year's Eve of 1624 when a fight broke out, was able to recall in remarkable detail the arrival at the establishment of a gentleman: 'there came in a gent in a green sattin doublett cutt and buttoned, and a scarfe about his necke, but noe sword hanginge in it'.[47] If the gentry made regular appearances in taverns and inns, and even on occasions mixed with lower-status clientele there, their irregular presence in an alehouse was an occurrence that left a deep impression.

If the gentry and the professional classes were rarely members of alehouse companies, the substantial yeomen farmers that made up such a crucial component of the local middling sort in many communities appear in alehouse company more often. Generally, however, they appear to have drunk amongst their own. Thomas Hanbury, John Tabor and Daniel Wiltshire, who were presented to the Essex quarter sessions in 1630 'for drinking and tippling at Thomas Mayes, one of our alehouses, at an unseasonable time about 10 of the clock at night', were a company consisting exclusively of Terling yeomen.[48] A company of two yeomen were 'in an alehouse in West Tilbury [Essex] drinking and talking in friendly manner' in an incident in 1650, when one accidentally shot and killed the other whilst jesting with a 'birding peece'.[49] At Hornchurch, in the same county, in 1686, the two yeomen John Tuttle and John Ballard were 'in company' with one another at 'the Red Lyon'.[50] Those designated with lower ranks of status likewise tend to appear in the

[45] ERO, 268/54, 55.
[46] *York Cast. Deps*, nos. CCLXIII, CCLXXL.
[47] Bettey (ed.), *The Case Book of Sir Francis Ashley*, pp. 81–2.
[48] ERO, Q/SR, 271/35, and p. 100 above.
[49] ERO, T/A 418/136/15.
[50] ERO, Q/SR, 449/92.

records primarily as drinking with their peers: a company of four men all described as husbandmen stopped off in a drinking establishment on the way back from a market at Knutsford, Cheshire, in 1684.[51] Two labourers from Great Clacton, Essex, were together at an alehouse 'in company' one Sunday in 1609 – before stealing some geese from a husbandman on their way home.[52] In 1629, at Peter de Cort's alehouse in Moulsham, Essex, two labourers were found drinking together and playing at 'slide groat'.[53] Such descriptors could, of course, obscure important differentials of wealth and status that were meaningful within a local community: two husbandmen could have quite divergent land holdings, or two labourers significant earning differentials, but it remains the case that sizeable distinctions in socio-economic status between drinking companions are rarely explicitly identified in these sources.

A similar pattern can be observed in relation to the more specific use of occupational descriptors. Alice Ballson described 'two Tinkers sittinge by the fyer drinkinge' before the well-dressed gentleman arrived at the Dorset alehouse on New Year's Eve of 1624.[54] A company of tailors mused on the downfall of the King over drinks in an establishment in Wells in 1649; another company of the same trade discussed the Monmouth Rebellion over glasses of ale in a Newcastle alehouse in 1685.[55] Two weavers kept company together at 'Symons alehouse' in Reading in 1623.[56] Tradesmen are not only identified as drinking with those of the same occupation though, and we commonly find companies that included men working in closely related trades or even different – though similar status – occupations.[57] In Wrington, Somerset, in 1663, a dyer and a cloth worker drank 'in Company', and in Rochford, Essex, in 1686 a tailor and a 'webster' (weaver) were drinking in an alehouse when the tailor expressed his view that the King was a Jesuit.[58] We find a yeoman and a blacksmith in company, and falling out over a claim that the Duke of Monmouth lived, in an alehouse in Kirkby Ravensworth,

---

51 CRO, QJF/112/3/140.

52 ERO, Q/SR/189/25.

53 ERO, Q/SR/267/20, and p. 000 above.

54 Bettey (ed.), *The Case Book of Sir Francis Ashley*, pp. 81–2.

55 SHC, Q/SR/81/87. *York Cast. Deps*, no. CCXLVI.

56 *Read. Boro. Recs*, II, pp. 143–4.

57 See Hailwood, 'Sociability, Work and Labouring Identity'; Hailwood, 'The Honest Tradesman's Honour'.

58 SHC, Q/SR/103/8; ERO Q/SR/449/85.

Yorkshire, in 1687.[59] In 1685, in the Wiltshire parish of North Bradley, a labourer and a brazier were drinking companions, and in one instance in Great Ilford, Essex, in the same year, a brickmaker and a warrener were 'drinking in company with some other men'.[60] Again, finer gradations of status within these trades are not discernible in these cases, but the dominant pattern that emerges is of small companies consisting of men of similar socio-economic status. Alehouse companies tended to be composed of relative peers, and in many cases were built upon occupational ties.

Historiographical preoccupation with the socio-economic status of alehouse patrons has arguably led to a relative neglect of other factors that linked those who chose to drink together. Ties of kinship, for instance, often operated within drinking companies. In 1625 the brothers Robert and Thomas Talbott, of Upwey, Dorset, had been together in an alehouse shortly before abusing the local constable, calling him a 'black rogue and black knave' whilst 'beating their breeches' and bidding him to 'come and kiss their tayles'.[61] In January of 1663 Roger Lowe went to an alehouse with his brother, and in March 1665 he and two companions went with 'Mr Edwrd Byrom and his two brothers . . . to an Ale house where we stayd drinkeinge a good while'.[62] Sibling socialising was not exclusively conducted between brothers. On Christmas Eve of 1681 Soloman Reddatt went to the 'sign of the Naggs Head' in Reading with 'his sister Elizabeth Reddatt, and George Parfitt'.[63] Tristram Strang and his sister Elizabeth were drinking at an alehouse in Stogursey, Somerset, in 1600.[64] In April of 1664 Lowe was invited to go to the alehouse with Ann Taylor and Elizabeth Taylor. The Taylor sisters had perhaps sought out Lowe as an 'approved male escort', for examples of sisters drinking together without male friends or relatives present are elusive.[65]

Husbands and wives drinking together represent the most common form of mixed-gender company amongst relatives. In 1656, a group comprising of two married couples and three single men visited a Lancashire alehouse and spent their time listening to a fiddler whilst they

[59] *York Cast. Deps*, no. CCLVIII.

[60] *Wilts. Q.S. Recs*, p. 271; ERO, Q/SR/449/87.

[61] Bettey (ed.), *The Case Book of Sir Francis Ashley*, p. 87.

[62] *Lowe*, pp. 14, 81.

[63] WSHC, D1/39/1/57/fols 132r–133r.

[64] SHC, D/D/Cd/32, Waterman v Elsworthie.

[65] *Lowe*, p. 58.

drank 'all the ale in the house'.[66] Roger Lowe spent an evening 'making merry' with John Hasleden and his wife Izibell in October of 1663, and in July 1666, 'Mr Hopwood and his wife' sent for Lowe to join them at John Jenkinson's alehouse.[67] In Lowe's social circle the practice of married couples drinking together appears to have been a fairly routine aspect of alehouse sociability, but this was not everywhere the case. Adam Eyre recorded taking his wife to an alehouse in 1647, where they met with three other married couples 'to be merry', but this reference to the presence of his wife in an alehouse was unique.[68] Indeed, Eyre had been forced to make a special arrangement to borrow a horse to carry himself and his wife there, and such a joint outing may have represented a special occasion rather than a social norm. In his more routine alehouse sociability Eyre kept company only with other men. As the contrasting experiences of Lowe and Eyre suggest, the regular presence of married couples in alehouses undoubtedly varied from one community or social circle to the next.

Kinship ties beyond the immediate relations of marriage or siblinghood also played a part in the formation of company.[69] Roger Lowe and his brother 'met Cozen Hugh Lowe' and went to the alehouse in January of 1663, and for his thirty-third birthday Adam Eyre went to hear a sermon before going to an alehouse where he 'drunk with my father-in-law and my coz'.[70] After the christening of his brother's child in October of 1664 Lowe, who was 'ingaged to be the one godfather', and Raph Falster, who was the other, 'stayd and drunke' all afternoon in an alehouse.[71] Maids and servants – considered in the period as kin of the broader 'household-family' in which they lived and worked – could also be included in company: Lowe and a male friend went to the alehouse with Anne Woods and her maid in January of 1665.[72] Such servants also formed companies of their own. On a Sunday in September 1664 Lowe 'was with Mr Sorowcold's servents in Ale house, and was merry'.[73] After a long day

---

66 Martin, *Alcohol, Sex and Gender*, p. 75; Clark, *The English Alehouse*, p. 131.

67 *Lowe*, pp. 42–3, 104.

68 *Eyre*, pp. 12–13.

69 See also the evidence from Pepys's diary: Archer, 'Social Networks in Restoration London', pp. 87–8.

70 *Lowe*, p. 14; *Eyre*, pp. 28–9.

71 *Lowe*, p. 74.

72 Naomi Tadmor, 'The Concept of the Household-Family in Eighteenth-Century England', *Past and Present* 151 (1996), pp. 111–40; *Lowe*, p. 79.

73 *Lowe*, p. 71.

of threshing in the August of 1615, Thomas Norman, a day labourer of Cerne Abbas, Dorset, invited his master's servant, Agnes Fiven, to join him and other 'young men and maids' to play cards and 'drinke and make merry with them' at a nearby alehouse.[74] Merriment between kinship groups was not always the preserve of the young, however, and inter-generational kinship-based companies also appear regularly in the records. We have seen that Adam Eyre drank with his father-in-law, and in February 1663 Roger Lowe went to the alehouse together with 'old John Jenkins and his soun Matthew'.[75] The company of Tickenham gold-diggers who had sought out a private chamber included a father and son, and the hell-raising Cheshire constable John Crosbie – encountered in Chapter 2 – visited the alehouse with his two sons, and ordered them to beat up an alehousekeeper.[76] Masters and mistresses might also on occasion drink together with their servants or apprentices, as in the case of Anne Woods and her maid, or an instance in Nantwich, Cheshire, in 1675, when a 22-year-old servant-in-husbandry and his master shared a drink 'at the signe of the Swanne' one Sunday.[77] As often as not though alehouse-going was a source of tension between master and apprentice: in 1633 the shoemaker Thomas Richards complained to the corporation in Reading that the alehousekeeper Symon Cane had allowed his apprentice to spend 10s 8d of his master's money, and had helped to conceal the offending apprentice in a cupboard when his master came to the alehouse to search for him.[78] An apprentice butcher from Moulsham, Essex, who ran away from an unpopular master in 1609, was found to have escaped to 'spend and play' for several days in a series of alehouses.[79]

If ties of kinship, service and apprenticeship played a key determining role in the composition of alehouse company, the role of neighbourhood is more ambiguous. The Somerset husbandman Thomas Cordent, who was a witness to the defamatory words spoken in an alehouse in Stogursey in 1600, deposed that he had been in Waterman's drinking establishment as he lived nearby and had 'for neighbourhood's sake' gone

[74] Bettey (ed.), *The Case Book of Sir Francis Ashley*, pp. 12–13. See also Steve Hindle, 'Below Stairs at Arbury Hall: Sir Richard Newdigate and his Household Staff, c.1670–1710', *Historical Research* 85 (2012), p. 82.

[75] *Lowe*, pp. 14–15.

[76] CRO, QJF/38/3/5, and pp. 86, 183 above.

[77] CRO, QJF/103/4/64.

[78] *Read. Boro. Recs*, III, pp. 186–7.

[79] ERO, Q/SR/189/28.

to drink with Waterman to 'keep him company'.[80] Roger Lowe also specified a number of instances of alehouse sociability that had been motivated by 'neighbourliness': in February of 1664 Thomas Atherton was
moving away from the neighbourhood, so Lowe 'was envited amongst
neighbours to go to the alehouse to drinke' to bid him farewell.[81] In April
of that year he recorded that 'the neighbourhood of Ashton [his home
town] envited me to goe with them to the Ale house this eveninge',
and on 7 October he 'was this night with Townmen of Ashton in Ale
house'.[82] Neighbours not only came together in company at their 'local';
an encounter with a neighbour on the road often led to the sharing
of a drink. In the May of 1665 Lowe had been travelling across Orrell
Moor, near Wigan, in the rain, when he 'mett with Devid Pendlebery,
an Ashton man', who he asked to join him for a 'flaggon' at 'Skenneing
John's', a nearby alehouse.[83] In 1656 a Somerset husbandman, Andrew
Miller, was attending the market at Glastonbury when he 'mett accidentally with one William Willis who together with [Miller] about one yeare
before lived in Croscombe ... whereupon the said William Willis desired
this exam[inate] to drink with him'.[84] Neighbours, even ex-neighbours,
might then go drinking together.

But in the case of both Lowe and Eyre drinking companions were
more often than not drawn from a wider network that extended beyond
the local village or parish. Lowe recorded making trips to the alehouse
with friends and acquaintances who had 'come to town' more often than
he mentioned drinking with his Ashton neighbours, and both Lowe and
Eyre regularly travelled to meet companions in alehouses outside of their
immediate locale. We have seen already that Eyre needed to borrow a
horse to carry himself and his wife to meet their friends at an alehouse,
and on one particularly boozy day out – 26 December 1647 – Eyre and a
fellow parliamentary soldier went 'to Thurleston, and there spent 4d; to
Cawthorn, and there spent 6d. Thence wee went by Rawroyd and called
on Capt. Shirt, who was gone before, and so meeting with my leiftenant
and cornett, wee went together to Netherton, and so to Bradford, in
all 16 myles; and there I spent 6d.'[85] Good fellows could, then, be a
relatively peripatetic breed, and we should not necessarily imagine the

80 SHC, D/D/Cd/32, Waterman v Elsworthie.
81 *Lowe*, p. 52.
82 *Lowe*, pp. 58, 74.
83 *Lowe*, p. 84.
84 SHC, Q/SR/95:2/133.
85 *Eyre*, p. 82.

alehouse as the locus for the tightly knit local community that the 'local' village pub is often hailed as in the modern era. Drinking companies were often constructed around ties that stretched over a wider network of neighbouring villages and market towns. We might, then, understand the role of 'neighbourhood' or 'locality' in shaping drinking companies to refer to this wider vicinity, rather than referring necessarily to proximate habitation in the same settlement or parish.

Travelling home after a bout of extramural drinking, either on foot or by horse, could be hazardous. In 1686 two husbandmen from Grays Thurrock, Essex, had to answer to the authorities after Henry Ruffin 'was lately slain by a fall from his horse occasioned by excess of drinking in their company'.[86] Some chose instead to take advantage of the lodging facilities that alehouses were required to offer. After his Boxing Day exploits Adam Eyre opted to 'lay all night at widow Thorpe's house' rather than attempt to journey home. John Lufkin, with whom this chapter opened, lodged overnight at the alehouse despite 'his own house being not above one quarter of a mile distant from the said alehouse'.[87] Such behaviour blurred the lines between the 'local' patrons of alehouses and those 'wayfaring people' for whom such accommodation was – as we saw in Chapter 1 – intended to cater, and many of the individuals who frequented alehouses would have been neither local parishioners nor longer-distance travellers, but people from nearby towns and villages. This practice was common enough that such patrons were likely to have been familiar faces to alehousekeepers: Lowe certainly knew the names of the proprietors, and made regular visits to, those alehouses within the wider network of towns and villages that he socialised in: Humphrey Cowley's alehouse at Billinge (roughly four miles from Ashton), William Anderton's at Pemberton (five miles), Skenneing John's at Orrell Moor (six miles).

Where though, if at all, did more genuine 'wayfarers' and 'strangers' – those without a firm connection to the locale in which they sought to patronise an alehouse – fit into the profile of alehouse companies? As we saw in Chapter 1 the two seamen who stopped to lodge at an alehouse in Shrewton, Wiltshire, in 1654, en route from Plymouth to Portsmouth, were bought drinks by a local husbandman, William Richards, who himself 'had a son at sea' – though the strangers quickly fell under suspi-

86 ERO, Q/SR, 354/84.
87 ERO, Q/SR, 170/3.

cion when Richards found that money had gone missing from his purse.[88] Thomas Jones – a 'singleman', with no home parish stated – stopped over to lodge at the alehouse of William Tomalin in Ramsden Bellhouse, Essex, in November 1677, where he 'called for a quart of beer, a penny loaf and a pennyworth of cheese and went to bed'. This functional and solitary experience was no doubt common for the lone traveller, but the following morning when Jones 'rose and was going away ... company coming in stopped him'. Jones ended up spending two further nights at the alehouse, subsequently spending 'all his money which was 5s. 5d'. Left in desperate poverty, Jones, 'being drove to necessity', attempted to steal a sheet off the bed by stuffing it in his trousers, an act that did not go unnoticed by the alehousekeeper.[89] The details of his drinking companions, and further detail about Jones, do not survive, but it seems plausible that here was a poor traveller who was nonetheless able to fall into the kind of sustained bout of good fellowship with which this chapter opened, among a group of men not previously known to him.

Of course, there may have been a mercenary motive at work behind this warm embrace of a stranger. John Coulsborrough, a royal messenger, was travelling through Wiltshire in 1617 when he stopped to lodge for the night at Widow Lunnatt's 'contry alehowse' in Ramsbury. Coulsborrough was invited to join in company with one Robert Humphries, a tinker, but this seemingly friendly encounter soon escalated into a bout of heavy gambling in which the tinker sought to fleece Coulsborrough, and threatened to strike him with a candlestick if he would not pay up.[90] That lone travellers – whether poor or in the King's employ – needed to be cautious about the company they kept is clear from the fact that Humphries demanded to know of Coulsborrough 'which way he rodd[e] the next morninge' and threatened to 'beat him and way lay him' on the road. One way to mitigate such risks was for those travelling from place to place to form companies with other travellers that endured both in the alehouse and on the road. In 1682 there were a number of sightings in the alehouses of Taunton of a 'strange woman' – suspected of stealing a gold ring from a local shop – who kept company with two male 'strangers' from Gloucester and 'did ride behind one of the men upon his ... horse'.[91] Three unemployed weavers who had each been independently

88 WSHC, 1654/M/200, and p. 41 above.
89 ERO, Q/SR, 438/86, 87.
90 *Wilts. Q.S. Recs*, p. 59.
91 SHC, Q/SR/152/4, 9.

'travelinge the cuntry to seeke worke' were found together in a Reading alehouse one night in 1623, and were accused of recently ganging together to beg and commit a string of thefts.[92] A Yorkshire-born spinster, Agnes Gregory, was also apprehended by the Reading authorities that year after joining in company with a group of travellers that moved from alehouse to alehouse, led by a suspected criminal known as 'Hampshire Will'.[93]

The archival record undoubtedly privileges those instances in which travellers in alehouses were met with suspicion and wariness, and it is possible that many received a warm welcome into company in the alehouses where they stopped overnight for beer, bread and a bed. Nonetheless, such examples are elusive even in the diary sources that offer us an insight into those more routine aspects of alehouse sociability that might fall below the radar of legal sources. It is surely telling that neither Lowe nor Eyre record drinking in company with complete strangers. It was not unheard of, but the picture that emerges from these records is one in which alehouse encounters between travellers and people from the 'local' vicinity – which included nearby towns and villages – were generally fraught, and there is a strong sense that 'strangers' and 'locals' formed distinct, rather than overlapping, drinking companies.

As the example of Agnes Gregory and Hampshire Will attests, contexts in which men and women might be found in mixed-gender company were not confined to those instances bound by kinship and marriage discussed above. Whilst these were perhaps the most common forms of bond that brought men and women into contact in the alehouse, they were certainly not essential prerequisites for mixed-gender company.[94] In November of 1663 Lowe was 'ingaged into Compenie' with Ann Barrow and James Naylor, none of whom were related to each other, and a year later drank in the Ashton alehouse 'Tankerfield's' with Richard Weinwright, Peter Buckstone and Ellin Scott, the latter of whom had come to town, seemingly alone, from nearby Bamfurlong (2.5 miles).[95] It may be that such instances of company involved courtship – another of the acceptable contexts for female patronage of alehouses – but this was not necessarily the case. In November 1663 Lowe noted in his diary that 'Jane Wright Mr Sorowcolds maid came to towne'. He bought her ale,

---

[92] *Read. Boro. Recs*, II, pp. 143–5.

[93] *Ibid.*, pp. 146–9.

[94] On mixed-gender sociability see also Archer, 'Social Networks in Restoration London', pp. 89–90.

[95] *Lowe*, pp. 43–4, 75.

and they 'ware very merry togather'. But the two seem to have simply been friends, rather than courting, for Lowe spent the remainder of the day's diary entry musing on his prospects with his two love interests Mary Naylor and Emm Potter.[96] In another instance of Lowe's alehouse company, in the March of 1664, there was certainly not a backdrop of respectable courtship: 'John Naylor's wife came to town and wish me to goe with her to Alehouse. I went.'[97] Here too, it seems, was a case of acquainted men and women drinking together without any ties of kinship, marriage or courtship.

This can be seen in a detailed church court case from Chester, in 1625, involving one Elizabeth Case. Case was a married woman, but from whom her husband was seeking the early modern English equivalent of a divorce in the sense of permission from the church to live separately. She regularly entered into alehouse company with unrelated men without her husband. Indeed, on one occasion at the alehouse of Henry Trafford she was invited to join in company with three men known to her who were already there, and she drank with them and remained with them as long as they stayed at the house. The three men later decided to relocate to the Swan in Foregate Street, and asked Elizabeth Case to go with them. She refused to be seen entering with them, but told them she would follow them later, arrive at the house proclaiming she was looking for her husband, and that they should then 'entreate her to sit down'. The plan went off without a hitch, and she sat with the men drinking 'until tenn of the clocke in the evening'.[98] This intriguing ploy suggests that a married woman could not always keep company among unrelated acquaintances with complete impunity, as does the fact that reports of this event were being collected as evidence of inappropriate behaviour for a married woman. Nonetheless, that Case was invited by the men to join them, that she did so, and that the pretence that this was a chance rather than premeditated encounter seemed worth cultivating, all point to the constraints on such behaviour being relative rather than absolute. It was not essential to have a related male chaperone, and in these cases ties of neighbourhood and acquaintance within a broadly conceived 'local' area again appear to have been an important factor in the composition of company. Neither single nor married women could enter into company as freely as men – a point to which we will return below – but

---

[96] *Lowe*, p. 45.

[97] *Ibid.*, p. 75.

[98] Addy, *Sin and Society*, pp. 189–95.

both participated in mixed alehouse companies that were by no means exclusively underpinned by ties of kinship and marriage.

If the range of ties that could underpin mixed-gender alehouse sociability was rather wider than the traditional historical orthodoxy allows, the degree of freedom afforded to women does not appear to have permitted the routine formation of all-female companies. Such instances are relatively rare in the records. It was not unheard of – we have seen above the case of the Sussex wives who went to the alehouse to 'make merry' after church in 1613 – but its occurrence does seem to have been limited in a number of respects, and there is some evidence that reinforces ballad representations of all-female sociability as occasional rather than regular. In early-seventeenth-century Twickenham, Middlesex, a group of women rioters met in an alehouse a year to the day after their protest, to boast of a 'valiant' deed worthy to be remembered 'in the Chronicles', and promised to hold a feast yearly for remembrance sake.[99] It is possible that all-female sociability was generally limited to special occasions such as this, though market days in some cases provided a more common 'occasion' for women to gather. In 1623 Elizabeth Wilson, of West Ham, deposed in a church court case that her routine was to bring her family's produce to sell at market in London, and at the end of the day's business she would drink a pint of wine with her 'friends' at the Kings Head before travelling home.[100]

Such behaviour may – in line with ballad evidence – have been more common in London and its environs than elsewhere, and Bernard Capp has found that female 'London street sellers, an independent breed, clearly enjoyed an alehouse culture which paralleled that of men', and that 'in London and perhaps other large towns women might drink together in alehouses or taverns on any day of the week'.[101] One example reveals three women who shared 'a pott of beere or two' in Hackney in 1590, and another a company of sailors' wives drinking together – on Twelfth Night, another festive occasion – at 'the Signe of the Unicorne' in Limehouse in 1670.[102] Yet if all-female drinking companies were a

[99] John Walter, 'Faces in the Crowd: Gender, Youth and Age in Early Modern Protest', in Helen Berry and Elizabeth Foyster (eds), *The Family in Early Modern England* (Cambridge, 2007), p. 123.

[100] Flather, *Gender and Space*, p. 117.

[101] Capp, *When Gossips Meet*, pp. 331–2.

[102] Gowing, *Domestic Dangers*, p. 241; London Metropolitan Archives, Diocese of London, Consistory Court, DL/C 236. My thanks to Professor Keith Wrightson for providing the reference to, and a transcription of, this example.

feature of the cultural world of London's alehouses, in the rural parishes and small market towns with which this book is concerned 'the alehouse remained primarily a milieu for men, courting couples, and sometimes mixed groups of friends'.[103] Despite their regular participation in mixed-gender alehouse sociability there is little evidence to suggest that women routinely frequented the alehouse in single-sex groups.

The practice of good fellowship

If the social and gender profile of alehouse companies bore a number of similarities to their depiction in good fellowship ballads, what about their character? What were the rituals around which bouts of drinking were structured and what were the meanings and values attached to drinking practices? The valorisation of heavy drinking is one aspect of the ballad idiom of good fellowship that was undoubtedly also manifested in its practice. A considerable amount of alcohol was consumed by two Somerset men who went drinking one Sunday afternoon in Nettlecombe in 1663. They started in one alehouse with 'a Jugg of Beer & from thence they went into a weyne house', where they 'drank about 2 or 3 juggs of beer', before continuing on to Chrystable Baker's alehouse where they continued 'drinkeinge for [th]e space of 2 houres'.[104] Three Dorchester men managed a similar Sunday session in 1617, spending nearly eight shillings – perhaps as much as two weeks' income for a wage labourer – on beer and tobacco in a single sitting that stretched from before morning prayer well into the evening.[105] Roger Lowe occasionally indulged in an all-day drinking session on a Sunday, and he recalled a time in 1663 when he spent 'all afternoone in [the] ale house'. One Monday night in 1664 Lowe 'was with John Potter with his friends that ware come from Winwicke in John Jenkins [an Ashton alehouse] I spent 10d and far in night I went to bed'.[106] Lowe may have consumed as many as ten pints of ale during this particular late-night binge. The alehouse-haunting constable John Lufkin, as we have seen, was reported to have been involved in many excessive drinking sessions in 1604. These often appear to have included drinking contests. In addition to

---

[103] Capp, *When Gossips Meet*, pp. 331–2.

[104] SHC, Q/SR/104/5.

[105] Cited in Shepard, '"Swil-bots and Tos-pots"', p. 111. See also Bettey (ed.), *The Case Book of Sir Francis Ashley*, p. 45.

[106] *Lowe*, pp. 26, 75.

the instance described above when he and Marsh attempted to drain 'Fowler', complainants against Lufkin reported an occasion when he had goaded fellow parishioner Henry Addams into a bout of competitive drinking, only to later confess – after he was spotted 'drying his hat by the fire, being within all wet' – that he had been surreptitiously pouring his own drink into his headgear.[107] An example from 1619 suggests that George Taylor, an alehousekeeper from Northfield, Worcestershire, was also keen on drinking contests, and 'falls out with his neighbours if they will not carouse and drink full cups with him calling them cowards and many other base words'.[108]

If refusing to imbibe liberally brought on accusations of cowardice, being renowned as a heavy drinker was a reputation good fellows could own with pride. A Nottingham man, known as Martin, was reported to the borough authorities in 1599 as the principal 'drawer on of drunkards togeather in this towne', a role and reputation that it was claimed he 'delytes cheifely in'.[109] The ability to consume heavily might even be respected in a female drinker, and the men with whom Elizabeth Case drank in Chester deposed, in a seemingly admiring tone, that although she had consumed a considerable quantity of drink in their company, she 'did speak directly and did goe [home] of herself' at the end of the evening. On another occasion she had been in company with Thomas Cowper, a shoemaker, and John Minshall, an ironmonger, during which time they consumed between six and nine pints of wine – they could not remember exactly – in a session that went on until 11.00p.m. Cowper described Elizabeth as 'somewhat spent in drinke' and offered to help her home, but as a matter of principle she refused, declaring that 'she scorned to be brought home', and was determined to show she had enough control to manage the journey unassisted. It seems as though she in fact fell and hurt her face, but it was clearly important to Elizabeth Case, as it was to many a ballad good fellow, not only to drink liberally but to insist on being able to do so without losing control.[110]

Indeed, the acknowledgement of a fine line between an optimum level of intoxicated merriment on the one hand and a descent into drunken oblivion on the other was an important feature of good fellowship.[111]

---

107 ERO, Q/SR 170/3.
108 *Worc. Q.S. Recs*, p. 310.
109 *Nott. Boro. Recs*, IV, p. 249.
110 Addy, *Sin and Society*, pp. 189–95.
111 See Hailwood, "'It puts good reason into brains'".

John Lufkin's drinking companion Thomas Marsh, who sat foaming at the mouth in his own effluent, was not alone in bringing shame upon himself for crossing that threshold. Adam Eyre regularly engaged in long bouts of alehouse sociability, but he too accepted that on rare occasions he had over-indulged. After going to church one morning in March of 1648 he confessed in his diary: 'I spent (God forgive mee) the after-noone in the alehouse, and spent in all 2s 6d … I had abused myself in drinking. God have mercy on me.' After his outing to an 'ale' the previous month he likewise noted that 'This day I abused myselfe with too much drink, God have mercy on mee and forgive mee.'[112] Eyre seems to have crossed this line only occasionally, for the many other instances in which he spent considerable time and money in the alehouse were recorded with no such admonishment. These more successful visits, for both Eyre and Lowe, were invariably described as 'merry', and the distinction between being 'merry' and having too much appears to have been a widely recognised idiom. In 1628, two deponents from court cases in Essex made explicit use of it: Grace Field admitted 'that some tymes she is merrie amongst her friends, and that one tyme she was somewhat overcome with drinkinge to[o] much'; William Hasley declared 'that some tymes hee is meerye but never so ill but that he can give a man an answer and to goe about his business'.[113]

If these individuals sought to stay on the 'merry' side of the line more often than not, others appear to have habitually crossed it. The Somerset yeoman, John Hole, gave testimony in 1681 that he had recently met with one 'John Lytton and one other of his neighbours' at the alehouse of Widow Feers in Croscombe, when their notoriously drunken local cler-gyman, 'Drunken Alisbury', had turned up looking for Lytton. At first, noting that Alisbury was already 'fudled', they were 'unwilling that he should come in' and join their company. Alisbury ignored their protests and took up a place at their table. After refusing the generous offer of a pipe of tobacco to smoke, Alisbury then proceeded to drink 'a pott being fild with ale', followed by 'three or four more' before he did smoke the pipe, 'and after that drank about 4 or 5 more of ale which none of the company drank any but himself', and 'at length he began to be very drunke'. Alisbury then gave an abusive speech against a former minister who had been dead for fifteen years – a man considered 'honest' by the company – before his companions could bear him no more and took

---

112   *Eyre*, pp. 107, 98.
113   Wrightson, 'Alehouses, Order and Reformation', p. 6.

their leave.[114] Alisbury was clearly not a good companion and fellow boozer, and the fact that his disposition was railing rather than jovial served to compound the reluctance of these Somerset men to tolerate the company of a man whom they clearly felt had gone beyond the optimal level of intoxication. That Alisbury was prepared to keep knocking back extra pots of ale that the rest of the company abstained from was not in this case regarded by his companions as a brave and impressive feat deserving of 'honour and glory', but an ill-advised bout of excess that was likely to end in an embarrassing state of stupor. Indeed, when he left Widow Feers's alehouse, Alisbury 'was so much overgon with drinking that he fell down and slept in the streats with a great many boyes and others about him where he lay an object of scandal and reproach'. Such was the fate of those who failed to tread the fine line between being 'merry' and 'overcome'.

As we saw in the previous chapter, the jovial and merry atmosphere to which good fellows aspired was in part fostered through song and music, and both appear regularly in the records as features of alehouse company. The writer Izaak Walton claimed in 1653 to have enjoyed the sound of a milkmaid singing ballads from memory in a country alehouse, but on many occasions such recitals were rather more boisterous and less bucolic. In 1637 a mixed-gender company drank through the night in an alehouse in Bridport, Dorset, while three of their number sang loudly 'wherby the neighbours could not sleepe'. In another 1630s case a group of parishioners skipped church on a Sunday afternoon to drink beer and play cards at an alehouse in Staunton, Nottinghamshire, where they performed their own ironic prayers by 'singing in ridiculous sort'.[115] A contemporaneous case from Dorchester reveals a group of apprentices who spent the evening at the alehouse, before cheerfully staggering home 'singing of songs'.[116] Instruments might also contribute to the soundscape of good fellowship. In 1657 a potential lodger opted not to stay at the Ship in Glastonbury because of a 'company ranting and drinking and

---

114 SHC, D/D/Cd/97, Office v Alisbury, and p. 104 above. On the growing role of tobacco in English drinking cultures at this time see Withington, 'Intoxicants and Society'; Jordan Goodman, *Tobacco in History: The Cultures of Dependence* (London, 1993); Jason Hughes, *Learning to Smoke* (London, 2003); Mary Norton, *Sacred Gifts, Profane Pleasures: A History of Tobacco and Chocolate in the Atlantic World* (London, 2008).

115 These examples are from Marsh, *Music and Society*, pp. 188–9.

116 Underdown, *Fire from Heaven*, p. 80.

drumming' there.[117] As we saw in Chapter 2, the Cheshire constable John Crosbie had invited a travelling tinker to join in a raucous instance of good fellowship in Nether Knutsford in 1609 as he was carrying a trumpet, and under instruction from Crosbie he blasted upon it to call together 'all drunkerdes'.[118] And we have already heard that in 1656 a mixed-gender company spent the day at a Lancashire alehouse listening to a fiddler whilst they drank all the ale in the house.[119] Such musicians were not always well received. In the same year a Glastonbury fiddler, Walter Hamlin, spent three or four hours at an inn in nearby Wedmore, only for the innkeeper and two other men to then beat him over the head with a flagon pot and burn his fiddle.[120]

If music and song helped to structure the practice of good fellow-ship, so too did a number of other marked ritual elements. Ceremonial drinking vessels, such as Fowler, were sometimes involved. Roger Lowe encountered a ritual drinking vessel in September of 1663 when 'John Hasleden was pretty merry' and called for '6d for ale': 'it was made in a jelly bowle and I was sent for to the drinkeing of'.[121] These vessels may have been wassail bowls – 'wassail' in Old English meant 'for your health' – which were passed around a drinking company, with each companion crying out 'Wassail' and taking a drink before passing the bowl onto the next person.[122] Lowe was engaged in such a drinking ritual – described

---

117 SHC, Q/SR/95:3/246. For more on both music and alehouses as noise nuisance in the early modern period see Emily Cockayne, *Hubbub: Filth, Noise and Stench in England* (New Haven, 2007).

118 QJF/38/3/5, and p. 86 above.

119 Clark, *The English Alehouse*, p. 131. For another instance of a drinking company being entertained by musicians see Withington, 'Company and Sociability', p. 304.

120 SHC, Q/SR/93:1/49.

121 *Lowe*, pp. 34–5. For more on the significance of the vessels used in early modern drinking rituals see Angela McShane, 'Material Culture and "Political" Drinking in Seventeenth-Century England', *Past and Present* 222, Supplement 9: *Cultures of Intoxication* (2014), pp. 247–76. My thanks to Dr McShane for allowing me to see a pre-publication version of this piece. Also Karen Harvey, 'Ritual Encounters: Punch Parties and Masculinity in the Eighteenth Century', *Past and Present* 214 (2012), pp. 165–203; Jasmine Kilburn-Toppin, '"Discords have arisen and brotherly love decreased": The Spatial and Material Contexts of the Guild Feast in Early Modern London', *Brewery History* 150 (2013), pp. 28–38.

122 See Hutton, *The Rise and Fall of Merry England*, pp. 13–14. Hutton records that by 1600 it had also become a custom on festive occasions for a wassail bowl to be taken from house to house in a village, offering drink from it and expecting money in return. Another adaptation of wassailing took place in orchards as a form of drinking the health of trees and crops.

as a 'wessell' – in mixed-gender alehouse company in the November of 1664.[123] Indeed, health-drinking regularly occurred in instances of good fellowship. In one of the more bizarre instances, two men appear to have drunk a health to each other in their own co-mingled urine. In a Dorset alehouse in 1617, a servant and a butcher, two of the three men who had spent two weeks' wages on a Sunday binge, 'piste both at once into a chamber pott and then dranke upp the one haulfe and thother the other haulfe'.[124] A more easily interpreted, if no less elaborate, health-drinking ritual occurred in the Essex parish of Corringham in 1599. John Smith of Corringham, Richard Cottes of Orsett, and George Landish of Barking, capped a bout of heavy alehouse drinking by heading to 'the field at the town's end' with 'four or six pots of beer'. There they did 'humbly kneel down' and 'kiss the pots', before drinking to each other and saying a prayer 'for the health of all true and faithful drunkards'. In particular they praised one 'Mr Andrew Browghton' as 'the maintainer and upholder of all true and faithful drunkards', and after exchanging kisses with each other each man made 'his mark upon an ashen tree that stood there' to provide an indelible 'memory of their worthy act'.[125] The behaviour of these 'true and faithful drunkards' certainly resonates with sentiments expressed in those good fellowship ballads such as *Heres to thee kind Harry*, which encouraged the drinking of healths with beloved alehouse companions.

Of course, less spectacular forms of health-drinking are less likely to find their way into legal records, but there is fragmentary evidence that the practice was not restricted to grand gestures such as these, and could take on a more routine character. A group of male Dorchester apprentices politely toasted the wife of a fellow townsman, though not of their company, who had entered the alehouse in which they were drinking one Sunday morning in 1631.[126] Two men drinking in the same company came to blows in the 'Green Dragon' at Alderbury, Wiltshire, in 1686, when one refused to drink a health to the other as he suspected the man of having an affair with his wife – an affair that was apparently being conducted primarily in discreet meetings in a back room of the same establishment.[127] Health-drinking did not always then take

[123] *Lowe*, p. 75.

[124] Bettey (ed.), *The Case Book of Sir Francis Ashley*, p. 45. For more on the possible meanings of this ritual see Shepard, '"Swil-bots and Tos-pots"', p. 111.

[125] Emmison, *Elizabethan Life: Morals and the Church Courts*, p. 70.

[126] Underdown, *Fire from Heaven*, p. 80.

[127] WSHC, D1/42/60/fols 110v–106v.

on elaborate forms, nor was it always a political statement of the sort of which we saw numerous examples in Chapter 2. It seems to have been a more routine feature of everyday drinking practices that could on occasion take on these extra characteristics. That said, from the middle of the seventeenth century examples of politically loaded health-drinking proliferate considerably. Chapter 2 documents a number of these, but it is worth reiterating the extent to which the issue of political allegiance was coming to play an increasingly prominent role in the ritual forms and dynamics of alehouse sociability. In Beverley in 1651 one William Bewick, a currier – a type of leather worker – proposed 'a health to Prince Charles, King of Scotts, and to his good successe into England, and to the confusion of all his enimies', and then drained 'a silver beaker full of ale'. He then urged his drinking companion Thomas Stockdale to do likewise, but Stockdale refused, whereupon 'Bewick puld of the said Stockdale's hatt from his head, saying it was a health that deserved to be uncovered'.[128]

If the issue of political allegiance was bringing drinking companions to blows, or at least close to blows, it also began to pervade the drinking songs that were so central to good fellowship, as we saw in Chapter 3. In December of 1656, at 'the Blackboy' in Ashcott, Somerset, William Higgons proposed to his drinking companions a loyal toast that took the form of a drinking song beginning, 'Let us drinke let us sing here's a health to our King & it will never [b]e well until wee have one againe.' When his companions refused, Higgons grew 'angry & fell out with' them.[129] By the time of the succession disputes of the early 1680s the politically charged atmosphere of health-drinking could, in some places, provide a spark for brawling and chanting in the streets. In Oxford in 1683 a confrontation developed in 'the Magpie' alehouse between townsmen who had been drinking healths to the Duke of Monmouth, and scholars who were drinking to the Duke of York. When the scholars left the Magpie the townsmen followed them, assaulted them, and ran up and down the High Street crying 'A Monmouth! A Monmouth! No York!'[130] Whilst the alehouse had always to some extent been a politicised space, the partisan dimension of good fellowship took on even greater prominence in the turbulent political decades of the middle and later seventeenth century.

---

128 *York Cast. Deps*, no. XLIII.

129 SHC, Q/SR/95:3/253.

130 See Tim Harris, *Restoration: Charles II and his Kingdoms* (London, 2006), p. 289.

Another area of resonance between good fellowship ballads and the evidence of 'practice' in depositions and diaries relates to the considerable importance accorded to the 'politics of payment'. Despite the emphasis on liberality in the idiom of good fellowship, drinking companions apparently kept a careful count of their own balance of payments. Both Adam Eyre and Roger Lowe routinely recorded in their diary entries the sum they had spent during a visit to the alehouse, and Lowe was a keen observer of the relative contributions drinking companions made to the collective 'score' or 'shot'. He noted that his bonding session with fellow godfather Raph Faster, in October 1664, had resulted in a total 'score' of 2s 6d, and on that occasion the two men had 'payd it jointly'.[131] On other days, Lowe was the recipient of that symbolic gesture of other men covering his share for him. In June of 1664 he had accompanied a male friend who was visiting a sister in a nearby village, Houghton, and on the way home they stopped at 'Astleys', an alehouse in Hindley (4.5 miles from Ashton). Here they met by chance one Robert Reynolds junior, an ex-neighbour, who was 'glad to see' Lowe, so they 'stayed drinkinge of 8d', and Lowe recorded that 'I paid not a 1d'.[132] In October of 1663, Lowe recorded a similar gesture, when 'Roger Naylor and Thomas Unsworth came to towne to me and envited me to ale house and Rogr said it should cost me nothing soe I went.'[133]

Occasionally Lowe himself paid for a companion, but when he did so his actions appear to have been more directly informed by a sense of duty to reciprocate a kind act than simply by selfless generosity. One afternoon in August 1664 Lowe had been 'quarrelling' with one Roger Naylor in an alehouse, when his regular drinking companion John Potter stepped in and 'vindicated my cause nobly'. Potter's reward was that later that day Lowe took him into another alehouse 'and spent 6d on him'.[134] Covering another's share of the shot could therefore be a symbol of altruistic affection, but it might also represent – or bring with it the expectation of – a reciprocal gesture, and insisting on redressing the balance was often a matter of pride, and a statement of honour, means and independence. This was true for female drinkers as well as male. Elizabeth Case was keen to demonstrate her equality with her male drinking companions and offered to buy them a pint of wine at William Conwaie's Chester

---

[131] *Lowe*, p. 74.
[132] *Ibid.*, pp. 63–4.
[133] *Ibid.*, p. 42.
[134] *Ibid.*, p. 70.

tavern. The men accepted, but then insisted that Elizabeth join them at Thomas Percival's alehouse so that they could return the favour.[135] In St Sepulchres, London, in 1633, a man and woman engaged in a defamation dispute met in an alehouse to make their peace, and pledged each other's health. The woman, Ellenor Meade, insisted on paying for her own can of beer to drink from rather than making the pledge from his, in order to ensure that the exchange was a truly equal one, and that they had both 'spent their ii d a peece in beere'.[136] Paying your own or another's share of the shot was, then, a symbolically charged gesture, and contemporaries were aware that there was a certain politics at work when it came to settling the score.[137]

If the settling of the score was intended to reinforce either affectionate or reciprocal bonds between drinking companions, it could just as often put a strain on any such bonds. John Rumbelow, a Devonian, had spent the night at a Somerset alehouse in Dulverton in 1661. The next day, however, there was 'a difference arising' between Rumblelow and 'others that had kept his Company all that night' about 'payment of the reconinge ... for beere'.[138] Henry Porter, an innkeeper from Taunton, received three guests in 1664 who called for 'some beer to be brought for them & when they had drunke as much as they would they fell at difference amongst themselves who of them should pay for it'. Porter's reaction suggests an awareness that the politics of payment could be highly charged, and he urged that 'rather than there should be any disturbance bred; he would have nothing for his beer'. Porter's son, however, disagreed, and the publicans ultimately came to blows with their customers.[139]

One way in which good fellows often sought to resolve the issue of who was responsible for paying the shot was to gamble over it. Though it was not a central feature of ballad depictions of good fellowship, the playing of competitive games was a ubiquitous characteristic of alehouse company. Whilst urban male elites, gathered in their taverns, engaged each other in contests of witty wordplay, extemporised versifying, or

---

[135] Addy, *Sin and Society*, pp. 191–2.

[136] Archdeaconry Court of London, GL MS 9057/1. My thanks to Professor Keith Wrightson both for this reference and a transcription of the case.

[137] The politics of payment surrounding drinking might usefully be considered within the paradigm of gift exchange. See Ilana Krausman Ben-Amos, *The Culture of Giving: Informal Support and Gift-Exchange in Early Modern England* (Cambridge, 2008).

[138] SHC, Q/SR/101/18.

[139] SHC, Q/SR/106/16.

competitive Latin and Greek, alehouse-goers of both genders vied to outdo each other at cards, dice, bowling, 'tables' – an ancestor of modern backgammon – and perhaps most popularly in games of shovel board or shove groat, a pastime that both Roger Lowe and Elizabeth Case apparently enjoyed.[140] Such games may on occasion have simply been played for fun, to pass the time, or as an extension of the competitive spirit that underpinned drinking contests, but when they appear in the records they are usually linked to forms of gambling. On a rainy day in September 1663 Roger Lowe took shelter in Watt's alehouse where he played 'a sett of Bowleinge', with the stakes set 'for each man [at] 2d in Ale'. Lowe 'was one to bowle and lost'.[141] In 1601, two men at an alehouse in Kilmington, on the Somerset and Wiltshire border, engaged in a game of tables which they 'played for drink'.[142] In 1623 three men who went to an alehouse in Wantage, Oxfordshire, decided that to 'parte the strife, whoe should paye for the bere', one of the men 'drewe fourth 3 dyce and would have the dyce to decyde the controversye by casting ten or above upon a wager of wynninge or losing the beere'.[143]

What values were enshrined in these prevalent rituals of gaming and gambling? Thomas Brennan found that such rituals were a prominent feature of the culture of drinking establishments in eighteenth-century Paris, and moreover that drinking companions invariably gambled only for the cost of drinks. This was small-scale rather than serious gambling, and Brennan argued that historians should avoid seeing gambling as yet another 'moral lapse' on the part of the labouring classes, or a consequence of their 'misery or their debauchery'. Instead he interpreted it as 'another way of sharing the cost of drink, like buying rounds', whereby 'the personal fortune or misfortune of the individuals contributed to the enjoyment of the group as a whole', and that 'wagering on games functioned in this way to reinforce the fellowship of a group and to distinguish it from others'.[144] Gambling only for expenses was common enough in early modern England too, and no doubt added an entertaining element of fortune or skill to the politics of payment and the dynamics of fellowship. But it could, equally, take on a more serious bent. After initially

---

[140] For instances of competitive Latin and Greek see Withington, 'Company and Sociability', p. 291; Nott. Boro. Recs, V, pp. 352–3. For the shuffle board examples see Lowe, p. 79; Addy, Sin and Society, p. 191.

[141] Lowe, p. 28.

[142] SHC, D/D/Cd/32, Simons v Edwardes.

[143] Read. Boro. Recs, II, pp. 138–40.

[144] Brennan, Public Drinking and Popular Culture, pp. 249–57.

throwing dice to settle the score, the gambling between the men in a Wantage alehouse began to escalate, with the stakes rising after each game until one man 'gave over and left the play' having claimed 'his owne money agayne and 18s over and above' – no small profit at a time when a day labourer's wages were in the region of 8d a day. Faced with such loses, one of his companions later complained that he had been cheated because the dice were 'false'.[145] The gambling that took place between the King's messenger and a tinker at an alehouse in Ramsbury, Wiltshire, in 1617, took on a similar high-stakes trajectory. The two men played at 'penny prick' – a game in which participants throw objects at a penny on a stick – for 40s, followed by a game of bowles for £10. This, too, ended in dispute when it came to paying up, and as we saw above the tinker threatened the King's messenger with assault.[146] The gambling that accompanied alehouse drinking was not always a modest affair intended as 'an adjunct to the basic aim of sociability'; it could at times involve high stakes and provoke violent conflicts, though the legal records are likely to over-represent such instances in relation to low-stakes, amicable affairs.[147]

Even if the stakes were regularly no more than a round of drinks, the close connection between alehouse sociability and gambling reminds us that participation in good fellowship could be a very costly pursuit. The flip side to good fellowship's celebrated atmosphere of liberality was that many who cried 'hang pinching' whilst in alehouse company found themselves ruefully counting the costs when settling their own accounts. In December 1647 Adam Eyre spent a day calculating his annual expenses, and came to the grim conclusion that he was living beyond his means. The finger was pointed at good fellowship, and he 'resolved herafter never to pay for any body in the alehouse, nor never to entangle myselfe in company so much again as I have done'.[148] Even tradesmen – depicted in ballads as drinking heavily precisely because they could comfortably afford to do so – in practice paid a heavy price for their conspicuous consumption. Richard Gough was certainly able to identify a number of tradesmen from Myddle whose commitment to good fellowship hampered their prosperity. Roger Jewks, a Shrewsbury shoemaker, 'was an excellent workman as any in town; he had a house and shop on his own land, and

---

145 *Read. Boro. Recs*, II, pp. 138–40.
146 *Wilts. Q.S. Recs*, p. 59.
147 Brennan, *Public Drinking and Popular Culture*, p. 250.
148 *Eyre*, p. 81.

a good fortune with his wife, and had no child; and yet being given to drink he was never rich'. Humphrey Hall was 'a silversmith in London, and is there married; he is a strong man, and a skillfull workman, but he loves his drink too well to be rich'. Likewise, his brother Andrew was a much sought-after glover and skinner in Shrewsbury, but he too 'was so addicted to drinking that he quickly got in debt in Shrewsbury so that he was forced to leave the town'.[149] One tailor who had spent beyond his means at an alehouse in Epping, Essex, in 1664, resorted to making a 'suit of new clothes' for the victualler to settle his score.[150] The financial obligations that accompanied the purchase of a 'good fellow's name' were, then, considerable, and ballad characters such as John Jarret's wife, who cautioned that alehouse-haunting could bring financial ruin, tapped into very real concerns.

They were not only the concerns of opponents of alehouse recreation. Eyre's resolution suggests that he too was well aware of the risks involved, and a month later he once more denounced good fellowship in his diary: 'God Almighty hath kept mee from danger, praised be His holy name therefore; but I have lived very vainely in idle company, and feasting and ryott. God Allmighty in mercy forgive mee, and lay not these sinnes to my charge.'[151] This did not, however, mark Eyre's defection to the ranks of those who opposed the alehouse. Two days after this self-admonishment he was back in the alehouse, and within two weeks, after an expensive trawl of several drinking establishments led to him behaving uncivilly, he was once more seeking forgiveness: 'When I came home, I was very angry, and caryed myselfe unsivilly. God forgive me this!' Eyre was undoubtedly like many of his contemporaries, caught between the allure of good fellowship on the one hand, and its considerable costs on the other. Indeed, we should think of the 'pro-drink' and 'anti-drink' sentiments that were so often set against each other in 'ballad banter' not necessarily as two competing ideologies each with their own followers, but as the twin faces of a Janus-like disposition that existed within many early modern individuals.

Of course, the pitfalls of good fellowship were not only financial. As we saw in Chapter 3, ballads often articulated tensions between alehouse-going and the expression of masculine identity, especially for those husbands and fathers whose patriarchal authority hinged on the

---

149 Gough, *The History of Myddle*, pp. 220, 222.
150 ERO, Q/SR/402/126.
151 *Eyre*, pp. 85–6.

performance of the values of thrift, moderation and provision. In part these heavy costs of good fellowship were at odds with the demands placed upon such men to provide for their wives and children, and both ballads and petitions complained that good fellows left their families crying at home for want of bread. Anxiety about patriarchs participating in recreational drinking had other sources too, not least of which was the assumption that alehouses often served as bawdy houses, and that male customers went there to procure the services of 'whores' or 'wenches' – a complaint we find echoed in depositions. On the night before Christmas, 1681, Debora Allen burst into the Nag's Head alehouse in Reading in search of her husband, and finding him there she flew into a rage, picking up a quart pot and throwing it at a window, before she 'levelled her passion' against Sara Newbury, the alewife. Debora Allen called Sara Newbury a whore and a bawd, and accused her of keeping a bawdy house.[152] In a defamation case from Stogursey, Somerset, in 1600, a man who was ejected from a drinking establishment for being abusive responded by shouting through the window for all the customers to hear that the alehousekeeper's wife 'selleth small pots and she fucketh in every corner with every knave that cometh to thy house'.[153]

This case may have simply been the misogynistic insult of a disgruntled alehouse customer, but its implication that sex could be had with female alehouse workers was not entirely unfounded – though more often than not it was serving maids, rather than alewives, who were thought to be sexually available.[154] There were undoubtedly cases involving a degree of complicity and consent, but serving maids were treated by many male customers as 'public property' for whom 'attempts on their virtue seem to have gone with the territory'.[155] This could lead to some terrifying experiences, including rape.[156] In one appalling incident that occurred in an alehouse in Snargate, Kent, in 1598, five men were found guilty of sexually assaulting the alewife and her maids, and gang-raping

[152] WSHC, D1/39/1/57/fols 132r–133r.

[153] SHC, D/D/Cd/32, Waterman v Elsworthie.

[154] For some suggestive examples see SHC, D/D/Cd/32, Simons v Edwardes; *Read. Boro. Recs*, III, p. 397; WSHC, 1629/T/136.

[155] Capp, 'Gender and the Culture of the Alehouse', pp. 107–9, Laura Gowing, *Common Bodies: Women, Touch and Power in Seventeenth-Century England* (London, 2003), pp. 60–1; the quote is from Brown, 'The Landscape of Drink', pp. 99–100.

[156] Brown, 'The Landscape of Drink', pp. 99–100. For other examples of misogyny and sexual assault directed at alehouse serving maids see also Tim Hitchcock, 'Sociability and Misogyny in the Life of John Cannon, 1684–1743', in Tim Hitchcock and Michele Cohen (eds), *English Masculinities, 1660–1800* (London, 1999), pp. 25–43.

one fourteen-year-old maid who later died of her injuries – actions that were initially dismissed by the local JP as 'but a trick of youth'.[157] The alehouse could, then, be pervaded by a sexually aggressive masculinity. A less dramatic but more commonplace feature of this was a culture of bragging about sexual conquests. John Harris of Huntspill, Somerset, sought to use the alehouse as an arena for displaying his sexual prowess when, in 1656, he boasted that he had slept with a woman who 'was a saint' and laid his 'carnal instrument' on the table to prove it.[158] Similarly, a company of men were gathered at the White Swan in Devizes, Wiltshire, in 1681, when one of the group bragged several times that his brother had had a Mrs Long 'by the Cunt'.[159] This brash culture of sexually aggressive masculinity may have had a particular appeal for young and unmarried men, who 'often boasted in alehouses about real or imagined sexual intimacies with prostitutes and maidservants to gain approval and admiration from their peers'.[160] Whilst married men may have been far more circumspect about advertising their sexual exploits, we should not assume that they did not contribute to the sexual instrumentalisation of female alehouse staff – Samuel Pepys, for one, regularly had sex with alehouse workers.[161]

If young men might revel in it, married men be tainted by association with it, and female staff be victimised by it, what was the effect of the relationship between sex and the alehouse for female patrons? Did attempts on women's virtue 'come with the territory' of visiting an alehouse as well as working in one? They might do. When Agnes Fiven, a servant, went to an alehouse in Cearne Abbas in 1615 with a mixed group of four or five 'men and maydes', she was subjected to one of the men, Thomas Dike, 'toyeing and playeinge with her', an unwelcome assault that 'made her to come away againe'.[162] Sexual assault was undoubtedly endemic in alehouse culture. There is, however, another side to the story of alehouse

---

[157] Though the case did later end up in Star Chamber, and full transcriptions of the depositions can be found in Louis A. Knafla (ed.), *Kent at Law, v.III, Star Chamber* (Kew, Surrey, 2012), pp. 11–24. The men were heavily fined.

[158] SHC, Q/SR/93:2/162, 163.

[159] WSHC, D1/39/1/57/fol. 134. Elizabeth Foyster has argued that after the Restoration a culture of sexual libertinism made the notion of sexual conquest as a way to acquire manhood more prevalent, so this aspect of alehouse culture may have become more pronounced. Elizabeth Foyster, *Manhood in Early Modern England: Honour, Sex and Marriage* (London, 1999), p. 41.

[160] Reinke-Williams, 'Misogyny, Jest-Books and Male Youth Culture', p. 330.

[161] Capp, 'Gender and the Culture of the English Alehouse', pp. 107–9.

[162] Bettey (ed.), *The Case Book of Sir Francis Ashley*, p. 12.

sexual culture. One May afternoon in Castle Cary, Somerset, in 1660, a man and women who had been drinking together at 'The Angel' slipped off to have sex in a ditch.[163] On a November evening in Inkberrow, Worcestershire, in 1602, Edward Pearce and a male companion enjoyed a meal of fresh herring with two women at an alehouse in the village. Afterwards, Pearce excused himself and 'went to his chamber and did set a candle lighted in his window and when he returned he said he had done as the scholars in Oxford did when they meant to do any exploit and light a candle that they may be thought to be at their books'. With this decoy in place, Pearce and his companion 'went abroad into the fields with the two women very suspiciously'.[164] Other than what they tell us about an early modern penchant for outdoor sex, the seductive qualities of a herring dinner, and the tricks of the trade of Oxford scholars, these examples offer some confirmation of the oft-cited ballad warning that mixed-gender sociability was often a precursor to sexual relations. What is less clear is that this represented a process of sexual commodification that necessarily victimised female participants in good fellowship. There is no implication that the sexual adventures in the field at Inkberrow or the ditch at Castle Cary were anything other than consensual, and this sexual dimension of mixed-gender sociability may have been part of the appeal of the alehouse to some women. Both single unmarried women, and perhaps even married ones, may have sought out alehouse sociability as a springboard for sexual adventures, in the same way that some men did.[165]

The connection between sex and the alehouse appealed to some, but was undoubtedly forbidding for others. There were also those, as we saw in ballads, who sought to dismiss or suppress that connection, and those cases of sexual boasting that survive in legal records come to light only because others present objected, and in the case of John Harris of Huntspill they went so far as to fetch the constable to have him arrested.[166] These objectors may have been echoing those married ballad good fellows who dismissed the association between the alehouse

---

[163] SHC, Q/SR/99/6.

[164] *Wilts. Q.S. Recs*, pp. 52–3.

[165] For a similar argument that 'even outside of marriage, a bit of sex between a consenting man and woman could be treated as an innocent, natural pleasure' by non-elite men and women in the seventeenth century, and for examples of alehouses providing a context for the same, see Faramerz Dabhoiwala, *The Origins of Sex: A History of the First Sexual Revolution* (Oxford, 2012), pp. 18–19.

[166] SHC, Q/SR/93:2/162, 163.

and sexual activity to allow them to claim that being a good fellow and being a good husband were compatible identities. For, as Jennifer Jordan has argued, 'whilst young and single men could engage in casual sexual encounters and brag amongst their peers about their sexual achievements – real or imagined – with relative impunity, once married this behaviour was no longer acceptable and could cause tensions within both family and community'.[167]

If challenging the sexually aggressive tone set by young male alehouse-goers was one way for married men to counter claims that participation in good fellowship jeopardised their patriarchal credentials, another – as we have seen – was to include their wives in their alehouse recreation. What can we tell about the character of alehouse company involving husbands and wives? For Adam Eyre it was a special occasion, but for others – such as those with whom Roger Lowe kept company – it appears to have been more routine, and it was not unusual for wives to be fully integrated into the rituals and spirit of good fellowship. John Lufkin included his wife in some of his alehouse high jinks. On one occasion Lufkin secretively dropped a stone that the two had seemingly used as a sex toy into another drinking companion's pot of beer, and then proposed a toast. As the toast was raised the stone was heard to 'clash against the pot side', upon which Lufkin revealed to all present, including his wife, that they had all drunk a toast to 'she knew where', whereupon 'she he and all the rest laughed'.[168] Richard Gough related in his history of Myddle that William Crosse and his wife went daily to the alehouse together, but noted also that 'soone after the cows went thither alsoe' – implying that they had to sell their land and cattle stock to maintain such a course.[169] If including wives in good fellowship could help to ease marital tensions, it was not necessarily a strategy that enhanced patriarchal provision.

Nathaniel and Mary Smith of Manningtree, Essex, were another couple who drank regularly together, and in 1627 their neighbours complained that they spent 'the service time in sleeping or drinking with his companions . . . they are most notorious drunkards, and swearers and railers', and were even running their own alehouse 'drawing people to spend their money; if they come in without money, if it be possible, they will make them pawn something for beer before they will let them go'.

167 Jordan, 'Her-story Untold', p. 579.
168 ERO, Q/SR 170/3.
169 Gough, The History of Myddle, p. 130.

The petitioners pleaded for action to be taken against them as 'for the better sort it is almost no living with them'.[170] Examples such as these reveal husbands and wives who routinely engaged together in alehouse good fellowship – spending and consuming liberally, raising toasts, sharing jokes and merriment – but they further complicate the conclusions that we can draw about the gendered meanings of alehouse recreation. Whilst these married men and women were clearly not participating in alehouse sociability characterised by a misogynistic bachelor culture that celebrated sexual conquest, we cannot easily categorise them as championing a respectable, patriarchal form of good fellowship either. Their co-drinking may have strengthened the bonds of marriage, but their prodigality, their absenteeism from church, and their lack of decorum, would all have called into question their status as respectable couples. These husbands would not have been heralded as successful patriarchs, nor their wives as living up to the expectations of female propriety. The gender identities that might be taken on by good fellows could then incorporate a wider range than those that lined up neatly on the same side of the binaries of married/unmarried, respectable/disreputable and chaste/unchaste.

Indeed, we have seen throughout this chapter that for both men and women alehouse company could take on a number of forms that were characterised by neither marital ties nor sex. Siblings and kin drank together; Lowe drank with other men's wives, and with single women who were merely friends; mixed groups of servants kept company without a sexual dimension always being implied; single-sex groups drank together; married or single women could play with men at shuffle board, display their own prowess at holding their drink, or drink with men as a symbol of reconciliation after a dispute. If the gendered forms of alehouse sociability were varied, its meanings and implications for gender relations were too. The practice of good fellowship could drive wedges between husbands and wives, but it could also strengthen marital ties; it could appeal to respectable patriarchal males, but it could also be an expression of values that were decidedly at odds with those expected of a good husband and father; it could take on a sexual dimension that for some was part of its appeal, but for others was something to oppose or avoid; or it could be an opportunity to revel in the idiom of good fellowship in ways that had little to do with sex, patriarchy, or respectable norms of gender behaviour. It is clear that women formed a significant

[170]   ERO, Q/SR 259/10.

minority of those who participated in alehouse sociability, and that they did so in a wide range of contexts. We no longer need to ask 'if' and 'when' women were involved in alehouse sociability. Historians should instead focus their attention on the multi-faceted ways in which gender informed the meanings, values and appeals of good fellowship to both women and men.

The bonds of good fellowship

So far this chapter has been concerned with questions of who kept company with whom in the early modern English alehouse, and with the character of that company – its ritual forms and meanings. This final section will examine the nature of the bonds that resulted from sharing a round of drinks, pledging each other's health, or combining to sing a good fellowship ballad. Did participation in the sociable rituals of good fellowship contribute to the formation of meaningful social bonds that endured beyond the context of a given instance of 'keeping company', or was involvement in a drinking company an opportunity to briefly escape from the bonds and obligations of wider society, and to simply enjoy a moment of fleeting liberation in company with individuals to whom connections were ephemeral and unobligating?

This issue is best addressed by considering the manner in which drinking companies formed. A common pattern was for instances of sociable alehouse recreation to develop out of the quotidian routines of worship, work and travel. Lowe's alehouse visits regularly occurred when he was 'gadding' to and from sermons or church. On one Sunday in July 1665, Lowe had gone to worship in Wigan (about five miles from Ashton) with Joshua Naylor and John Hasleden, and recorded that 'when we came to Eles Leighe's we stayd and had each a cupp of ale, and then I left them drinkeing and I went into church'.[171] If Lowe kept this visit functional whilst his companions opted to make theirs a recreational one, this was not always the pattern of his worship-related alehouse visits. In August 1664 he went to Newton, near Wigan, to hear 'Mr Blakeburn' preach, and afterwards the preacher invited him and his companion William Hasleden to an alehouse where they 'had 2 pints of wine which he would have paid for but I would not suffer it'.[172] On a January Sunday in 1648, Adam Eyre recorded that 'after evening prayer

171 *Lowe*, p. 88.
172 *Lowe*, p. 68.

I drunk at Ernshaw's [an alehouse] with Richard Micklethwayte and Edward Hinchcliffe'.[173] If co-worship provided a context for the formation of drinking company, so too did co-working. In January of 1647 Adam Eyre spent the day 'running errands' with his fellow parliamentarian soldier Captain Rich, after which they stopped for refreshment in Wakefield, 'where we stayd all night at the Mearemayd, and spent 3s'.[174] No doubt many post-work calls for refreshment at the alehouse developed into such bouts of recreational good fellowship. Lowe also drank with those to whom he was tied through work. In October 1663 a fellow mercer from Warrington came to town, and he and Lowe headed for the alehouse to 'talk about tradeinge' – but the visit soon developed into a bout of recreation, and the conversation turned to 'how to gett wives'.[175] In March of 1665 Lowe had been assisting some men in sealing a lease, after which they went together 'to an Ale house where we stayd drinkeinge a good while'.[176]

As we saw in the case of neighbours, chance encounters with acquaintances on the road might also prompt the formation of a drinking company. In January 1647 Eyre had been with a companion travelling through 'Denby Green' when they passed an alehouse 'where were our two Peniston vicars and some others, who called us in to drink; and wee spent either of us 6d'.[177] The weather could play a part in transforming such instances from a simple courtesy of sharing one round to a more extended recreational session. In May 1665 Roger Lowe met fellow Ashton man David Pendlebury on the road and agreed to 'go spend 1d' with him at a nearby alehouse. Lowe then records that 'we ware no sooner gotten into house and had a flaggon but Mr Leigh schoolmaster of Ashton came in', and a drink was shared with him too – and as it was 'a rainy day' they 'stayd 2 or 3 flaggons' before heading home.[178] If many instances of recreational alehouse drinking grew out of more functional alehouse stops, that were in turn part of the routines of work, worship, travel and neighbourliness, others were more explicitly intent on merrymaking from the outset. If this was rarely admitted in legal records, it is clear enough from the diary evidence. Lowe recorded occasions when acquaintances came to his door to invite him to the alehouse to drink,

173 Eyre, p. 86.
174 Eyre, pp. 6–7.
175 Lowe, p. 37.
176 Ibid., p. 81.
177 Eyre, pp. 7–8.
178 Lowe, pp. 84–5.

as in March 1664 when 'Mr Maddocke came with Roger Naylor and envited me to the alehouse', and in April that year 'the neighbourhood of Ashton envited me to goe with them to the Ale house this eveninge'. A more purposeful recreational intent was also evident on occasions when Lowe was 'sent for' to join in a bout of good fellowship that was intended to run long into the night. In June 1664 'Thomas Jameson was in Jenkins [an Ashton alehouse] and sent for me to come to drinke with hime and we stayed late in night', and in January 1665 Thomas Tickle and John Hasleden were 'at John Jenkins drinkinge they sent for me and I went but it cost me nothinge for Ralph and John spent either of them 12d'.[179]

Instances of alehouse sociability could develop out of functional or routine visits to the alehouse, or be embarked upon by companies with a clear intent to 'make merry', but the key point here is that in both cases they were generally founded upon *pre-existing* ties between those who became drinking companions. Bouts of good fellowship were conducted between men and women who had more often than not entered the alehouse together, or been invited to meet each other there. Alehouse-goers did not go to the alehouse in search of company: companies went in search of alehouses. This reinforces the point that the appeal of alehouse-going for many contemporaries was more about sociability than it was about the individual pursuit of narcotic oblivion, but perhaps more significantly it also reiterates the point that people tended to choose as drinking companions those to whom they were already connected through ties of kin, marriage, work, worship, neighbourhood, and even politics. Good fellowship did not serve as an escape from such bonds, it served to reinforce them.

It might be more appropriate then to label the bonds of good fellow-ship as something more enduring than fleeting 'comradeship'. Contem-poraries would have recognised such bonds as 'friendship', for the word 'friend' had a wide application in the early modern period that encom-passed kin, business associates, religious and political fellow-travellers, and spouses.[180] We might object, however, that the bonds of good fellow-ship do not quite match up to *modern* definitions of friendship, which social scientists define in relation to the criteria of voluntary 'emotion-ally close, proximate, frequently seen, non-work or non kin-relation-

---

[179] *Lowe*, pp. 54, 58, 64, 78.

[180] See Naomi Tadmor, *Family and Friends in Eighteenth-Century England: Household, Kinship and Patronage* (Cambridge, 2001), p. 167.

ships'.[181] The friendships that were expressed and maintained through participation in good fellowship may have been more significant than fleeting or ephemeral bonds of comradeship, but it could be argued that they were nonetheless closer to being instrumental rather than affectionate relationships. The friends people drank with were very often in some sense useful people to maintain good relations with – colleagues, kin, neighbours – rather than individuals who fell outside of work, kin and neighbourly circles. But such relationships could also have a sentimental dimension. Naomi Tadmor's analysis of the friendships of the eighteenth-century Sussex shopkeeper Thomas Turner, for instance, argued that whilst early modern 'friends' often 'worked together and for each other, lent and borrowed money and goods, bought and sold to and from each other … and exchanged many other "favours" and "services"', 'sentimentality and instrumentality often went hand in hand' in their relationships.[182]

A similar argument can be advanced about the bonds between good fellows. Roger Lowe, for instance, spent a considerable amount of time in company with one John Potter, and Adam Eyre with both Captain Rich and Edward Mitchell. In each case there were instrumental ties between the men – Lowe was courting, and would eventually marry, Potter's daughter; Eyre had military ties to Rich, and appears to have leased land to Mitchell – but the frequency with which these men kept company went beyond what was necessary to simply oil the wheels of purely functional relationships. There is further evidence that suggests a degree of genuine affection between these good fellows. In May 1667 Lowe called on Potter 'meerly out of love' to see if he would 'take part of 2d in beere' with him. When Potter refused, Lowe observed that he 'seemed as if he ware angry which troubled me very sore'.[183] A rejection of the offer of good fellowship could, then, be felt deeply, and there was clearly an emotional charge to such relations. In a diary entry from November 1663, Lowe penned a furious reaction to finding out that another regular drinking companion, James Naylor, was interfering in his attempts to woo James's sister Mary. Lowe claimed that 'this stinkinge Rascall betrayed his one sister and me', despite the fact that Lowe was 'allwayes with [him] and spent monys for his sake', calling him 'a seeminge prtende friend'.[184]

181   *Ibid.*, p. 211.
182   *Ibid.*, p. 212.
183   *Lowe*, p. 114.
184   *Ibid.*, pp. 46–7.

Lowe may well have been hoping that buying drinks for James would have encouraged the latter to play an instrumental role in encouraging his relationship with Mary, but his emotional reaction suggests that the bond between the two men was indeed one where 'sentimentality and instrumentality' went hand in hand.

Perhaps the most poignant example of how emotionally meaningful the bonds of good fellowship could be comes from a story told by Richard Gough about his fellow parishioner John Gossage. Gossage used to drink regularly with one Richard Eaton in Shrewsbury, but on one occasion Eaton 'beestowed pretty store of ale upon Gossage, butt had occasion to goe home that night, and told Gossage soe'. However, 'Gossage did not beeleive, but conceited hee told him this onely on purpose to shirke him off, and in that drunken humour went and bought arsenicke, and poysened himselfe, and dyed before morning'.[185] The relationship between these two drinking companions had clearly been one imbued with deep personal significance for John Gossage.

The bonds forged by good fellowship were, then, both an expression and reinforcement of personal and lasting bonds of early modern 'friendship'. The flip side of the social cohesion produced by good fellowship was that the internal solidarity of drinking companies often found expression in conflict with 'outsiders', and alehouse sociability could prove divisive within certain manifestations of community at the same time as bolstering other manifestations. It could often, for instance, disrupt attempts to keep the local peace, as it threatened to in an earlier case involving John Gossage described by Richard Gough. William Tyler, a parishioner of Myddle, had refused to settle a debt he owed to a fellow parishioner, which had led to an ongoing feud in which Tyler ultimately turned violent and was arrested by local officials. As they led Tyler out of town towards the gaol, they encountered 'John Gossage and severall others of Tyler's drunken companions, with a paleful of ale'. Gossage and the other drinking companions were prepared to 'fall on' to rescue their fellow drinking companion from custody, but Tyler called them off from the potential ruckus.[186] The bonds forged between these regular drinking companions were clearly powerful enough that these men would contemplate risking arrest themselves to save one of their own.

Similarly, as we saw in Chapter 1, the 'cup companions' of Calne were prepared to close ranks and risk the wrath of the local authorities, and

---

[185] Gough, *The History of Myddle*, pp. 102–3.
[186] *Ibid.*, p. 178.

refused to testify against each other as drunkards. The bonds between good fellows were not so ephemeral as to disintegrate in the face of authority. The same was true in another incident in Pensford, Somerset, in 1656. When a victualler and his wife refused to keep serving drink to a company that 'had been very unruly and required more drinke', the company forced their way into the butter store and 'drew beere them-selves'. The parish constable was called, and commanded the drinking companions to leave, but on their way out one Richard Sledge struck the proprietor 'two or three blowes on the face'. The constable commanded the rest of the company to 'ayd him to keepe the peace' and carry Sledge 'to the stocke', but 'none of them would assist him'. Not only did the drinking companions remain loyal to their fellow drinker, but when the proprietor's servant tried to intervene, he 'was greivously beaten & brused by them'.[187]

If a drinking company might close ranks against alehousekeepers and local officers, their internal cohesion could also embolden them into acts of aggression against other outsiders. In 1649, a troop of soldiers were quartered at an alehouse in Croscombe, Somerset. They were disturbed from their sleep one night when 'they herd some company in the house that were very uncivill, and they herd the woman of the howse disier them to be civill for theyre weare some gent[lemen] in bed that would be disturbed by theyre noyse'. Upon hearing this complaint, 'one of the company demanded what they weare that was in bed, the woman answered that they weare soldiers, one of them replyed and said com let us goe up and cut theyre throtes'. The soldiers rose from bed and stood guard, and the tension seems to have dissipated.[188] Again though, this example provides evidence that drinking companies could have enough confidence in their collective strength to encourage them to acts of violence or aggression – also including, as we saw above, epsi-odes of sexual violence. Spurred on by both intoxication and a sense of solidarity that was manifested through highly charged boundaries of inclusion and exclusion, these drinking parties might begin to act and feel rather like a closely knit military company.[189] The resultant clashes could even take on an element of class hostility. The company of tinkers who had been drinking on New Year's Eve of 1624 in a Dorset alehouse

187 SHC, Q/SR/93:2/164,165.
188 SHC, Q/SR/81/80.
189 See also SHC, Q/SR/165/4, 5.

became riled after a gentleman and his entourage arrived at the establishment. They complained of a lack of service, 'sayinge that now gents were come they neglected their old guests that had spent the most money'. The gentleman's company was equally combative however, and one of his men 'threw a glasse of beere that he had in his hand in one of their faces, uppon which they all fell together by the eares'.[190] Another clash of companies resulted in a 'great tumult' in Cheshire in 1615. An alehouse brawl occurred 'which occasioned a great uproar in the town of Malpas, so that most of the town were disquieted and arose forth of their beds to appease the tumult'. Not only did the clash serve to disturb the local community, it had the potential to polarise it, and the constable reported that 'if the night had not been very dark much harm would have ensued for the people began to take sides'.[191] If sociable drinking could bind individuals into a tightly knit band of good fellows, it could simultaneously create fragmentation within the wider community.

Conclusion

This chapter has analysed gleanings from diaries, depositions and other legal records to reconstruct the everyday practice of good fellowship in the early modern English alehouse. Such good fellowship usually occurred within relatively small groups – most commonly containing two to four people, and rarely a number in double figures – referred to by contemporaries as 'companies', and it was not uncommon for a given alehouse to be populated by multiple companies at any given time. A company was generally composed of relative socio-economic peers, and whilst the majority would have been all-male, mixed-gender companies were not uncommon. All-female companies were relatively rare. Those engaged in an alehouse company were likely to be connected to each other by one or more pre-existing tie of kinship, marriage, co-worship, neighbourhood – involving a wider network than the immediate settlement in which they lived – political allegiance, work or occupation. Those who drank together usually knew each other, and companies were more likely to form outside of the alehouse than inside.

Once formed, companies might simply pay a short visit to an alehouse for refreshment, or to break up a long journey. Often, however, they

---

[190] Bettey (ed.), *The Case Book of Sir Francis Ashley*, p. 82.
[191] *Ches. Q.S. Recs*, p. 74.

engaged in more prolonged stays – whether this was their initial intention or not – which took on the characteristics of a bout of good fellowship. They consumed liberal amounts of alcohol whilst trying to avoid being overcome by drink; they drank each other's health – and, as the seventeenth century progressed, increasingly that of monarchs or pretenders; they sang songs; they played shuffle board to determine who would pay for the drinks; they generously offered to pay for the drinks of their 'true and faithful' companions; they quarrelled and came to blows when someone looked to shirk their share of the shot. They slipped off for sexual adventures in nearby ditches; they boasted about their sexual conquests; they were condemned by other drinkers for doing so. They went home, counted the costs of their merry bouts, vowed to forgo good fellowship in future, and within days returned to the alehouse for more of the same. These activities could appeal to different types of men, and different types of women, in different ways, and not all would have appealed to all alehouse-goers – though none were necessarily easily avoidable. Such activities were, after all, part of a series of behavioural conventions and expectations. Taken together, their appeal had a considerable reach, and men and women, young and old, labourer and substantial farmer – even the occasional gentleman – ventured into the alehouse to participate in them. Central to this appeal was the fact that good fellowship was both an expression of, and served to reinforce, meaningful and enduring bonds of 'friendship' – a relationship both instrumental and affectionate – between those who participated in it together.

If good fellowship had a broad appeal, and enhanced social bonds, its overall contribution to social cohesion in this society was ultimately ambivalent. Participation in good fellowship brought drinking companions closer together, but at the same time it tended to bring them into conflict with those outside of the company – whether that was the authorities, other drinking companies, alehouse workers, or hostile groups of the local chief inhabitants. Inclusion and cohesion came with exclusion and conflict, and given the relatively small size of drinking companies those on the inside rather than the outside were only ever a very narrow segment of the wider community. Despite the widespread appeal of good fellowship, then, the alehouse was not a place in which a vast swathe of the local community came together and developed stronger ties by sharing a drink. This was not the communal drinking of the churchyard or church house, but a rather more fragmented drinking culture that both reflected and reinforced more narrowly based forms of community. This, of course, is often seen as one of the distinctive developments of the sixteenth and seventeenth centuries in England – that the basis of 'community' was ever narrowing.[192]

But we need to take care to avoid some of the baggage that often comes with discussions of this historical development: that a meaningful sense of community was 'declining', or 'corroding'; that the history of the alehouse in early modern England reflects the death 'of a once vital popular culture', which left only 'truncated remains' in the form of 'a culture of poverty and petty disorder'.[193] There was rather more vitality to good fellowship than this, and for those contemporaries who made it a central activity in their daily lives, there would have been little sense that the social bonds they forged and maintained in the alehouse were in some sense inferior to those enjoyed by their forebears. Instead, they experienced good fellowship as an activity that was the lifeblood of friendship and that defined networks that were every bit as important to them as their membership of wider forms of community – whether that was of the village, the parish, or of overarching classes or sorts – that historians tend to privilege. The bonds and networks of friendship, to which good fellowship was so important for many early modern men and women, deserve to be accorded the prominent place in historical analysis that they occupied in the lives and identities of our subjects.

[192] See, for instance, Keith Wrightson, 'Mutualities and Obligations: Changing Social Relationships in Early Modern England', *Proceedings of the British Academy* 139 (2006), pp. 157–94.
[193] Wrightson, 'Alehouses, Order and Reformation', p. 21.

Conclusion

Good fellowship – a practice centred on recreational drinking in alehouses – was a widespread, meaningful, and potent form of social bonding in early modern England. Yet it was not an activity in which participation was an uncontested right for all. Those who looked to the alehouse – as opposed to the inn or tavern – as the principal site for the practice of recreational sociability, did so in contravention of the laws of the land. In the years between 1550 and 1630 a national system of alehouse regulation was established on the principle that whilst alehouses were an essential component of community infrastructure, this status was conditional upon them serving their 'true and principal uses' – lodging travellers, and providing victuals to the local poor – and refusing to permit any forms of recreational drinking. To fully appreciate the significance of good fellowship, therefore, we need to acknowledge a point of wider importance for the study of the cultural lives of relatively humble men and women in the past to which this book has sought to contribute: the need to 'integrate popular cultural experiences with the power structures that variously encouraged, permitted, and suppressed them'.[1]

If there was a power struggle over good fellowship in this society it was not a straightforward fight between 'elite' and 'popular' cultures. The lines of allegiance were rather messier than that, and it was too fiercely contested to represent a process whereby a ruling elite confidently asserted its hegemony through the suppression of the activities of subordinates. The central government certainly felt that this was a two-way fight, and regulatory hostility to alehouse sociability was to a considerable extent stoked by fears that the institution posed as much of a threat to the established structures of authority as vice versa. The authorities imagined alehouse-goers huddled around the alebench, plotting the downfall of church and state. It was a paranoid vision, but not a complete fantasy. The alehouse was a space in which the burning matters of church and state affairs were regularly discussed, but as often as not it was in an atmosphere of dispute and disagreement, rather than of consensus and

---

1   Griffin, 'Popular Culture in Industrialising England', p. 627.

solidarity that might have fomented a radical plebeian revolution. The fractious character of the political culture of the alehouse became even more pronounced in those divisive years of the 1640s and 1650s, and through the period of the 'birth of party' that followed in the later years of the century. But it had been a forum for political debate long before the emergence of the coffeehouse and the supposed genesis of the 'public sphere' in its mature form after the Restoration. The political culture of the alehouse may have only been a rough and ready manifestation of a public sphere – with the emphasis on rough – but its part in that story deserves to be acknowledged.[2]

Those tasked with enforcing the legislation against alehouse sociability were no more united in the positions they adopted than were alehouse patrons debating matters of church and state. Many magistrates, ministers and local office-holders took up the campaign against the alehouse with zeal. Many others did not. Foot-dragging on the part of magistrates may have owed more to notions of patronage, paternalism and profit, but for many ministers and local office-holders a reluctance to wage war on good fellowship was a result of their own routine involvement in it. Some members of the middling sort were becoming assimilated to the values of their social superiors, and to the teachings of the 'hotter sort of Protestant' ministers. As a result they simultaneously attacked and withdrew from the cultural world of their poorer neighbours. But this process of social polarisation was not uniform, and many of those chief inhabitants of local communities, including those that held local office, made use of the same recreational space as their lower-status neighbours – the alehouse – as a forum for their own sociability. As a result, they threw a spanner in the machinery of state, and remind us that the expansion of state authority in this period – reliant as it was on the participation of local middling sorts in the business of government on the ground – continued to ebb and flow, and perhaps faltered nowhere more clearly than in the ambitious attempt to micro-manage the recreational sociability of the alehouse-goer. It did so not only because many office-holders themselves cherished good fellowship, but because the patrons and proprietors of alehouses mobilised considerable levels of everyday forms

---

[2] For a model of the development of a public sphere in England that acknowledges its pre-1640 roots whilst nonetheless recognising the significance of developments in the second half of the seventeenth century, see Peter Lake and Steve Pincus, 'Rethinking the Public Sphere in Early Modern England', *The Journal of British Studies* 45:2 (2006), pp. 270–92.

of resistance in those cases where local officials did mount a determined attack.

Why were so many early modern contemporaries so firmly attached to alehouse sociability? Through seeking for areas of resonance across a range of source types – from broadside ballads (a form of print embedded in the practice); through various legal records (especially witness testimonies); to diary material containing accounts of quotidian drinking habits – it has been possible to reconstruct the forms and meanings of good fellowship in early modern England.[3] It was an activity structured by a number of rituals – toasting, drinking contests, games and gambling, songs – and by a series of behavioural conventions that encouraged liberal spending, heavy but controlled drinking, and the maintenance of a jovial – or 'merry' – disposition and atmosphere. These rituals and conventions expressed a number of values: courage, self-control, loyalty, financial prosperity and independence, a pride in hard work, a bold defiance of dominant gender norms. It did not, of course, mean all of these things to all participants at all times: its stock forms could be appropriated by different individuals and groups to express different values. Consequently its appeal was broad, and men and women, young and old, married and unmarried, poor and middling sort, servants and masters, apprentices and master craftsmen, could all find an attraction in the practice of good fellowship, and it could play a role in the expression of a range of identities. This reinforces a point that has been emphasised in the recent work on the cultural history of drinking, which has argued that the role played by routine, heavy drinking in the formation of elite identities in early modern England should correct a tendency to instinctively and exclusively associate such an activity with the poor and downtrodden. Indeed, we need to recognise that it was an activity central to the social and cultural lives of a considerable cross-section of early modern English society, from the tavern sociability of civic and literary

---

[3] For more on the notion of looking for resonance across sources as a means of strengthening conclusions, see Dror Wahrman, 'Change and the Corporeal in Seventeenth- and Eighteenth-Century Gender History: Or, Can Cultural History Be Rigorous?', *Gender and History* 20:3 (2008), pp. 584–602. Wahrman sees this approach primarily as a way to improve the rigour of cultural history, looking for the appearance of idioms within and across a range of printed genres to assess their prevalence in early modern society. Here I have expanded on this idea to look for areas of resonance across both social and cultural history sources – legal records, diaries, print – as a means of uncovering prevalent idioms *and* practices of good fellowship. I hope readers find the result amounts to more than just the kind of 'weak collage' of fragments of evidence that Wahrman rightly criticises.

elites to the alehouse-based good fellowship of the yeoman farmer, petty tradesman or agricultural labourer. Significantly, it should be acknowledged that although this society configured this activity as inherently more problematic and circumscribed for women than for men, many women nonetheless found ways of participating in good fellowship that carried for them more benefits than stigma. Most interesting, perhaps, are those contexts in which men and women drank together, often in ways that seem to have carried a similar appeal for both male and female participants, and served to express values that were shared by both genders. Contexts in which voluntary mixed-gender social activities took place in early modern England have not loomed large in analyses of gender relations in this society, though they could potentially provide a counterpoint to some of the highly conflictual portraits to which such relations are often subjected.

That good fellowship had a broad appeal does not mean it fostered broad forms of community. It was generally conducted in relatively small 'companies', tightly bound to each other – often by pre-existing ties of various forms of friendship – but often hostile to outsiders. That good fellowship could mean different things to different groups in society reinforced its tendency to underpin narrow forms of community. The bonds both expressed through and reinforced by co-participation in alehouse sociability were, then, more constrained than those associated with the kind of church-ale sociability characteristic of the late medieval period, with its wider basis of communal participation. It risks anachronism, however, to overstress the degree of decline involved in the changing parameters of those communities expressed through forms of recreational sociability: to contemporaries the bonds of good fellowship were not tarnished by their narrowness. Instead, these were among the bonds of collectivity most deeply felt by early modern men and women. Voluntary forms of association have long been seen as significant forms of community, especially in relation to the development of the associational culture of the eighteenth century, and now they are beginning to attract attention in attempts to revise our understanding of the key collective bonds operating in the seventeenth century.[4] These expressions of community were not only conducted in assembly rooms and guild halls – they had their equivalent in the more humble world of the alehouse.

---

[4]   See in particular Withington, *Society in Early Modern England*; Withington, 'Company and Sociability'; and also Peter Clark, *British Clubs and Societies 1580–1800: The Origins of an Associational World* (Oxford, 2000).

It was this connection between the alehouse and meaningful practices of social bonding that enabled the institution to overcome official hostility and to win its central place in seventeenth-century English society. It is a victory reflected in a relative decline of such official hostility around the turn of, and on into, the eighteenth century, as government came to grudgingly accept that place. Even the Society for the Reformation of Manners recognised that recreational drinking was largely beyond reform, and concentrated their energies elsewhere.[5] There were other important developments in the history of the alehouse in these years too. It underwent a process of 'improvement', reflected in an enhancement of its material culture, and – it has been argued – in the 'respectability' of its clientele.[6] The difference between an improved alehouse and a smaller inn became less distinct, and the term 'public house' began to emerge as an umbrella term for both. Larger inns, however, became grander than before, and the eighteenth century brought them into a 'golden age' in which they became an even more important focus of elite sociability.[7] The improvement of both alehouses and inns can be seen as part of a broader urban renaissance in this period, in which both the number and range of establishments available as sites of recreational sociability in England's urban centres boomed.[8] New commodities, most of which had become available in the sixteenth and seventeenth centuries but which began to be mass consumed in the eighteenth, also emerged. Coffee and coffeehouses, gin and dram-shops, tea and parlours – tea was generally consumed domestically, though not entirely without rituals of sociability attached – might all be seen as forms of competition to the traditional intoxicants ale and beer and the sociable forum of the

---

5   The Society for the Reformation of Manners did make some effort to keep the regulatory pressure on recreational drinking at this time, but even in their most active year, 1708, less than 5% of the prosecutions they initiated targeted drunkenness, a total of 150 prosecutions. In no other year between 1693 and 1738 did they initiate more than 46 total prosecutions for drunkenness in London. See Robert Shoemaker, 'Reforming the City: The Reformation of Manners Campaign in London, 1690–1738', in L. Davison, T. Hitchcock, T. Keirn and R. Shoemaker (eds), *Stilling the Grumbling Hive: The Response to Social and Economic Problems in England, 1689–1750* (Stroud, 1992), pp. 99–120, esp. p. 105.

6   Clark, *The English Alehouse*, chs 9–10.

7   Everitt, 'The English Urban Inn'; John Chartres, 'The Eighteenth-Century English Inn: A Transient "Golden Age"?', in Kümin and Tlusty (eds), *The World of the Tavern*, pp. 205–26.

8   Peter Borsay, *The English Urban Renaissance: Culture and Society in the Provincial Town, 1660–1770* (Oxford, 1989).

alehouse.[9] Levels of beer consumption fell in the eighteenth century as the consumption of spirits and hot drinks rose.[10] The improvement of the alehouse may have been part of a desperate attempt to keep up with this growing competition.

If the place of alehouse sociability in England's social and cultural life was being squeezed in an increasingly crowded market of intoxicants and sites of sociability in the eighteenth century, questions remain over the extent to which this development extended beyond the largest urban centres. In country towns and villages, and no doubt even in large urban centres, smaller 'unimproved' alehouses persisted – sometimes referred to as pot-houses – where there were no coffeehouses to compete with, and where gin was often sold in existing alehouses rather than rival establishments. Domestic tea consumption may, though, have represented a serious rival, and diary evidence suggests that this was becoming an important feature of the round of recreational sociability, especially for women.[11] The role played by the alehouse in the social and cultural lives of those non-elite men and women who lived outside of the major urban centres – the subjects of this book – remains to be fully explored for the eighteenth century, though it seems likely that there would be rather more continuities with the picture outlined in this study than is allowed by the emphasis on expansion, improvement and competition in existing studies of intoxicants and sociability in the eighteenth century.[12] But some significant changes are unmistakeable. Of crucial importance is that some of the meanings attached to alehouses and good fellowship in contemporary discourses had shifted. Whereas in the formative century

[9] Cowan, The Social Life of Coffee; Ellis, The Coffee House; Woodruff D. Smith, 'From Coffeehouse to Parlour: The Consumption of Coffee, Tea and Sugar in North-Western Europe in the Seventeenth and Eighteenth Centuries', in Jordan Goodman et al. (eds), Consuming Habits: Drugs in History and Anthropology (London, 1995), pp. 142–57; Peter Clark, 'The "Mother Gin" Controversy in the Early Eighteenth Century', Transactions of the Royal Historical Society, 5th series 38 (1988), pp. 63–84; Jessica Warner, Craze: Gin and Debauchery in an Age of Reason (New York, 2004); John Burnett, Liquid Pleasures: A Social History of Drinks in Modern Britain (London, 1999), chs 3–4, 8.

[10] Spring and Buss, 'Three Centuries of Alcohol'; Burnett, Liquid Pleasures, p.77.

[11] On pot-houses in the eighteenth century see Jennings, The Local, p. 30. On tea-drinking and recreational sociability see David Vaisey (ed.), The Diary of Thomas Turner, 1754–1768 (Oxford, 1984); Ronald Blythe (ed.), A Country Parson: James Woodforde's Diary, 1758–1802 (Oxford, 1985).

[12] There are two valuable studies of the recreational lives of such subjects for the eighteenth century, though neither has much to say about alehouses: Robert Malcolmson, Popular Recreations; Emma Griffin, England's Revelry: A History of Popular Sports and Pastimes, 1660–1830 (Oxford, 2005).

between 1550 and 1650 the alehouse had been associated by its opponents with political subversion, reckless prodigality, the breakdown of households, the transgression of gender norms, and indeed all manners of disorder, by 1750 a number of these connotations had migrated to other institutions. The coffeehouse was now the site of political disloyalty and sedition; beer-drinking was a loyal activity. But much more so than coffee it was gin that had taken the heat off the alehouse. In his famous prints of 1750, William Hogarth depicted 'Gin Lane' as the place where poverty, disorder and transgression were rife. Its companion print, 'Beer Street', depicted an alehouse scene in which prosperous tradesmen and market women drank wholesome beer, and read from broadsides together. It was, in essence, a positive portrayal of good fellowship. It is one that would have struck a chord with the good fellows of a century earlier, but it would have seemed unimaginable to them that their recreational drinking could be held up in public discourse as a model of appropriate behaviour to be contrasted with the evils of the excessive drinking of the poor. It is an indication that the struggle for the legitimacy of alehouses and good fellowship had been a triumph.

Bibliography

Manuscript sources

Cheshire Record Office (CRO)
CRO, QJB/2–3
CRO, QJF/34–112

Essex Record Office (ERO) – consulted at <http://seax.essexcc.gov.uk/>
ERO, Q/SR/159–449
ERO, T/A 418/136/15

Henry E. Huntington Library
Hastings Manorial Records (HAM), Box 2, Folder 1

London Metropolitan Archives
Archdeaconry Court of London, GL MS 9057/1
Diocese of London, Consistory Court, DL/C 236

Norfolk Record Office
NRO, C/S 3/42A(2)
NCR, 12 B (1), 1684–89 – consulted at http://www.webarchive.org.uk/wayback/
    archive/20051206120000/http://virtualnorfolk.uea.ac.uk/index.html

Somerset Heritage Centre (SHC)
SHC, Q/SR/2–198
SHC, D/D/Cd/32, Waterman v Elsworthie
SHC, D/D/Cd/32, Poines v Evans
SHC, D/D/Cd/32, Simons v Edwardes
SHC, D/D/Cd/97, Office v Alisbury

West Yorkshire Archive Service
WYAS, QS/1/15/3/7/1

Wiltshire and Swindon History Centre (WSHC)
WSHC, 1604/M–1683/T
WSHC, D1/39, 42
WSHC, D1/39/1/57/fols 132r–133r
WSHC, D1/39/1/57/fol.134
WSHC, D1/42/60/fols110v–106v

Ballad collections

Bodleian Library Ballad Collection: facsimiles accessed online at <http://eebo.chadwyck.com/home> (Early English Books Online)

British Library Ballad Collection: facsimiles accessed online at <http://eebo.chadwyck.com/home> (Early English Books Online)

Ebsworth, J.W. (ed.), *The Bagford Ballads*, Vol.II (Hertford, 1878)

Euing Ballads Collection: facsimiles accessed online at <http://ebba.english.ucsb.edu/> (English Broadside Ballad Archive, University of California, Santa Barbara)

Houghton Library Ballad Collection: facsimiles accessed online at <http://eebo.chadwyck.com/home> (Early English Books Online)

Pepys Ballad Collection: facsimiles accessed online at <http://ebba.english.ucsb.edu/> (English Broadside Ballad Archive, University of California, Santa Barbara)

Roxburghe Ballad Collection: facsimiles accessed online at <http://ebba.english.ucsb.edu/> (English Broadside Ballad Archive, University of California, Santa Barbara)

Printed primary sources

Ashley, Sir Francis, *The Case Book of Sir Francis Ashley, J.P.: Recorder of Dorchester, 1614–1635*, ed. J.H. Bettey (Dorchester: Dorset Record Society, 1981)

Baber, A.F.C. (ed.), *Court Rolls of the Manor of Bromsgrove and King's Norton, 1491–1504* (Kineton: Worcestershire Historical Society, 1963)

Baker, T.W. (ed.), *Records of the Borough of Nottingham: Being a Series of Extracts from the Archives of the Corporation of Nottingham*, Vol. V, 1625–1702 (London, 1900). See also Stevenson, W.H. below.

Bates Harbin, E.H. (ed.), *Quarter Sessions Records for the County of Somerset*, Vol. I, James I, 1607–1625; Vol. II, Charles I, 1625–1639; Vol. III, Commonwealth, 1646–1660 (London: Somerset Record Society, 1907–12). See also Dawes, M.C.B. below.

Bateson, Mary; Stevenson, W.H., and Stocks, J.E. (eds), *Records of the Borough of Leicester, Being a Series of Extracts from the Archives of the Corporation of Leicester*, Vol. III: 1509–1603; Vol. IV: 1603–1688 (Cambridge, 1905–23)

Bennett, J.H.E., and Dewhurst, J.C. (eds), *Quarter Sessions Records, with other Records of the Justices of the Peace for the County Palatine of Chester, 1559–1760* (Chester: Record Society of Lancashire and Cheshire, 1940)

Bettey, J. H. (ed.), *Calendar of the Correspondence of the Smyth Family of Ashton Court, 1548–1642* (Bristol: Bristol Record Society, 1982)

Coleman, M. Clare (ed.), *Court Roll of the Manor of Downham 1310–1327* (Cambridge: Cambridgeshire Records Society, 1996)

Cressy, David, and Ferrell, Lori Anne (eds), *Religion and Society in Early Modern England: A Sourcebook* (London, 1996)

Cunnington, E.B.H. (ed.), *Records of the County of Wilts: Being Extracts from the Quarter Sessions Great Rolls of the Seventeenth Century* (Devizes, 1932)

Dalton, Michael, *The Countrey Justice* (London, 1619)

Dawes, M.C.B. (ed.), *Quarter Sessions Records for the County of Somerset*, Vol. IV, Charles II, 1666–1677 (London, 1919). See also Bates Harbin, E.H. above.

Dent, Daniel, *A Sermon Against Drunkenness* (London, 1628)

Earle, John, *Micro-cosmographie* (London, 1628)

Eyre, Adam, 'A dyurnall, or catalogue of all my accions and expences from the 1st of January, 1646–[7]', ed. H.J. Morehouse, in *Yorkshire Diaries and Autobiographies in the Seventeenth and Eighteenth Centuries* (Durham, 1877)

Gascoigne, George, *A Delicate Diet for Dainty-mouthed Drunkards* (London, 1576)

Gough, Richard, *The History of Myddle*, ed. David Hey (Harmondsworth, 1981)

Guilding, J.M (ed.), *Reading Records: Diary of the Corporation*, Vol. II, 1603–1629; Vol. III, 1630–1640; Vol. IV, 1641–1654 (London, 1895–96)

Hale, W.H. (ed.), *A Series of Precedents and Proceedings in Criminal Causes, Extending from the Year 1475 to 1640; Extracted from the Act-Books of Ecclesiastical Courts in the Diocese of London, Illustrative of the Discipline of the Church of England* (London, 1847)

Holcroft, William, *William Holcroft His Booke: Local Office Holding in Late Stuart Essex*, ed. J.A. Sharpe (Chelmsford, 1986)

Hughes, P.L., and Larkin, J.F. (eds), *Stuart Royal Proclamations*, Vol. I (Oxford, 1973)

Le Hardy, William, and Reckitt, Geoffrey L. (eds), *Calendar to the Sessions Records, County of Buckingham, II, 1694–1705* (Aylesbury: Buckinghamshire County Council, 1936)

Lowe, Roger, *The Diary of Roger Lowe*, ed. William Sachse (London, 1938)

Mabbs, A.W. (ed.), *Guild Stewards' Book of the Borough of Calne, 1561–1688* (Devizes: Wiltshire Archaeological and Natural History Society, 1953)

Mews, Peter, *The Ex-Ale-Tation of Ale* (London, 1671)

Noy, David (ed.), *Winslow Manor Court Books, 1327–1377, 1423–1460* (Aylesbury: Buckinghamshire Record Society, 2011)

Prynne, William, *Healthes: Sickness* (London, 1628)

Rabelais, François, *The Histories of Gargantua and Pantagruel*, trans. J.M. Cohen (Harmondsworth, 1955)

Raine, James (ed.), *Depositions from the Castle of York; Relating to Offences Committed in the Northern Counties in the Seventeenth Century* (Durham: Publications of the Surtees Society, 1861)

Rawlidge, Richard, *A Monster Late Found Out and Discovered* (Amsterdam, 1628)

Roberts, S.K. (ed.), *Evesham Borough Records of the Seventeenth Century, 1605–1687* (Worcester: Worcestershire Historical Society, 1994)

Robinson, F.N. (ed.), *The Complete Works of Geoffrey Chaucer*, 2nd edn (Oxford, 1976)

Stevenson, W.H. (ed.), *Records of the Borough of Nottingham: Being a Series of Extracts from the Archives of the Corporation of Nottingham*, Vol.IV, King Edward VI to King James 1, 1547–1625 (London, 1889). See also Baker, T.W. above.

Sowernam, E., *Ester hath hang'd Haman: Or An Answere to a lewd Pamphlet, entituled, The Arraignment of Women* (London, 1617)

Vaisey, David (ed.), *The Diary of Thomas Turner, 1754–1768* (Oxford, 1984)

Willis Bund, J.W. (ed.), *Worcestershire County Records: Calendar of the Quarter Sessions Papers*, Vol.1, 1591–1643 (Worcester: Worcestershire County Council, 1900)

Woodforde, James, *A Country Parson: James Woodforde's Diary, 1758–1802*, ed. Ronald Blythe (Oxford, 1985)

Young, Thomas, *Englands Bane: or, The Description of Drunkennesse* (London, 1617)

Younge, Richard, *The Blemish of Government, Shame of Religion, Disgrace of Mankinde, or a Charge drawn up against Drunkards* (London, 1655)

Secondary sources

Achilleos, Stella, 'The *Anacreontea* and a Tradition of Refined Male Sociability', in Smyth (ed.), *A Pleasing Sinne*, pp. 21–35

Addy, John, *Sin and Society in the Seventeenth Century* (London, 1989)

Amussen, Susan, *An Ordered Society: Gender and Class in Early Modern England* (New York, 1993)

Archer, Ian, 'Social Networks in Restoration London: The Evidence of Samuel Pepys's Diary', in Alexandra Shepard and Phil Withington (eds), *Communities in Early Modern England* (Manchester, 2000), pp. 76–94

Bakhtin, Mikhail, *Rabelais and His World*, trans. Helene Iswolsky (Cambridge, MA, 1968)

Bellany, Alastair, 'Libels in Action: Ritual, Subversion and the English Literary Underground, 1603–42', in Harris (ed.), *The Politics of the Excluded*, pp. 99–124

Ben-Amos, Ilana Krausman, *The Culture of Giving: Informal Support and Gift-Exchange in Early Modern England* (Cambridge, 2008)

Bennett, Judith, *Ale, Beer and Brewsters in England: Women's Work in a Changing World, 1300–1600* (Oxford, 1996)

Bennett, Judith, 'Conviviality and Charity in Medieval and Early Modern England', *Past and Present* 134 (1992), pp. 19–41

Berridge, Virginia, 'Dependence: Historical Concepts and Constructs', in Griffith Edwards and Malcolm Lader (eds), *The Nature of Drug Dependence* (Oxford, 1990), pp. 1–18

Berry, Helen, and Foyster, Elizabeth (eds), *The Family in Early Modern England* (Cambridge, 2007)

Borsay, Peter, *The English Urban Renaissance: Culture and Society in the Provincial Town, 1660–1770* (Oxford, 1989)

Braddick, Michael J., *State Formation in Early Modern England, c.1550–1700* (Cambridge, 2000)

Braddick, Michael J., and Walter, John (eds), *Negotiating Power in Early Modern Society: Order, Hierarchy and Subordination in Britain and Ireland* (Cambridge, 2001)

Brennan, Thomas, *Public Drinking and Popular Culture in Eighteenth-Century Paris* (Princeton, 1988)

Brennan, Thomas, 'Towards the Cultural History of Alcohol in France', *Journal of Social History* 23 (1989), pp. 71–92

Brewer, John, and Styles, John (eds), *An Ungovernable People: The English and their Law in the Seventeenth and Eighteenth Centuries* (New Brunswick, 1980)

Brown, James, 'Alehouse Licensing and State Formation in Early Modern England', in Herring *et al.* (eds), *Intoxicants and Society*, pp. 110–32

Brown, James, 'Drinking Houses and the Politics of Surveillance in Pre-Industrial Southampton', in Kümin (ed.), *Political Space in Pre-Industrial Europe*, pp. 61–80

Brown, Pamela Allen, *Better a Shrew than a Sheep: Women, Drama, and the Culture of Jest in Early Modern England* (Ithaca, NY, 2003)

Bryson, Anna, *From Courtesy to Civility: Changing Codes of Conduct in Early Modern England* (Oxford, 1998)

Burke, Peter, *Popular Culture in Early Modern Europe* (London, 1978; Farnham, 2009)

Burnett, John, *Liquid Pleasures: A Social History of Drinks in Modern Britain* (London, 1999)

Capp, Bernard, *England's Culture Wars: Puritan Reformation and its Enemies in the Interregnum, 1649–1660* (Oxford, 2012)

Capp, Bernard, 'Gender and the Culture of the Alehouse in Late Stuart England', in Korhonen and Lowe (eds), *The Trouble with Ribs*, pp. 103–27

Capp, Bernard, 'Popular Literature', in Reay (ed.), *Popular Culture*, pp. 198–243

Capp, Bernard, *When Gossips Meet: Women, Family, and Neighbourhood in Early Modern England* (Oxford, 2003)

Capp, Bernard, *The World of John Taylor the Water-Poet* (Oxford, 1994)

Carlile, Diane, '"A comon and sottish drunkard you have been": Prosecutions for Drunkenness in the York Courts c.1660–1725', *York Historian* 16 (1999), pp. 32–44

Chartier, Roger, 'Culture as Appropriation: Popular Cultural Uses in Early Modern France', in Steven L. Kaplan (ed.), *Understanding Popular Culture: Europe from the Middle Ages to the Nineteenth Century* (Berlin, 1984), pp. 229–54

Chartres, John, 'The Eighteenth-Century English Inn: A Transient "Golden Age"?', in Kümin and Tlusty (eds), *The World of the Tavern*, pp. 205–26

Clark, Peter, 'The Alehouse and The Alternative Society', in Pennington and Thomas (eds), *Puritans and Revolutionaries*, pp. 47–72

Clark, Peter, *British Clubs and Societies 1580–1800: The Origins of an Associational World* (Oxford, 2000)

Clark, Peter, *The English Alehouse: A Social History, 1200–1830* (London, 1983)

Clark, Peter, 'The "Mother Gin" Controversy in the Early Eighteenth Century', *Transactions of the Royal Historical Society*, 5th series 38 (1988), pp. 63–84

Clark, Peter, and Slack, Paul (eds) *Crisis and Order in English Towns 1500–1700* (London, 1972)

Clark, Peter, and Slack, Paul, *English Towns in Transition, 1500–1700* (Oxford, 1976)

Clark, Sandra, 'The Broadside Ballad and the Woman's Voice', in Cristina Malcolmson and Mihoko Suzuki (eds), *Debating Gender in Early Modern England, 1500–1700* (Basingstoke, 2002), pp. 103–20

Cockayne, Emily, *Hubbub: Filth, Noise and Stench in England* (New Haven, 2007)

Collinson, Patrick, 'From Iconoclasm to Iconophobia: The Cultural Impact of the Second English Reformation', in Peter Marshall (ed.), *The Impact of the English Reformation, 1500–1640* (London, 1997), pp. 278–307

Collinson, Patrick, *The Religion of Protestants: The Church in English Society, 1559–1625* (Oxford, 1982)

Connell, R.W., *Masculinities* (Cambridge, 1995)

Coster, Will, and Spicer, Andrew (eds), *Sacred Space in Early Modern Europe* (Cambridge, 2005)

Courtwright, David, *Forces of Habit: Drugs and the Making of the Modern World* (Harvard, 2001)

Cowan, Brian, *The Social Life of Coffee: The Emergence of the British Coffeehouse* (London, 2005)

Cressy, David, *Dangerous Talk: Scandalous, Seditious and Treasonable Speech in Pre-Modern England* (Oxford, 2010)

Cressy, David, 'Levels of Illiteracy in England, 1530–1730', *The Historical Journal* 20:1 (1977), pp. 1–23

Crick, Julia, and Walsham, Alexandra (eds), *The Uses of Script and Print, 1300–1700* (Cambridge, 2004)

Cust, Richard, and Lake, Peter, 'Sir Richard Grosvenor and the Rhetoric of Magistracy', *Bulletin of the Institute of Historical Research* 54 (1981), pp. 40–53

Dabhoiwala, Faramerz, *The Origins of Sex: A History of the First Sexual Revolution* (Oxford, 2012)

Davies, M.G., *The Enforcement of English Apprenticeship: A Study in Applied Mercantilism* (Cambridge, 1956)

Davis, Natalie Zemon, *Fiction in the Archives: Pardon Tales and their Tellers in Sixteenth-Century France* (Stanford, 1987)

Davis, Natalie Zemon, *Society and Culture in Early Modern France* (Stanford, 1975)

Davison, L.; Hitchcock, T.; Keirn, T., and Shoemaker, R. (eds), *Stilling the Grumbling Hive: The Response to Social and Economic Problems in England, 1689–1750* (Stroud, 1992)

Dougall, Alastair, *The Devil's Book: Charles I, The Book of Sports and Puritanism in Tudor and Stuart England* (Exeter, 2011)

Douglas, Mary (ed.), *Constructive Drinking: Perspectives on Drink from Anthropology* (Cambridge, 1987)

Duffy, Eamon, *The Voices of Morebath: Reformation and Rebellion in an English Village* (London, 2001)

Earnshaw, Steven, *The Pub in Literature* (Manchester, 2000)

Elias, Norbert, *The Civilizing Process*, trans. Edmund Jephcott (Oxford, 2000)

Ellis, Markman, *The Coffee House: A Cultural History* (London, 2004)

Emmison, F.G., *Elizabethan Life: Morals and the Church Courts* (Chelmsford, 1973)

Everitt, Alan, 'The English Urban Inn, 1560–1760', in Alan Everitt (ed.), *Perspectives in English Urban History* (London, 1973), pp. 91–137

Ferentzy, Peter, 'From Sin to Disease: Differences and Similarities between Past and Current Conceptions on "Chronic Drunkenness"', *Contemporary Drug Problems* 28 (2001), pp. 362–90

Flather, Amanda, *Gender and Space in Early Modern England* (Woodbridge, 2007)

Fletcher, Anthony, *Reform in the Provinces: The Government of Stuart England* (London, 1986)

Fletcher, A.J., and Stevenson, J. (eds), *Order and Disorder in Early Modern England* (Cambridge, 1985)

Fox, Adam, 'Ballads, Libels and Popular Ridicule in Jacobean England', *Past and Present* 145 (1994), pp. 47–83

Fox, Adam, *Oral and Literate Culture in England, 1500–1700* (Oxford, 2000)

Foyster, Elizabeth, 'A Laughing Matter? Marital Discord and Gender Control in Seventeenth-Century England', *Rural History* 4 (1993), pp. 5–21

Foyster, Elizabeth, *Manhood in Early Modern England: Honour, Sex and Marriage* (London, 1999)

Frearson, Michael, 'The Distribution and Readership of London Corantos in the 1620s', in Robin Myers and Michael Harris (eds), *Serials and their Readers, 1620–1914* (Winchester, 1993), pp. 1–25

French, Henry and Barry, Jonathan (eds), *Identity and Agency in England, 1500–1800* (Basingstoke, 2004)

Fumerton, Patricia, 'Not Home: Alehouses, Ballads, and the Vagrant Husband in Early Modern England', *Journal of Medieval and Early Modern Studies* 32:3 (2002), pp. 493–518

Fumerton, Patricia; Guerrini, Anita, and McAbee, Kris (eds), *Ballads and Broadsides, 1500–1800* (Farnham, 2010)

Gammon, Vic, *Desire, Drink and Death in English Folk and Vernacular Song, 1600–1900* (Aldershot, 2008)

Gaskill, Malcolm, 'Reporting Murder: Fiction in the Archives in Early Modern England', *Social History* 23 (1998), pp. 1–30

Goldie, Mark, 'The Unacknowledged Republic: Officeholding in Early Modern England', in Harris (ed.), *The Politics of the Excluded*, pp. 153–94

Goodman, Jordan; Lovejoy, Paul E., and Sherratt, Andrew (eds), *Consuming Habits: Drugs in History and Anthropology* (London, 1995)

Goodman, Jordan, *Tobacco in History: The Cultures of Dependence* (London, 1993)

Gowing, Laura, *Common Bodies: Women, Touch and Power in Seventeenth-Century England* (London, 2003)

Gowing, Laura, *Domestic Dangers: Women, Words and Sex in Early Modern London* (Oxford, 1999)

Gowing, Laura; Hunter, Michael, and Rubin, Miri (eds), *Love, Friendship and Faith in Europe, 1300–1800* (Basingstoke, 2005)

Griffin, Emma, *England's Revelry: A History of Popular Sports and Pastimes, 1660–1830* (Oxford, 2005)

Griffin, Emma, 'Popular Culture in Industrialising England', *The Historical Journal* 45 (2002), pp. 619–35

Griffiths, Paul, *Youth and Authority: Formative Experiences in England, 1560–1640* (Oxford, 1996)

Griffiths, Paul; Fox, Adam, and Hindle, Steve (eds), *The Experience of Authority in Early Modern England* (Basingstoke, 1996)

Habermas, Jürgen, *The Structural Transformation of the Public Sphere: An Inquiry into a Category of Bourgeois Society*, trans. Thomas Burger with the assistance of Frederick Lawrence (Cambridge, 1989)

Hailwood, Mark, 'Alehouses, Popular Politics and Plebeian Agency in Early Modern England', in Fiona Williamson (ed.), *Locating Agency: Space, Power and Popular Politics* (Newcastle, 2010), pp. 51–76

Hailwood, Mark, '"Come hear this ditty": Seventeenth-Century Drinking Songs and the Challenge of Hearing the Past', *The Appendix: A New Journal of Narrative and Experimental History* 1:3 (August 2013), pp. 31–5; available at <http://theappendix.net/issues/2013/7/come-hear-this-ditty-seventeenth-century-drinking-songs-and-hearing-the-past>

Hailwood, Mark, 'The Honest Tradesman's Honour: Occupational and Social Identity in Early Modern England', *Transactions of the Royal Historical Society*, 6th series 24 (2014), forthcoming

Hailwood, Mark, '"It puts good reason into brains": Popular Understandings of the Effects of Alcohol in Seventeenth-Century England', *Brewery History* 150 (January, 2013), pp. 39–53

Hailwood, Mark, 'John Jarret and Roaring Dick of Dover: Popular Attitudes toward Drinking in Seventeenth-Century England', in Karen Christianson (ed.), *Intersecting Disciplines: Approaching Medieval and Early Modern Cultures* (Chicago, 2010); available at <http://www.newberry.org/sites/default/files/text-page-attachments/2010Proceedings.pdf>

Hailwood, Mark, 'Sociability, Work and Labouring Identity in Seventeenth-Century England', *Cultural and Social History* 8:1 (2011), pp. 9–29

Harris, Tim (ed.), *The Politics of the Excluded, c.1500–1850* (Basingstoke, 2001)

Harris, Tim, *Restoration: Charles II and his Kingdoms* (London, 2006)

Harris Sacks, David, 'Searching for "Culture" in the English Renaissance', *Shakespeare Quarterly* 39:4 (1988), pp. 465–88

Harvey, Karen, 'Ritual Encounters: Punch Parties and Masculinity in the Eighteenth Century', *Past and Present* 214 (2012), pp. 165–203

Heal, Felicity, *Hospitality in Early Modern England* (Oxford, 1990)

Herring, Jonathan; Regan, Ciaran; Weinberg, Darin, and Withington, Phil (eds), *Intoxicants and Society: Problematic Pleasures of Drugs and Alcohol* (Basingstoke, 2013)

Hill, Christopher, 'The Many-Headed Monster in Late Tudor and Early Stuart Political Thinking', in C.H. Carter (ed.), *From the Renaissance to the Counter-Reformation: Essays in Honour of Garrett Mattingley* (New York, 1965)

Hindle, Steve, 'Below Stairs at Arbury Hall: Sir Richard Newdigate and his Household Staff, c.1670–1710', *Historical Research* 85 (2012), pp. 71–88

Hindle, Steve, 'Exhortation and Entitlement: Negotiating Inequality in English Rural Communities, 1550–1650', in Braddick and Walter (eds), *Negotiating Power*, pp. 102–22

Hindle, Steve, *On the Parish? The Micro-Politics of Poor Relief in Rural England c.1550–1750* (Oxford, 2004)

Hindle, Steve, 'Power, Poor Relief and Social Relations in Holland Fen, c.1600–1800', *The Historical Journal* 41 (1998), pp. 67–96

Hindle, Steve, 'The Shaming of Margaret Knowsley: Gossip, Gender and the Experience of Authority in Early Modern England', *Continuity and Change* 9:3 (1994), pp. 391–419

Hindle, Steve, *The State and Social Change in Early Modern England, 1550–1640* (Basingstoke, 2000)

Hindle, Steve; Shepard, Alexandra, and Walter, John (eds), *Remaking English Society: Social Relations and Social Change in Early Modern England* (Woodbridge, 2013)

Hitchcock, David, 'A Typology of Travellers: Migration, Justice, and Vagrancy in Warwickshire, 1670–1730', *Rural History* 23:1 (2012), pp. 21–39

Hitchcock, Tim, 'Sociability and Misogyny in the Life of John Cannon, 1684–1743', in Hitchcock and Cohen (eds), *English Masculinities*, pp. 25–43.

Hitchcock, Tim, and Cohen, Michele (eds), *English Masculinities, 1660–1800* (London, 1999)

Holt, Mack (ed.), *Alcohol: A Social and Cultural History* (New York, 2006)

Hughes, Jason, *Learning to Smoke* (London, 2003)

Hunt, Arnold, *The Art of Hearing: English Preachers and Their Audiences, 1590–1640* (Cambridge, 2010)

Hunter, Judith, 'English Inns, Taverns, Alehouses and Brandy Shops: The Legislative Framework, 1495–1797', in Kümin and Tlusty (eds), *The World of the Tavern*, pp. 65–82

Hunter, Michael (ed.), *Printed Images in Early Modern Britain: Essays in Interpretation* (London, 2010)

Hutton, Ronald, *The Rise and Fall of Merry England: The Ritual Year, 1400–1700* (Oxford, 1994)

Jackson, Christine, 'A Town "Governed by a company of geese in furred gowns": Political and Social Conflict in Reading c. 1620–40', *Southern History* 29 (2007), pp. 29–58

Jackson, Matthew, 'A Contested Character: The Female Publican in Early Modern England and France', *Brewery History* 150 (2013), pp. 16–27

Jennings, Paul, *The Local: A History of the English Pub* (Stroud, 2007)

Jordan, Jennifer, 'Her-story Untold: The Absence of Women's Agency in Constructing Concepts of Early Modern Manhood', *Cultural and Social History* 4:4 (2007), pp. 575–83

Kaplan, Steven L. (ed.), *Understanding Popular Culture: Europe from the Middle Ages to the Nineteenth Century* (Berlin, 1984)

Keblusek, Maria, 'Wine for Comfort: Drinking and the Royalist Exile Experience, 1642–1660', in Smyth (ed.), *A Pleasing Sinne*, pp. 55–68

Kent, Joan, 'The English Village Constable, 1580–1642: The Nature and Dilemmas of the Office', *Journal of British Studies* 20 (1981), pp. 26–49

Key, Newton '"High feeding and smart drinking": Associating Hedge-Lane Lords in Exclusion Crisis London', in McElligott (ed.), *Exclusion and Revolution*, pp. 154–73

Kilburn-Toppin, Jasmine, '"Discords have arisen and brotherly love decreased": The Spatial and Material Contexts of the Guild Feast in Early Modern London', *Brewery History* 150 (2013), pp. 28–38

King, W.J., 'Regulation of Alehouses in Stuart Lancashire: An Example of Discretionary Administration of the Law', *Transactions of the Historic Society of Lancashire and Cheshire* 129 (1980 for 1979), pp. 31–46

Korhonen, Anu and Lowe, Kate (eds), *The Trouble with Ribs: Women, Men and Gender in Early Modern Europe*, Collegium: Studies across Disciplines in the Humanities and Social Sciences 2 (Helsinki, 2007)

Kümin, Beat, *Drinking Matters: Public Houses and Social Exchange in Early Modern Central Europe* (Basingstoke, 2007)

Kümin, Beat, 'Public Houses and their Patrons in Early Modern Europe', in Kümin and Tlusty (eds), *The World of the Tavern*, pp. 44–62

Kümin, Beat, 'Sacred Church and Worldly Tavern: Reassessing an Early Modern Divide', in Coster and Spicer (eds), *Sacred Space in Early Modern Europe*, pp. 17–38

Kümin, Beat, *The Shaping of a Community: The Rise and Reformation of the English Parish, c.1400–1560* (Aldershot, 1996)

Kümin, Beat and Tlusty, B. Ann (eds), *The World of the Tavern: Public Houses in Early Modern Europe* (Aldershot, 2002)

Lake, Peter, and Pincus, Steve, 'Rethinking the Public Sphere in Early Modern England', *The Journal of British Studies* 45:2 (2006), pp. 270–92

Lemon, Rebecca, 'Compulsory Conviviality in Early Modern England', *English Literary Renaissance* 43:3 (2013), pp. 381–414.

Malcolmson, Cristina and Suzuki, Mihoko (eds), *Debating Gender in Early Modern England, 1500–1700* (Basingstoke, 2002)

Malcolmson, Robert, *Popular Recreations in English Society, 1700–1850* (Cambridge, 1973)

Malcolmson, Robert, '"A set of ungovernable people": The Kingswood Colliers in the Eighteenth Century', in Brewer and Styles (eds), *An Ungovernable People*, pp. 85–127

Marsh, Christopher, *Music and Society in Early Modern England* (Cambridge, 2010)

Marsh, Christopher, 'The Sound of Print in Early Modern England: The Broadside Ballad as Song', in Crick and Walsham (eds), *The Uses of Script and Print*, pp. 171–90.

Martin, A.L., *Alcohol, Sex, and Gender in Late Medieval and Early Modern Europe* (Basingstoke, 2001)

Martin, A.L., *Alcohol, Violence and Disorder in Traditional Europe* (Kirksville, MO, 2009)

Martin, A.L., 'Drinking and Alehouses in the Diary of an English Mercer's Apprentice, 1663–1674', in Holt (ed.), *Alcohol: A Social and Cultural History*, pp. 93–105

McElligott, Jason (ed.), *Exclusion and Revolution: The Worlds of Roger Morrice, 1675–1700* (Aldershot, 2006)

McIntosh, M.K., *Controlling Misbehavior in England, 1370–1600* (Cambridge, 1998)

McRae, Andrew, *Literature and Domestic Travel in Early Modern England* (Cambridge, 2009)

McShane, Angela, 'The Extraordinary Case of the Flesh Eating and Blood Drinking Cavaliers', in McShane and Walker (eds), *The Extraordinary and the Everyday in Early Modern England*, pp. 192–210

McShane, Angela, '"Ne sutor ultra crepidam": Political Cobblers and Broadside Ballads in Late Seventeenth-Century England', in Fumerton, Guerrini and McAbee (eds), *Ballads and Broadsides*, pp. 207–28

McShane, Angela, 'Material Culture and "Political Drinking" in Seventeenth-Century England', *Past and Present* 222, Supplement 9: *Cultures of Intoxication* (2014), pp. 247–76

McShane, Angela, and Backhouse, Claire, 'Top-Knots and Lower Sorts: Popular Print and Promiscuous Consumption in Late Seventeenth-Century England', in Hunter (ed.), *Printed Images in Early Modern Britain*, pp. 337–57

McShane, Angela, and Walker, Garthine (eds), *The Extraordinary and the Everyday in Early Modern England* (Basingstoke, 2010)

McShane Jones, Angela, 'Roaring Royalists and Ranting Brewers: The Politicisation of Drink and Drunkenness in Political Broadside Ballads from 1640 to 1689', in Smyth (ed.), *A Pleasing Sinne*, pp. 69–87.

Morrill, J.S., *Cheshire 1630–1660: County Government and Society during the English Revolution* (Oxford, 1974)

Muldrew, Craig, *The Economy of Obligation: The Culture of Credit and Social Relations in Early Modern England* (Basingstoke, 1998)

BIBLIOGRAPHY

Muldrew, Craig, *Food, Energy and the Creation of Industriousness: Work and Material Culture in Agrarian England, 1550–1780* (Cambridge, 2011)

Nicholls, James, *The Politics of Alcohol: A History of the Drink Question in England* (Manchester, 2009)

Nicholls, James, 'Vinum Britannicum: The "Drink Question" in Early Modern England', *The Social History of Alcohol and Drugs* 22: 2 (2008), pp. 6–25

Norton, Mary, *Sacred Gifts, Profane Pleasures: A History of Tobacco and Chocolate in the Atlantic World* (London, 2008)

O'Callaghan, Michelle, *The English Wits: Literature and Sociability in Early Modern England* (Cambridge, 2007)

O'Callaghan, Michelle, 'Tavern Societies, the Inns of Court, and the Culture of Conviviality in Early Seventeenth-Century London', in Smyth (ed.), *A Pleasing Sinne*, pp. 37–51

Pennell, Sara, '"Great quantities of gooseberry pye and baked clod of beef": Victualling and Eating Out in Early Modern London', in Paul Griffiths and Mark Jenner (eds), *Londonopolis: Essays in the Cultural and Social History of Early Modern London c.1500–c.1750* (Manchester, 2000), pp. 228–59

Pennington, Donald and Thomas, Keith (eds), *Puritans and Revolutionaries: Essays in Seventeenth-Century History Presented to Christopher Hill* (Oxford, 1978)

Pincus, Steve, '"Coffee politicians does create": Coffeehouses and Restoration Political Culture', *Journal of Modern History* 67 (1995), pp. 807–83

Porter, Roy, 'The Drinking Man's Disease: The Pre-History of Alcoholism in Georgian Britain', *British Journal of Addiction* 80 (1985), pp. 385–96

Reay, Barry (ed.), *Popular Culture in Seventeenth-Century England* (London, 1985)

Reinke-Williams, Tim, 'Misogyny, Jest-Books and Male Youth Culture in Seventeenth-Century England', *Gender and History* 21 (2009), pp. 324–39

Reinke-Williams, Tim, 'Women, Ale and Company in Early Modern London', *Brewery History* 135 (2010), pp. 88–106

Richards, Jennifer, 'Health, Intoxication and Civil Conversation in Renaissance England', *Past and Present* 222, Supplement 9: *Cultures of Intoxication* (2014), pp. 168–86

Roberts, S.K., 'Alehouses, Brewing and Government under the Early Stuarts', *Southern History* 2 (1980), pp. 45–71

Rollison, David, *A Commonwealth of the People: Popular Politics and England's Long Social Revolution, 1066–1649* (Cambridge, 2010)

Rollison, David, 'Exploding England: The Dialectics of Mobility and Settlement in Early Modern England', *Social History* 24 (1999), pp. 1–16

Sandall, Simon, *Custom and Popular Memory in the Forest of Dean, c.1550–1832* (Saarbrücken, 2013)

Scodel, Joshua, *Excess and the Mean in Early Modern English Literature* (Princeton, 2002)

Scott, James C., *Domination and the Arts of Resistance: Hidden Transcripts* (London, 1990)

Scott, James C., *Weapons of the Weak: Everyday Forms of Peasant Resistance* (New Haven, 1985)

Scott, Joan W., *Gender and the Politics of History* (New York, 1988)

Shagan, Ethan, *Popular Politics and the English Reformation* (Cambridge, 2003)

Shagan, Ethan, *The Rule of Moderation: Violence, Religion and the Politics of Restraint in Early Modern England* (Cambridge, 2011)

Sharpe, James, 'Plebeian Marriage in Stuart England: Some Evidence from Popular Literature', *Transactions of the Royal Historical Society*, 5th series 36 (1986), pp. 69–90

Sharpe, Pamela, *Population and Society in an East Devon Parish: Reproducing Colyton, 1540–1840* (Exeter, 2002)

Shepard, Alexandra, 'Honesty, Worth and Gender in Early Modern England, 1560–1640' in French and Barry (eds), *Identity and Agency in England*, pp. 87–105

Shepard, Alexandra, 'Manhood, Credit and Patriarchy in Early Modern England, c.1580–1640', *Past and Present* 167 (2000), pp. 75–106

Shepard, Alexandra, '"Swil-bols and Tos-pots": Drink Culture and Male Bonding in England, c.1560–1640', in Gowing, Hunter and Rubin (eds), *Love, Friendship and Faith in Europe*, pp. 110–30

Shoemaker, Robert, 'Reforming the City: The Reformation of Manners Campaign in London, 1690–1738', in Davison *et al.* (eds), *Stilling the Grumbling Hive*, pp. 99–120

Shrank, Cathy, 'Beastly Metamorphoses: Losing Control in Early Modern Literary Culture', in Herring *et al.* (eds) *Intoxicants and Society*, pp. 193–209

Simpson, Claude, *The British Broadside Ballad and its Music* (New Brunswick, 1966)

Slack, Paul, 'Poverty and Politics in Salisbury, 1597–1666', in Clark and Slack (eds) *Crisis and Order in English Towns*, pp. 164–203.

Slack, Paul, *Poverty and Policy in Tudor and Stuart England* (New York, 1988)

Smith, Woodruff D., 'From Coffeehouse to Parlour: The Consumption of Coffee, Tea and Sugar in North-Western Europe in the Seventeenth and Eighteenth Centuries', in Goodman *et al.* (eds), *Consuming Habits*, pp. 142–57

Smyth, Adam (ed.), *A Pleasing Sinne: Drink and Conviviality in Seventeenth-century England* (Cambridge, 2004)

Smyth, Adam, *Profit and Delight: Print Miscellanies in England, 1640–1682* (Detroit, 2004)

Snell, Keith, 'The Culture of Local Xenophobia', *Social History* 28 (2003), pp. 1–30

Spaeth, Donald, *The Church in an Age of Danger: Parsons and Parishioners, 1660–1740* (Cambridge, 2001)

Spring, J.A., and Buss, D.H., 'Three Centuries of Alcohol in the British Diet', *Nature* 270 (1977), pp. 567–72

Spufford, M., 'Puritanism and Social Control', in Fletcher and Stevenson (eds), *Order and Disorder in Early Modern England*, pp. 41–57

Spufford, Margaret, *Small Books and Pleasant Histories: Popular Fiction and its Readership in Seventeenth-Century England* (Cambridge, 1981)

Stedman Jones, Gareth, *Languages of Class: Studies in English Working Class History, 1832–1982* (Cambridge, 1983)

Stretton, Tim, *Women Waging Law in Elizabethan England* (Cambridge, 1998)

Tadmor, Naomi, 'The Concept of the Household-Family in Eighteenth-Century England', *Past and Present* 151 (1996), pp. 111–40

Tadmor, Naomi, *Family and Friends in Eighteenth-Century England: Household, Kinship and Patronage* (Cambridge, 2001)

Tadmor, Naomi, 'Where was Mrs Turner? Governance and Gender in an Eighteenth-

Century Village', in Hindle, Shepard and Walter (eds), *Remaking English Society*, pp. 89–111

Thomas, Keith, *The Ends of Life: Roads to Fulfilment in Early Modern England* (Oxford, 2009)

Thomas, Keith, 'The Place of Laughter in Tudor and Stuart England', *Times Literary Supplement* (21 January 1977), pp. 77–81

Thomas, Keith, *Religion and the Decline of Magic* (London, 1971)

Thompson, E.P., *Customs in Common: Studies in Traditional Popular Culture* (London, c.1991)

Thompson, E.P., 'Eighteenth-Century English Society: Class Struggle without Class?', *Social History* 3 (1978), pp. 133–65

Thompson, E.P., 'Time, Work-Discipline, and Industrial Capitalism', *Past and Present* 38 (1967), pp. 56–97

Tlusty, B.A., *Bacchus and Civic Order: The Culture of Drink in Early Modern Germany* (Charlottesville, 2001)

Tobriner, Alice, 'Old Age in Tudor-Stuart Broadside Ballads', *Folklore* 102 (1991), pp. 149–74

Tosh, John, 'What Should Historians do with Masculinity?', *History Workshop Journal* 38 (1994), pp. 179–202

Underdown, David, *Fire from Heaven: Life in an English Town in the Seventeenth Century* (London, 1992)

Underdown, David, *Revel, Riot and Rebellion: Popular Politics and Culture in England* (Oxford, 1985)

Waddell, Brodie, *God, Duty and Community in English Economic Life* (Woodbridge, 2012)

Waddell, Brodie, 'Governing England through the Manor Courts, c.1550–1850', *Historical Journal* 55:2 (June 2012), pp. 275–315

Wahrman, Dror, 'Change and the Corporeal in Seventeenth- and Eighteenth-Century Gender History: Or, Can Cultural History Be Rigorous?', *Gender and History* 20:3 (2008), pp. 584–602

Walker, Garthine, *Crime, Gender and Social Order in Early Modern England* (Cambridge, 2003)

Walter, John, 'Faces in the Crowd: Gender, Youth and Age in Early Modern Protest', in Berry and Foyster (eds), *The Family in Early Modern England* (Cambridge, 2007), pp. 96–125

Walter, John, 'Public Transcripts, Popular Agency and the Politics of Subsistence in Early Modern England', in Braddick and Walter (eds), *Negotiating Power*, pp. 123–48

Walter, John, '"The pooremans joy and the gentlemans plague": A Lincolnshire Libel and the Politics of Sedition in Early Modern England', *Past and Present* 203 (2009), pp. 29–67

Walter, John, and Wrightson, Keith, 'Dearth and The Social Order in Early Modern England', *Past and Present* 71 (1976), pp. 22–42

Warner, Jessica, *Craze: Gin and Debauchery in an Age of Reason* (New York, 2004)

Warner, Jessica, '"Resolv'd to drink no more": Addiction as a Preindustrial Concept', *Journal of Studies on Alcohol* 55 (1994), pp. 85–91

Watt, Tessa, *Cheap Print and Popular Piety, 1550–1640* (Cambridge, 1991)

Westhauser, Karl E., 'Friendship and Family in Early Modern England: The Sociability of Adam Eyre and Samuel Pepys', *Journal of Social History* 27 (1994), pp. 517–36

Withington, Phil, 'Company and Sociability in Early Modern England', *Social History* 32 (2007), pp. 291–307

Withington, Phil, 'Intoxicants and the Early Modern City', in Hindle, Shepard and Walter (eds), *Remaking English Society* (Woodbridge, 2013, pp. 135–63

Withington, Phil, 'Intoxicants and Society in Early Modern England', *The Historical Journal* 54:3 (2011), pp. 631–57

Withington, Phil, *The Politics of Commonwealth: Citizens and Freemen in Early Modern England* (Cambridge, 2005)

Withington, Phil, 'Renaissance Drinking Cultures and Popular Print', in Herring *et al.* (eds), *Intoxicants and Society*, pp. 135–52

Withington, Phil, *Society in Early Modern England* (Cambridge, 2010)

Withington, Phil, and McShane, Angela (eds), *Past and Present* 222, Supplement 9: *Cultures of Intoxication* (Oxford, 2014)

Wood, Andy, 'The Place of Custom in Plebeian Political Culture: England, 1550–1800', *Social History* 22 (1997), pp. 46–60

Wood, Andy, *The Politics of Social Conflict: The Peak Country, 1520–1770* (Cambridge, 1999)

Wood, Andy, '"Poore men woll speke one daye": Plebeian Languages of Deference and Defiance in England, c.1520–1640', in Harris (ed.), *The Politics of the Excluded*, pp. 67–98

Wood, Andy, 'Subordination, Solidarity and the Limits of Popular Agency in a Yorkshire Valley, c.1596–1615', *Past and Present* 193 (2006), pp. 41–72

Wrightson, Keith, 'Alehouses, Order and Reformation in Rural England, 1590–1660', in Yeo and Yeo (eds), *Popular Culture and Class Conflict*, pp. 1–27

Wrightson, Keith, *English Society, 1580–1680* (London, 1982; 2nd edn, Bury St Edmunds, 2003)

Wrightson, Keith, 'Mutualities and Obligations: Changing Social Relationships in Early Modern England', *Proceedings of the British Academy* 139 (2006), pp. 157–94

Wrightson, Keith, 'The Politics of the Parish in Early Modern England', in Griffiths, Fox and Hindle (eds), *The Experience of Authority in Early Modern England*, pp. 10–46

Wrightson, Keith, 'Two Concepts of Order: Justices, Constables and Jurymen in Seventeenth-Century England', in Brewer and Styles (eds), *An Ungovernable People*, pp. 21–46

Wrightson, Keith, and Levine, David, *Poverty and Piety in an English Village: Terling, 1525–1700* (London, 1979)

Wrigley, E.A., and Schofield, R.S., *The Population History of England 1541–1871: A Reconstruction* (London, 1981)

Wurzbach, Natascha, *The Rise of the English Street Ballad* (Cambridge, 1990)

Yeo, Eileen, and Yeo, Stephen (eds), *Popular Culture and Class Conflict 1590–1914: Explorations in the History of Labour and Leisure* (Brighton, 1981)

Unpublished secondary sources

Brown, James, 'The Landscape of Drink: Inns, Taverns and Alehouses in Early Modern Southampton' (Ph.D. diss., University of Warwick, 2008)

Hailwood, Mark, 'Everyday Life and the Art of the Dutch Masters: A Social Historian's Perspective' (Lincoln, 2013), reproduced at <http://manyheaded-monster.wordpress.com/2013/06/28/everyday-life-and-the-art-of-the-dutch-masters-a-social-historians-perspective/>

Hailwood, Mark, and Waddell, Brodie (eds), *The Future of History from Below: An Online Symposium* (2013) <http://manyheadedmonster.wordpress.com/history-from-below/>

Hitchcock, David, 'The Experience and Construction of the Vagabond in England, 1650–1750 (Ph.D. diss., University of Warwick, 2012)

Jackson, Matthew, 'Cultures of Drink: A Comparative Case Study of Early Modern Bristol and Bordeaux' (Ph.D diss., University of Warwick, in progress)

McShane Jones, Angela, '"Rime and Reason": The Political World of the English Broadside Ballad, 1640–1689' (Ph.D diss., University of Warwick, 2004)

Index

INDEX

Earnshaw, Steven 1
East Hoathly (Sussex) 56
East Pennard (Somerset) 104–5
Eastbourne (Sussex) 184
elites
    attitudes to the alehouse 19–22, 24,
        54–8, 61–3, 81–3, 100–1, 116, 118,
        169–70, 221, 223–4
    drinking 2, 55–7, 118–120, 179, 185–6,
        220, 225, 227
Elizabeth I, Queen 62
Emborough (Somerset) 94
Epping (Essex) 208
Essex 79
Everitt, Alan 55
Evesham (Worcestershire) 53
Eyre, Adam 175, 182–220

festive culture 5, 19, 62, 102, 116, 155,
    182
Fiddington (Somerset) 86
Flather, Amanda 179–81, 185
Fletcher, Anthony 21, 36, 80, 95, 101
friendship 136, 176–8, 216–18, 221–2,
    226
Fumerton, Patricia 134–5
functions (of drinking houses) 2, 17–58
    food 11, 20, 72, 171, 193, 211
    lodging 2, 11, 20, 25, 192, 223
    recreation 2, 5, 6, 21, 22, 25, 27, 36–8,
        100, 113–14, 223, 229
    refreshment for travellers 2, 25, 32,
        34–5, 39–46, 192–4, 223
    venue for parish/civic administration
        37, 56
    victualling for the poor 20, 25, 35–7,
        39–46, 81, 223
Fyfett (Somerset) 183–4

gambling see games
games 24, 96, 97, 187, 103, 190, 130, 193,
    205–7, 221, 225
gender 7, 152–167, 179–81, 194–7,
    208–14, 226, 228–9
    attitudes to female drinkers 154–163,
        226
    attitudes of female drinkers 153–70,
        198, 204–5, 211, 221, 226
    all-female sociability 157–60, 184–5,
        196–7, 220
    mixed-gender sociability 160–3, 183,
        188–90, 194–6, 201–2, 210–11, 220,
        226

patriarchal/masculine values and
    drinking 140–1, 149, 154–7,
    163–70, 173, 208–9, 212–14,
    tension between patriarchal provision
        and drinking 44–6, 47, 130,
        163–8, 207–8, 212, 229
    see also alehousekeepers, marital
        relations, patrons, sex, widows, wives
Germany
    Augsburg 55
Gifford, George 104
gin 227–9
Glastonbury (Somerset) 32–3, 191, 200–1
Goldhanger (Essex) 92–3
good fellowship 2, 9, 98, 100, 105,
    113–222, 223, 229
    broad appeal of 149–50, 167–9, 172–3,
        213–14, 221, 225
Gough, Richard 115, 117, 207–8, 212, 218
Grays Thurrock (Essex) 192
Great Clacton (Essex) 187
Great Coggeshall (Essex) 96–7
Great Durnford (Wiltshire) 66
Great Ilford (Essex) 67, 188
Green Oar (Somerset) 94
Grosvenor, Sir Richard 19–20, 81

Habermas, Jürgen 69
Hackleton (Wiltshire) 35, 52
Hadleigh (Essex) 84
Haselbury Plucknett (Somerset) 93
health-drinking 63, 71–3, 120, 135, 145,
    150, 151, 156, 158, 161, 166, 168,
    202–3, 205, 212, 221, 225
Henry VIII, King 61, 71
Hereford (Herefordshire) 63
Herrick, Robert 119
Hindley (Lancashire) 204
Hinton (Wiltshire) 31
historiography 7–10
    alehouse political culture 63–5
    battle over the alehouse 18–22
    decline of community 221–2
    emergence of cultural history of drinking
        116–121
    gender and drinking 152–7, 179–81,
        226
    hegemonic nature of the law 88–9,
        100–1
    literary studies 118–121
    power relations 74–5
    two concepts of order 84–5, 100–1
        as applicable to clergy 104

249

STUDIES IN EARLY MODERN CULTURAL,
POLITICAL AND SOCIAL HISTORY

XXIII
British Travellers and the Encounter with Britain, 1450–1700
John Cramsie

XXIV
Domestic Culture in Early Modern England
Antony Buxton

Printed and bound by CPI Group (UK) Ltd, Croydon, CR0 4YY

09/06/2025

14685713-0004